SPIRITUALITY IN ECUMENICAL PERSPECTIVE

SPIRITUALITY IN ECUMENICAL PERSPECTIVE

E. Glenn Hinson
Editor

Westminster/John Knox Press
Louisville, Kentucky

Scripture quotations from the Revised Standard Version of the Bible are copyrighted 1946, 1952, © 1971, 1973 by the Division of Christian Education of the National Council of the Churches of Christ in the U.S.A. and are used by permission.

Scripture quotations from the New Revised Standard Version of the Bible are copyright 1989 by the Division of Christian Education of the National Council of the Churches of Christ in the U.S.A., and are used by permission.

Scripture quotations marked JB are from *The Jerusalem Bible,* Copyright © 1966, 1967, 1968 by Darton, Longman & Todd, Ltd., and Doubleday & Co., Inc. Used by permission of the publishers.

Grateful acknowledgment is made to The Upper Room for permission to quote material from Douglas V. Steere, *Gleanings: A Random Harvest* (Nashville: Upper Room, 1986).

Book design by Susan E. Jackson

Cover design by Aavidar Design Inc.

First edition

Published by Westminster/John Knox Press
Louisville, Kentucky

This book is printed on acid-free paper that meets the American National Standards Institute Z39.48 standard. ∞

PRINTED IN THE UNITED STATES OF AMERICA

9 8 7 6 5 4 3 2 1

Library of Congress Cataloging-in-Publication Data

Spirituality in ecumenical perspective / E. Glenn Hinson, editor. —
1st ed.
    p.   cm.
Includes index.
ISBN 0-664-25385-7 (pbk. : alk. paper)

1. Spirituality.   2. Steere, Douglas Van, 1901–   . I. Hinson, E. Glenn.
BV4510.2.S665   1993
248—dc20   93-19483

In honor of
Douglas and Dorothy Steere,
beloved friends

CONTENTS

Contributors   xi

Preface   xiii

1
Ecumenical Spirituality   *E. Glenn Hinson*   1

The Benedictine Connection   1
Features of an Ecumenical Spirituality   3
Spirituality's Ecumenical Future   10

2
Theological Perspectives on Spirituality   *Morton T. Kelsey*   15

Steere's Introduction to von Hügel   16
The Worldview von Hügel Addressed   19
Von Hügel's Solution   23

3
Listening in the Rule of Benedict   *Doris Donnelly*   33

Silence   34
Ways of Listening   37
Where God Speaks   38
Obstacles to Listening: "Motion Words" in *The Rule*   42

4
Spirituality in the Dialogue of Religions   *Mary Lou Van Buren*   51

Points of Meeting   51
Points of Struggle   55

Meeting at the Crossroads   58
A Call for Help and Signs of Hope   59
Into the Future—A Life of Thanksgiving   61

5
Action and Contemplation: Two Ways
Toward the Ultimate Reality   *Jean Leclercq, O.S.B.*   63

Ancient World   64
The Monastic Middle Ages   68
After the Twelfth Century   74
On the Eve of the Twenty-first Century   78

6
Contemplation and Work   *Richard Luecke*   83

Elements of Work   85
Worlds of Work   86
Modes of Contemplation   90
Work and Contemplation Together   95

7
Discernment: An Ignatian Perspective
on John Woolman's Journal   *Thomas E. Clarke, S.J.*   101

John Woolman's *Journal*   103
Woolman and Ignatius   104
Woolman and Modern Jesuit Perspectives   112

8
Eucharist: Joy and the Beams of Love   *Edward J. Farrell* 115

Eucharist: A Catholic Perspective   115
Catholic Eucharistic Spirituality Complemented
    by the Quaker Spirituality of Presence   122

9
Centering Prayer and the Friends   *Basil Pennington, O.C.S.O.* 129

Centering Prayer   131
Centering Prayer and the Friends   132

10
Spiritual Perspectives on Peacemaking   *Tilden Edwards*   141

The Human and Spiritual Quest to Become Fully Alive   141
The Thrust of Scripture Toward a Lively Shalom   143
The Divided Response of the Church in History   145
The Spiritual Attraction of War   146
The Interior Orientation of the Peacemaker   148
The Practice of Peacemaking   149
Suggestions for Peacemaking   154

11
Letters for Spiritual Guidance   *E. Glenn Hinson*   161

Two Masters   162
Qualities of Literary Master Guides   164
Principles of Spiritual Guidance Through Letters   165
Minding a Serious Calling   174

12
Along the Desert Road:
Notes on Spiritual Reading   *John S. Mogabgab*   177

Philip and the Eunuch   178
Recognizing a Hunger   179
Finding a Community   181
Receiving a Blessing   190
Traveling with Confidence   194

Index   197

CONTRIBUTORS

Thomas Clarke, S.J., is a staff member of Christ the King Retreat House, Syracuse, New York. He has written numerous books and articles on spirituality and social justice.

Doris Donnelly is a professor in the Department of Religious Studies at John Carroll University in Cleveland, Ohio. Formerly a professor at Princeton Theological Seminary, she is the author of a searching study, *Forgiveness*, and many other essays.

Tilden Edwards is an ordained Episcopal priest and the founder of Shalem Institute for Spiritual Formation, Washington, D.C. He is the author of numerous books on spirituality and spiritual direction, including the widely used *Spiritual Friend.*

Edward Farrell is an ordained Roman Catholic priest who has served many years as pastor of an inner city parish in Detroit. Author of several books on spirituality and a popular retreat director, he now teaches theology at Sacred Heart Seminary in Detroit.

E. Glenn Hinson is Professor of Spirituality, Worship and Church History at the Baptist Theological Seminary at Richmond. A specialist in Patristics, he has written several books on spirituality, including *A Serious Call to a Contemplative Lifestyle.*

Morton T. Kelsey is Emeritus Professor of Theology at the University of Notre Dame. An ordained Episcopal priest, he has written more than twenty-five books on spirituality, including *The Other Side of Silence,* on the practice and theology of spirituality.

Jean Leclercq, O.S.B., is a monk of the Abbaye Saint-Maurice, Luxembourg. An internationally recognized authority on Bernard of

Clairvaux and on the history of Christian spirituality in the Middle Ages, he was a close personal friend of Thomas Merton.

Richard Luecke is Director of Studies for the Community Renewal Society in Chicago. An ordained Lutheran minister, he has written extensively about spirituality and contemporary urban society.

John S. Mogabgab, an Episcopal layperson, is the editor of the award-winning journal *Weavings.*

Basil Pennington, O.C.S.O., is a monk of Saint Joseph's Abbey, Spencer, Massachusetts. A prolific author, he is a major interpreter of the Benedictine tradition and popular lecturer.

Mary Lou Van Buren was formerly on the staff for spiritual and theological concerns in the Women's Division of the General Board of Global Ministries of the United Methodist Church, New York City. She is a deacon in the United Methodist Church.

PREFACE

This book is about spirituality as it is emerging in the present ecumenical climate in the United States and around the world. It owes its origin to the lifetime ecumenical endeavors of Douglas and Dorothy Steere. The themes developed in it by well-known contemporary contributors to spirituality are themes Douglas Steere has articulated in his writings and in his own labors as a leader not only within his own communion, the Friends, but within the church universal.

All the contributors are members of the Ecumenical Institute of Spirituality, which Douglas Steere and Godfrey Diekmann conceived in 1965 after boredom at the Second Vatican Council drove them to the coffee shop. From its first meeting at St. John's Abbey in Collegeville, Minnesota, the institute has brought together a roughly equal number of Roman Catholic and Protestant scholars to talk about the horizons of spirituality as it impinges on all aspects of life.

In the first chapter I have tried to give some insight into "ecumenical spirituality" as I have discerned it in the life and work of two persons who have blazed a trail for us in the last half of this century—Thomas Merton, O.C.S.O., and Douglas Steere. Their insights plug into the tradition going back to Benedict of Nursia (c. 480–547). Tradition is very important in the spirituality of both Merton and Steere, and it will gain in importance in the ecumenical future.

In the second chapter Morton T. Kelsey presents theological perspectives on spirituality drawn particularly from the writings of Baron Friedrich von Hügel, whose thought has impacted that of Douglas Steere heavily. Von Hügel, Kelsey argues, helps us to rectify the schism between science and religion caused by rationalism.

In the third chapter Doris Donnelly draws on the Rule of Benedict to elucidate a theme Douglas Steere has made a significant contribution to in his classic on Quaker worship, *On Listening to Another.* The Quaker and the Benedictine traditions share a concern for silence, not as doing nothing but as the condition for doing the most important thing human beings can do, that is, being attentive to God. From the Rule of Benedict, Donnelly furnishes very practical insight into ways to listen, where God speaks, and how to deal with obstacles to listening.

In chapter 4 Mary Lou Van Buren examines points of meeting and points of struggle in dialogue among persons of different faiths and directs us toward some hopeful signs. She suggests that spirituality may help the world's religions "make music together to delight, to heal, and to let loose the life that is waiting to be born."

In chapter 5 Jean Leclercq, O.S.B., traces the historical path of "action and contemplation" and indicates how the need for contemplation and the need for action have been effectively reconciled in our time in the thought of Thomas Merton, O.C.S.O. Christians found ways to harmonize the two in other eras, but the modern era poses new challenges that Merton addressed with unusual insight.

In chapter 6 Richard Luecke updates and extends insights of Douglas Steere's Rauschenbusch Lectures at Colgate Rochester Divinity School in 1952 on the topic of "work and contemplation." He has shown how contemplation may create a frame of meaning for work that is, all too often, detached from such a frame.

In chapter 7 Thomas E. Clark, S.J., examines, from the perspective of Ignatius Loyola, John Woolman's concept and practice in reaching decisions about critical social issues. Although he recognizes divergences, he finds numerous points of agreement that differences in language cannot obscure. According to Fr. Clarke, Jesuits today would find several other points of convergence regarding social, political, and economic responsibility.

In chapter 8 Edward J. Farrell finds in the thought of Douglas Steere some enrichments for Catholic eucharistic thought and practice.

In chapter 9 Basil Pennington, O.C.S.O., explores whether the simple prayer long practiced in the Benedictine tradition, centering prayer, is analogous to the prayer practice of the Friends. Although he discerns differences, he believes the two traditions can enrich one another.

In chapter 10 Tilden Edwards searches for insight into the human quest for peace in spirituality. The church has not had a consistent witness in peacemaking or lived up to its own deepest perceptions, but present world circumstances force us to apply in new ways the insight and the reality that are ours.

In chapter 11, I have sought to draw from the practice of Baron von Hügel and Douglas Steere some perspectives on spiritual guidance through letter writing. Both masters greatly enlarged the range of their gifts to others through the pen. Explanation for that lies partly in the writer, the kind of person each was, and partly in the way they wrote. Spirituality, nonetheless, stood at the center as they irradiated the lives of others with their own.

In the final chapter John S. Mogabgab offers practical counsel on reading for spiritual growth. He interweaves reflections on the use of varied kinds of devotional literature with a penetrating understanding of meditating on scriptures.

E. GLENN HINSON

1
Ecumenical Spirituality

E. GLENN HINSON

"Ecumenical spirituality" is a very comprehensive subject. Lest I cast a net too far and make no catch at all, therefore, I would like to relate the topic to the contribution of the contemplative tradition stemming from Benedict of Nursia to ecumenical spirituality as reflected in the lives and works of two pioneers, Douglas V. Steere and Thomas Merton. In doing so, I emphasize *tradition*, so important for both of them and for any spirituality that will endure and prosper and serve future generations. Like Thomas Merton, I would differentiate tradition from convention. Convention is the external, tradition the internal. Convention is the outer shell, tradition the vital inner core.

The Benedictine Connection

Before delineating the features of ecumenical spirituality in the thought of Steere and Merton, I had better establish the Benedictine connection of each. Merton's connection is obvious, for the Trappist order to which he belonged practices strict observance of the Rule of Benedict. Because many thought of Merton as a deviate from this tradition and possibly a wrecker of it, however, it is important to reiterate his commitment to tradition, to the essence and not the external—his excursions with Zen Buddhism and other Eastern religions or his engagements with the world notwithstanding. Merton saw no conflict between his Cistercian vocation and his interest in Eastern religions, and he tested everything by the measuring rod of tradition.[1]

The impact of the Benedictine tradition on Merton was not superficial. Quite the contrary, the best of that tradition is what he sought to communicate to an ever-widening range of readers. Although he "mertonized" everything he fed through his gifted and fertile mind, he did not do violence, as some have suggested, to the essence of the tradition. In a 1955 review of *No Man Is an Island*, Aelred Graham, who two years earlier had panned Merton as "a modern man in reverse," perceptively described him as attaining "an all but completely achieved maturity" that included "an instinctive sense of the orthodox blended with the originality, not of one who must think differently from other people, but of one who thinks for himself."[2] As I have pointed out elsewhere, Merton's traditionalism stands out in the central features of his theology of prayer, in his language, in his recommendations about methods of prayer, and in proposals he made for monastic reform. I agree with Jean Leclercq, O.S.B., that Merton immersed himself in history in preparation for the present and brought his own tradition to bear on every subject.[3]

Even if some may doubt how seriously Merton took his vocation as a monk, therefore, the Benedictine connection is fairly obvious. That of Douglas Steere, a Quaker, requires more explication. Douglas Steere's interest in this tradition surfaced in 1933 when he made a one-month spiritual retreat at Maria Laach, the Benedictine monastery that spawned the liturgical renewal movement in the Roman Catholic Church earlier in this century.[4] In 1938 Douglas may have shown a bit of his debt to the Benedictine tradition when he published his first book, *Prayer and Worship*. In fact, he complimented the monks of Maria Laach for their sense of community generated by an active consciousness of "working for God and one another, and of participating in a state of mutual interdependence as members of a Christian family."[5] In addition, he cited Bernard of Clairvaux several times, ending his brief book on a note from Bernard.[6]

Douglas Steere renewed ties with Benedictines at the Second

Vatican Council when he and Godfrey Diekmann met in a coffee shop and decided to establish the Ecumenical Institute of Spirituality.[7] The institute held its inaugural meeting, one week before the opening of the final session of Vatican II, at St. John's Abbey in Collegeville, Minnesota, center for the Catholic liturgical movement in the United States. Had his abbot approved, Thomas Merton would have attended the meeting. In brief opening remarks Douglas Steere tied the new venture directly to the monastic tradition in delineating its three goals: seek "a real engagement that will leave none of us as we are," "take a penetrating look at the nature and role of ascetic theology in our time" in order to "try to determine where fresh work needs to be undertaken," and "assess the inner and outer situations of our time into which our concern for a vital spiritual tradition must come."[8] The Ecumenical Institute of Spirituality has included one or more Benedictine monks (presently Jean Leclercq, O.S.B., and Basil Pennington, O.C.S.O.) throughout its history, though it is designed to represent the spectrum of Roman Catholic religious orders as well as Protestant traditions.

Features of an Ecumenical Spirituality

Having established the Benedictine connection of both Merton and Steere, the next task is to sketch some of the main features of the spirituality that has transcended or knocked down so many of the barriers that have kept Christians apart from one another and from non-Christians for centuries.

Mutual Appreciation

The first feature is *mutual appreciation,* namely, appreciation for one's own tradition and for that of others. Thomas Merton had to grow in this regard to attain what I have called "expansive catholicism."[9] In *Seven Storey Mountain* (1948) he found little good in Quaker or Anglican churches he had once attended, everything good in the Roman Catholic Church. By the late fifties and early sixties this "ghetto Catholic" mentality embarrassed him. In *Conjectures of a Guilty Bystander,* gleanings from his journal that he put together in 1965, while still expressing a preference for his own church, he wrote, "I will be a better Catholic not if I can *refute* every shade of

Protestantism, but if I can affirm the truth in it and still go further."[10] Vis-à-vis other religions, he concluded in a 1962 article that the West must seek solutions for some of its problems in Oriental religions.

> At least this much can and must be said: the "universality" and "catholicity" which are essential to the Church necessarily imply an ability and a readiness to enter into dialogue with all that is pure, wise, profound and humane in every kind of culture. In this one sense at least a dialogue with Oriental wisdom becomes necessary. A Christian culture that is not capable of such a dialogue would show, by that very fact, that it lacked catholicity.[11]

Merton himself set out on that quest for "Oriental wisdom" on the trip to Bangkok that ended in his death. He unabashedly paid tribute to Gandhi, not only because Gandhi understood the gospel better than most Christians but because he actually applied it.[12] Merton's appreciation extended outward to include even nonbelievers. In the late sixties he condemned narrow understandings of catholicity. "The 'Catholic' who is the aggressive specimen of a ghetto Catholic culture, limited, rigid, prejudiced, negative, is precisely a non-Catholic, at least in the cultural sense. Worse still, he may be anti-Catholic in the cultural sense and perhaps even, in some ways, religiously, without realizing it."[13]

Douglas Steere has operated on essentially the same wavelength as the mature Merton. From his first writings on, there is nothing but the most sensitive appreciation for other traditions, both Christian and non-Christian. He wrote his doctoral dissertation on Friedrich von Hügel and published a collection of the latter's writing, *Spiritual Counsel and Letters*, in 1964. His own writings overflow with wisdom drawn from Christian, Jewish, Islamic, Buddhist, Hindu, and other traditions, and he has absorbed much from what he likes to character- ize as "wisdom in human hide." His wonderfully sensitive biography of Arthur Shearly Cripps, the great Anglican missionary to Rhode- sia,[14] reveals clearly the way his appreciation of persons transcends all religious barriers.

In a statement of a Quaker view of ecumenism titled *Mutual Irradiation*, he rejected three widely practiced approaches to ecumenism: destroying or burying others, syncretism, or mere coexistence. He urged instead an effort "to provide the most congenial setting possible for releasing the deepest witness that the Buddhist or Hindu or Muslim might make to a Christian companion, and that the Christian might in turn share with a non-Christian friend," or Christians with other Christians.[15] He found the vision of Pope John XXIII exciting not merely because the latter tried to knock down negatives but because he called Christians to witness, in Steere's words, "the operative presence, here and now, of this fathomless love and concern that is at the heart of things; a presence which is already actively at work in the unconscious life of every part of the creation."[16]

Cosmic Christology or Pneumatology

Behind such mutual appreciation in ecumenical spirituality lies a cosmic christology or pneumatology. Emmanuel Sullivan, S.A., has correctly observed that mutual appreciation depends on recognition of "the continuing activity of the Holy Spirit over long periods of separation among churches."[17] Both Merton and Steere would agree, I am confident, with Abraham Joshua Heschel's conviction

> that the most significant basis for meeting of men of different religious traditions is the level of fear and trembling, of humility and contrition, where our individual moments of faith are mere waves in the endless ocean of mankind's reaching out for God, where all formulations and articulations appear as understatements, where our souls are swept away by the awareness of the urgency of answering God's commandment, while stripped of pretension and conceit we sense the tragic insufficiency of human faith.[18]

In the essay "The Power and Meaning of Love," Thomas Merton gently chastised persons with narrow understandings of Christ. Invoking the parable of kingdom righteousness in Matthew 25:31–46, he urged an expansive view: "I must learn that my fellow man, just as he is, whether he is my friend or my enemy, my brother or a stranger from the other side of the world, whether he be wise or foolish, no matter what may be his limitation, *'is Christ.'* " If Christians find this difficult, Merton went on to suggest, they need to unite themselves with the Spirit of Christ. Christian faith is not some kind of "radio-electric eye" used to examine consciences but rather "the needle by which we draw the thread of charity through our neighbor's soul and our own soul and sew ourselves together in one Christ."[19]

Thomas Merton tipped his hand on the christological base of ecumenism in a reflection on Barth's dream about Mozart and Barth's comment that "it is a child, even a 'divine child,' who speaks in Mozart's music to us."

> Fear not, Karl Barth! Trust in the divine mercy. Though you have grown up to become a theologian, Christ remains a child in you. Your books (and mine) matter less than we might think! There is in us a Mozart who will be our salvation.[20]

It is the ubiquity of Christ that motivates openness to others. The Christian life, and especially the contemplative life, he decided, "is a continual discovery of Christ in new and unexpected places."[21] As he matured, this christological perspective enabled him to relax and enjoy the discovery of light in more and more corners of a widening world.

Douglas Steere has not composed an essay on Christology, but those who know him and his writings will discern behind his remarkable openness the reality of a living, universal Christ. In his little pamphlet on ecumenism, *Mutual Irradiation*, he challenged Quakers to respond to Teilhard de Chardin's query in *The Divine Milieu* as to whether developments in the Western world have eclipsed the Christ we have known. Their reply should derive not from theory but from experience:

> that having felt inwardly in the presence of the living Christ both the joy and the misery of the world and having felt our arms being opened to the whole creation, while we may not ourselves at this point be able adequately to formulate a view of the universal Christ, we can be among those who are most open to it. For this universal burst of the limitless love of God has brought us not only to a Jesus Christ who is a "man for others," but to one who is "a man for all others," and to sense that his very uniqueness is grounded in his universality.[22]

The most basic tenet of the Society of Friends is the conviction that the living Christ is present everywhere to every person. George Fox, founder of the Friends' movement, found the answer to a most earnest religious search: "There is one, even Christ Jesus, that can speak to thy condition."[23] Quakers speak of Christ or the Spirit, sometimes without distinction, as the Light Within. In his classic, *Testament of Devotion,* edited by Douglas Steere, Thomas Kelly underlines that the Light Within has to do more with experience than with a concept.

> It is a dynamic center, a creative Life that presses to birth within us. It is a Light Within which illumines the face of God and casts new shadows and new glories upon the face of men. It is a seed stirring to life if we do not choke it. It is the Shekinah of the soul, the Presence in the midst. Here is the Slumbering Christ, stirring to be awakened, to become the soul we clothe in earthly form and action. And He is within us all.[24]

The last statement merits underscoring, for from that spring streams the powerful Quaker tradition of social service and action.

Person-Centered Approach to Unity

If neither Merton nor Steere had tipped us off to their affinity for the contemplative tradition in mutual appreciation of all traditions and cosmic Christology, they clearly do so when they share insights into Christian unity. Both reflect the suspicion of political solutions to divisions and the confidence in the power of the Spirit to work through persons that characterize contemplatives throughout the history of Christianity.

Merton was blunt about the superiority of the personal to the political. In *Conjectures of a Guilty Bystander,* he described his plan:

> If I can unite *in myself* the thought and the devotion of Eastern and Western Christendom, the Greek and the Latin Fathers, the Russians with the Spanish mystics, I can prepare in myself the reunion of divided Christians. From that secret and unspoken unity in myself can eventually come a visible and manifest unity of all

Christians. If we want to bring together what is divided, we can not do so by imposing one division upon the other or absorbing one division into the other. But if we do this, the union is not Christian. It is political, and doomed to further conflict. We must contain all divided worlds in ourselves and transcend them in Christ.[25]

The mature Merton who emerged from what he considered a false sense of solitude in the fifties experienced a unity that transcended all diversities, beginning with differences among Christians, but extended outward beyond those separating humankind.

Every other man is a piece of myself, for I am a part and a member of mankind. Every Christian is a part of my own body, because we are members of Christ. What I do is also done for them and with them and by them. What they do is done in me and by me and for me. But each one of us remains responsible for his share in the life of the whole body.[26]

In notes jotted down for a paper he was to have delivered in Calcutta in October 1968, on monastic experience and East-West dialogue, Merton contended that true communication must take place "beyond the level of words, . . . in authentic experience which is shared not only on a 'preverbal' level but also on a 'postverbal' level."[27] He raised a caution flag against "wrong ways" of doing dialogue: (1) reducing dialogue to talk, (2) facile syncretism, (3) ignoring of real differences, (4) neglect of the goal of the monk: "true self-transcendence and enlightenment," and (5) preoccupation with institutional structure, monastic rule, and so on, or not paying proper heed to them.[28] The goal ought to be true communication, indeed, "communion," something the contemplative can supply to modern persons. "Above all, it is important that this element of depth and integrity—this element of inner transcendent freedom—be kept intact as we grow toward the full maturity of the universal man."[29]

Merton himself possessed unusual gifts for such communion. He easily and naturally came in on the wavelength of other persons. Yet I am convinced that it was his experience at the Abbey of Gethsemani that equipped him. Early in *The Waters of Siloe*, a treatise on the monastic vocation published in 1949, he explained that solitude and silence enabled him to get in touch with the will of God wherein, by love, he found himself united with all others in the same love of God. Communion with the Spirit, "Who is the common life of the monastic community and of the whole Church of God," unites. "The closer the contemplative is to God, the closer he is to other men. The more he loves God, the more he can love the men he lives with. He does not withdraw from them to shake them off, to get away from them, but in the truest sense, to *find* them. *Omnes in Christo unum sumus.*"[30]

Douglas Steere, viewing ecumenism from the standpoint of the Quaker tradition, which has often thought of itself as a "third stream," that is, neither Catholic nor Protestant "but part of the Christian mystical stream that has nurtured them all,"[31] has proposed "a functional ecumenism that begins with all of us encouraging each other to practice our own religious tradition to the hilt and to share our experiences with each other in every creative way we can devise."[32] Like the tradition from which Thomas Merton spoke, the Quaker tradition also has some disdain for structures, especially those which might put a damper on responsiveness to the Spirit. As Douglas Steere has defined it,

> a truly functional ecumenism wants to witness to the world how much God cares, and if this means stopping a war; or trying to learn how to share more equitably the world's material resources; or meeting an emergency human need, or joining the poor; or sending brotherly teachers and companions to live and share with those in another area; or teaching one another how to meditate, or how to pray, or how to kindle corporate adoration, or how to grow in the life of devotion, or how to use the lives of past saints and heroes to re-kindle our commitment; or how great art, painting, sculpture and therapy may release the deeper life in us; or how the world of plants and animals and water and wind can temper our souls; a functional ecumenism will open us in these and in other areas to the witness of our fellows, whether Christian or the adherents of other world religions.[33]

In Steere, as in Merton, we see priority assigned to a universal experience of union "at the level of fear and trembling." John 3:16, Steere chides, did not say "God so loved *the Church*" but rather "God so loved *the world.*" This means that Christians will not be the only persons with some light to irradiate others; they too can learn from persons of other religious persuasions—Buddhists, Hindus, Muslims, as well as other Christians. The Friends, he has argued, "are naturally oriented to start at the right end of this ecumenical endeavor— namely to begin from within and to draw the whole ecumenical process in this direction. Yet their inward sense of being joined both to Him and to all the living, means a witness against violence and for the unlimited liability that we owe to each other."[34]

In this comment Douglas Steere has supplied a clue to the *modus operandi* of ecumenical spirituality in his own life. The Quaker tradition belongs to the same contemplative tradition that nurtured Thomas Merton. For centuries a liturgy of silence has united Friends with the Presence whose Center is everywhere, whose circumference is nowhere and thus with all humankind, just as the *Opus Dei* has done in Benedictine monasteries. It has furnished Douglas Steere himself with unusual gifts at both irradiating and receiving the beams of love pouring on us all.[35]

Spirituality's Ecumenical Future

Ecumenical spirituality, rooted in tradition, therefore, is characterized by mutual appreciation, cosmic christology or pneumatology, and person-centered approaches to Christian unity. Major exponents and contributors to it such as Thomas Merton and Douglas Steere probably would not want to claim exclusive viability for this approach or to negate more structured approaches through bilateral or multilateral dialogues, mergers, and cooperation. They would discern, rather, a special contribution for the contemplative way so admirably embodied in the Benedictine and Quaker traditions, that is, to be a sort of avant garde for the ecumenical movement in the areas of contemplation and community.

It is contemplation, namely the life of prayer, that has equipped both Thomas Merton and Douglas Steere in an unusual way for ecumenical engagement not merely with other Christians but with persons of other religious commitments and indeed with humankind. Both Douglas Steere and the mature Merton have exhibited a remarkable quality of openness and sensitivity. Those who know

Douglas Steere have often commented on a capacity for listening that encourages others to open up and disclose their own deepest insights. Steere possesses a kind of evocative presence, something that has made others seek him out when they dare to undertake to leap over human barriers.[36] For years he participated in a colloquium of eminent thinkers composed of such notables as Reinhold Niebuhr, Paul Tillich, George Buttrick, and John Oliver Nelson. Quakers called on him to represent them in dialogue with Zen Buddhists and Hindus. In the Ecumenical Institute of Spirituality he has inspired a colloquy that combines mind-blowing scholarly presentations and dialogue with a style of intimate caring unequalled in anything except a sustained community such as the monastery Merton himself lived in.

Many have noted Merton's gifts as a unifier. Shortly after his death Rosemary Haughton lauded him as "a bridge between two cultures" (European and American). A. M. Allchin labeled him "a liberator" and "a reconciler." John Moffit saw in him "a bridge between East and West." James T. Baker described him as a link between the City of God and the Secular City.[37] I remember him personally as "a transformer who could take any voltage input, measure it, and discharge it at exactly the right output for whatever appliance anyone attached."[38]

Today the question that interests us most is: How do we explain their ecumenical sensitivities? What prepared them for engagement with other people, Christian and non-Christian?

To begin with, let's not forget the natural gifts of both Steere and Merton. Steere was a Rhodes Scholar at Oxford. He received his Ph.D. in philosophy from Harvard. Before his retirement in 1964 he had a long and distinguished career at Haverford College. Many Quakers would recognize in him one of the key interpreters of their tradition. Merton, too, was precocious. A child of bright, artistic parents, he qualified for study at Cambridge, although a wild social life caused his guardian to yank him out of school and bring him to the United States. He earned a master's degree at Columbia University and would have attained a Ph.D. had he not heard the call to Gethsemani. Although he is not without his critics, few can doubt his gifts as writer, poet, and prophet as he reached maturity during the sixties.

Both Steere and Merton experienced Christianity in an ecumenical way through most of their lives. Steere attended several different churches—Reformed, Methodist, and so on—and did not become acquainted with Quakers until he went to Oxford in 1927. Merton's mother was a Quaker, his father an Episcopalian. Early on, he experienced the lure of Oriental religions, but some helpful advice from the Hindu Bramachari set him on a deeper quest in Christianity.

Both contributed to and benefited from the emerging ecumenical spirit of the mid-twentieth century. Liturgical studies, biblical studies, the Una Sancta Movement that developed in concentration camps during World War II, the New Pentecost of Pope John XXIII, and the Second Vatican Council have changed forever relations between Christians and, indeed, of Christians toward all humankind. Such a day as all of us who revel in Christian unity have been rejoicing in was made for persons like Douglas Steere and Thomas Merton. They have piped and we have danced to the new song. They have been the free spirits who dared to go on before the rest of us who could not yet venture into unknown places.

It is really their sense of freedom and openness to the unknown that may supply the main clue to the question we are asking. How do we explain their boldness? The answer surely lies in great part in the contemplative element at the very center of the traditions that nurtured both Steere and Merton, or, better said, in the love that those who take this route may experience at the center. The Quaker tradition is a contemplative tradition, just as the Benedictine tradition is. The aim of both is love of God, who is love, and, in the discovery of that love, union with others, first those around us but then in an ever-widening circle the whole of humankind and indeed the whole creation. In a foreword to Thomas Merton's *Contemplative Prayer*, Douglas Steere has cited a line from William Blake to sum up Merton's concept of prayer, a line that is equally fitting for Douglas Steere's own vocation. And it characterizes well the aim of ecumenical spirituality. "We are put on earth for a little space that we may learn to bear the beams of love." Ecumenical spirituality ought always to underline those words, lest we get so caught up in the "doings" and "fixings" of ecumenism that we forget why we are engaged in it.

Notes

1. E. Glenn Hinson, "The Catholicizing of Contemplation: Thomas Merton's Place in the Church's Prayer Life," *Cistercian Studies* 10 (1975): 180–81.

2. Aelred Graham, "The Mysticism of Thomas Merton," *Commonweal* 62 (May 13, 1955): 155–59.

3. Jean Leclercq, O.S.B., introduction to *Contemplation in a World of Action* (Garden City, N.Y.: Doubleday & Co., 1971), xiv.

4. Douglas V. Steere, "Common Frontiers in Catholic and Non-Catholic Spirituality," in *Protestants and Catholics on the Spiritual Life,* ed. Michael Marx, O.S.B. (Collegeville, Minn.: Liturgical Press, 1965), 45. Joseph A. Jungmann, S.J., *Liturgical Renewal in Retrospect and Prospect,* trans. Clifford Howell, S.J. (London: Burns & Oates, 1965), 15–18, attributes the initiation of the movement to a Benedictine monk from the Abbey of Mont César, Louvain, Lambert Beauduin (d. 1960), but adds that Maria Laach monastery had a central influence under Ildephonse Herwegen, abbot when Steere went there. Ernest B. Koenker, in *The Liturgical Renaissance in the Catholic Church* (Chicago: University of Chicago Press, 1954), 12, dates the movement from the first Liturgical Week held for lay persons at Maria Laach during Holy Week of 1914, the year after Herwegen became abbot.

5. Douglas V. Steere, *Prayer and Worship* (New York: Association Press, 1938), 51. Note, however, the reservations he expressed thirty years later concerning Abbot Herwegen's overemphasis on the Benedictine "family" and de-emphasis on individual effort, in "Common Frontiers," 46.

6. *Prayer and Worship,* 68; cf. also pp. 1, 10, 59.

7. On this organization see E. Glenn Hinson, "Jubilee of the Ecumenical Institute of Spirituality," *Ecumenical Trends* 19 (Dec. 1990): 169–70.

8. Douglas V. Steere, "Opening Address," in *Protestants and Catholics on the Spiritual Life,* ed. Marx, 1.

9. E. Glenn Hinson, "Expansive Catholicism: Ecumenical Perceptions of Thomas Merton," *Religion in Life* 47 (1979): 63–76.

10. Thomas Merton, *Conjectures of a Guilty Bystander* (Garden City, N.Y.: Doubleday & Co., Image Books, 1966), 144.

11. Thomas Merton, "Christian Culture Needs Oriental Wisdom," *Catholic World* 195 (May 1962): 72–79.

12. Thomas Merton, *Seeds of Destruction* (New York: Macmillan Publishing Co., 1967), 160, 164.

13. Ibid., 187–88.

14. Douglas V. Steere, *God's Irregular: Arthur Shearly Cripps* (London: SPCK, 1973).

15. Douglas V. Steere, *Mutual Irradiation: A Quaker View of Ecumenism* (Wallingford, Pa.: Pendle Hill Publications, 1971), 8.

16. Ibid.

17. Emmanuel Sullivan, S.A., "Ecumenical Spirituality," in *The Westminster Dictionary of Christian Spirituality*, ed. Gordon S. Wakefield (Philadelphia: Westminster Press, 1983), 126.

18. Abraham Joshua Heschel, "No Religion Is an Island," *Union Seminary Quarterly Review* 21 (1966): 122. Heschel corresponded with Merton from Dec. 17, 1960, on, and he visited Gethsemani on July 13, 1964.

19. Thomas Merton, *Disputed Questions* (New York: Mentor-Omega Books, 1965), 100.

20. Merton, *Conjectures*, 12.

21. Thomas Merton, journal entry for March 3, 1950, in *The Sign of Jonas* (New York: Harcourt, Brace & Co., 1953), 275.

22. Steere, *Mutual Irradiation*, 29.

23. George Fox, *Journal*, ed. J. Nickalls (Cambridge: Cambridge University Press, 1952), 11.

24. Thomas R. Kelly, *A Testament of Devotion* (New York: Harper & Row, 1941), 29.

25. Merton, *Conjectures*, 21.

26. Thomas Merton, *No Man Is an Island* (Garden City, N.Y.: Doubleday & Co., Image Books, 1967), 16.

27. Thomas Merton, *The Asian Journal*, ed. Naomi Burton, Patrick Hart, and James Laughlin (New York: New Directions, 1968), 315.

28. Ibid., 316f.

29. Ibid., 317.

30. Thomas Merton, *The Waters of Siloe* (Garden City, N.Y.: Doubleday & Co., Image Books, 1962), 362–63.

31. Steere, *Mutual Irradiation*, 12.

32. Ibid., 15.

33. Ibid., 16.

34. Ibid., 27.

35. Cf. E. Glenn Hinson, "Douglas V. Steere: Irradiator of the Beams of Love," *Christian Century* 102 (April 24, 1985): 416–19.

36. Cited by E. Glenn Hinson, "Merton's Many Faces," *Religion in Life* 42 (Summer 1973): 158–59.

37. Ibid., 160.

38. E. Glenn Hinson, "Merton's Many Faces," 161.

2
Theological Perspectives on Spirituality

MORTON T. KELSEY

Von Hügel wrote that the best way to study mysticism is to study a mystic. The best way to study the theological perspectives on spirituality may be to look at the lives of people who struggled with the basic theological underpinnings of spirituality in our own time. Three leaders in the recent renewed interest in spiritual practice have also been perceptive philosophers and theologians. They wrote widely and come from different religious traditions. Douglas Steere was a Quaker; Baron von Hügel a leader in the Modernist Movement in the Catholic church; Evelyn Underhill a devout and influential Anglican. The life, thought, and practice of von Hügel made a profound impact on the other two.

Douglas Steere has had a rich and varied life. He is probably best known for his books on the many aspects of the human encounter with the Divine. He has also interpreted the spiritual experience of Quakers to a wide readership. His ecumenical interest resulted in his being invited to the Second Vatican Council as an observer. There he made friends among the leaders of the council. This led to the formation of the Ecumenical Institute of Spirituality; his interest in and support of the group has been constant for twenty-five years. He has traveled the globe, often as one of the first outsiders on the scene in countries ravaged with war and other catastrophes. We sometimes forget that in the midst of all these activities his actual profession was that of professor of philosophy at Haverford College, where he taught for thirty-five years. His academic training and degree were in philosophy and his doctoral dissertation for Harvard was on the thought of Baron von Hügel. Let us look at Douglas Steere's philosophical background and see how the thinking of von Hügel and Evelyn Underhill influenced his life, devotional practice, and philosophy of religion. Steere considered Underhill the Baron's most able, intellectual follower.

Let us look, first of all, at Douglas Steere's introduction to these two great interpreters of religious experience. Fortunately, in his recent book *Gleanings: A Random Harvest,* he has provided us with important autobiographical data on this very subject. Then let us look at the philosophical world to which von Hügel was writing and at what he offered to religious searchers, and also describe briefly von Hügel's thought on the subject of mature religious life. We will conclude with Steere's description of von Hügel's method of spiritual direction as revealed in his relationship with Evelyn Underhill. This account reveals the many similarities among von Hügel, Underhill, and Steere.

Steere's Introduction to von Hügel

Douglas Steere was first introduced to the real meaning of the Quaker faith in England where he was studying at Oxford University. Up to that time it was, for him, an interesting religious movement of the seventeenth century. Through a Quaker doctor, he was introduced to the Quaker fellowship there. Steere describes an experience that was to have great consequence in his thinking and life:

> I attended an hour's silent Quaker meeting at Old Jordan's Hostel.
> It was there that I first felt the power of Christ's indwelling spirit
> sweep through me and that I came to experience what the Quakers
> call a "gathered" or a "covered" meeting. It was through Dr. Gillett
> that I was invited to spend the night with Rufus Jones at Haverford
> College when, after spending the summer in America, I was on my

way back to England for my third year at Oxford. And it was from this visit that I was invited to join Rufus Jones a year later as his junior colleague and to teach philosophy at Haverford College for what turned out to be the rest of my professional life.

With this growing hunger to understand better the inner experience of divine guidance that had come to me, I decided in my final year at Oxford (1927–28) to bury myself in the writing of the Roman Catholic philosopher and theologian, Baron von Hügel, and to prepare myself to write a doctoral thesis for Harvard on his thought. In the course of that year, only two years after the baron's death in 1925, I came to know a number of his closest friends. Professor Percy Gardiner, the baron's literary executor, generously gave me access to von Hügel's unpublished papers.

In the course of these visits I came to know Evelyn Underhill. Although she was and remained an Anglican, for the last three years of von Hügel's life she had been under his spiritual direction, and her life had been immeasurably deepened by him. In the next decade her books were treasures that I especially prized.[1]

Steere had been well prepared for his exposure to von Hügel. Originally trained in an agricultural college, he met a professor there who truly listened to him and confirmed his deepest longings and also encouraged him to do graduate study in philosophy at Harvard. His eagerness to study philosophy was undoubtedly "to find a frame for the inner guidance" that had drawn him away from agriculture. He writes:

> Instead of giving me this longed-for frame for my faith and experience, however, my study of philosophy wiped out what little faith I had. By spring of my first year at Harvard, I touched bottom and saw little to live for.[2]

At Harvard, Steere met a Chinese student who told him of his conversion to Christianity and away from communism, to which he had been attracted. One morning Steere woke suddenly and saw Jesus Christ standing beside his bed. During the same period he met some students from the Episcopal Theological School who gathered for silent prayer at noontime. That school was placed near Harvard's campus for the very purpose of reaching searching students. Steere never became an integral part of the group, but this fellowship opened to him the reality of prayer. "By the end of my first Harvard year, I had been inwardly renewed in my faith. The renewal had come to me through silent prayer, into which I could bring anything."[3]

My first acquaintance with Douglas Steere was through two books he edited and for which he wrote introductions, Thomas Kelly's *Testament of Devotion* and Søren Kierkegaard's *Purity of Heart Is to Will One Thing*. I was deeply moved by both of them. It was only later when I came to know Douglas and his wife, Dorothy, that I realized what an affinity I felt for his thought and devotional practice. I knew that von Hügel had been an important source of inspiration for him. However, not until I had read *Gleanings* did I realize how similar were the roads we had traveled. I too had gone for graduate studies in philosophy shortly after the death of my mother, but my work was done at Princeton. I had hoped that this study would make some meaning of a life where some of the finest people die prematurely and with great suffering. Instead, I found total agnosticism, and then in a tutorial I read Kant's *Critique of Pure Reason* and was given the task of rendering this work into simple and meaningful English. During that year I truly hit the bottom. I struggled on in the darkness for a year and then decided that I would go to the Episcopal Theological School to see if, by any chance, the Christian religion could give meaning to me in the abyss in which I found myself. I found two Christian writers who were more profound and philosophically sound than my agnostic professors at Princeton. One was A. E. Taylor. We had used his commentary on Plato in graduate school. In Taylor's Gifford Lectures, *The Faith of a Moralist,* he presented a philosophical framework for a religious life that made rigorous philosophical sense.

And then I began to read Baron Friedrich von Hügel. I met a mind of enormous depth and breadth. Here was a philosophical giant who knew ancient and modern philosophy, modern science, and scientific method, and who proposed a view of reality in which there was a place for religious experience, for acquaintance with God. Even though his English was difficult (von Hügel thought in German and wrote in English), I drank in both series of his *Essays and Addresses on the Philosophy of Religion.* They were water for the parched ground of my mind and soul. I also read the magnificent opening introduction to his magnum opus, *The Mystical Element of Religion as Studied in the Life of St. Catherine of Genoa and Her Friends*. I purchased all the rest of his published works and have read them through the years. At the same time I found a group of students who met for half an hour before the 8:00 A.M. chapel services for silent prayer, and prayer became meaningful for the first time. Now I had a philosophical and theological framework that made sense of the Divine-human encounter.

The Worldview von Hügel Addressed

In his introduction to Kelly's *Testament of Devotion,* Douglas Steere writes, "He seemed to be expounding less as one possessed of 'knowledge about' and more as one who had unmistakable 'acquaintance with'."[4] The Christian gospel maintains that individuals are not limited to a mere intellectual knowledge about God but can personally experience a relationship with God. Much of the modern church, however, had generally ceased to be a channel for men and women to experience the power of Christ. The rationalism and materialism that have permeated Western civilization, including the church, are based on a worldview that precludes belief in the existence of a nonmaterial, or spiritual, reality. If the modern person is really to encounter God, he or she must have a worldview that allows belief in a spiritual reality.

How did we arrive at such a thoroughly secularized worldview and how can we find a new one that will permit us honestly to set about being acquainted with, not merely knowledgeable about, God?

The Schism Between Science and Religion

In 1543 the ideas of Nicolaus Copernicus fell into the neatly ordered medieval cosmology like an explosion. Copernicus's well-supported hypothesis simply stated that the sun, not the earth, was the center of the solar system.

For those of us who have not struggled with doubts about our place in the universe, it is difficult to imagine the impact this theory had upon the entire Christian world. It shook the religious foundations of the medieval conception of the universe, for if the earth were no longer its center, then the whole schema collapsed.

Understanding the implications of Copernicus's hypothesis, the church reacted violently, declaring him a heretic after his death and exhuming and burning his body. Giordano Bruno, burned at the stake in 1600 for views similar to Copernicus's, spoke the truth in his last statement: "Ye who pass judgment over me feel, maybe, greater fear than I upon whom it is passed." On June 22, 1633, Galileo was forced to either deny his belief in the sun's centrality to the solar system or suffer the same fate as Bruno.

That the philosophical foundations of the church were shaken by Copernicus's hypothesis and subsequent scientific ideas clearly demonstrates that the church feared its beliefs could be disproven. The furor caused by the intrusion of scientific discovery exposed the fact that the church was based on a rationalistic theology. To understand how this rationalistic basis for belief occurred, it is necessary to take a look at the ideas of Plato and Aristotle and briefly trace the development of Western philosophical thought.

Platonic Thought in the Early Church

Plato believed that human beings are not limited to experiencing a merely physical reality but have access to a spiritual reality as well. He also maintained that there are four ways of knowing—that the source of humankind's knowledge is not reason and sense experience alone but also prophecy, healing (cleansing), artistic inspiration, and love. Plato believed that an individual's psyche has a spiritual element, and thus he or she can have experiences that transcend logical thought and sense experiences alone. Note that if we accept Plato's methods of knowing, we must realize that knowledge is never certain or final; rather, our conclusions are always tentative and subject to new revelation.

One of the early church fathers, Justin Martyr (150 C.E.), realized that Plato's philosophical ideas gave an intellectual expression to what Christ lived and taught. Since Plato gave the clearest, most systematic account of how human beings could know both the spiritual and the physical worlds, Justin began a great theological tradition joining the essential categories of Platonic thinking and Christian experience.

This Platonic point of view was expressed by all the major church fathers, including Irenaeus, Tertullian, and Cyprian in the West, and Clement, Origen, and Athanasius in Alexandria. In the Eastern and Greek side of the empire, Basil the Great, Gregory of Nyssa, Gregory of Nazianzus, and John Chrysostom based their works on Platonic thinking. Ambrose, Augustine, Jerome, and Gregory the Great laid a Platonic foundation for thinking in the West for almost a thousand years.

How Aristotle's Worldview Affected the Church

With the development of medieval Western Christianity and a new culture, Platonic thought was displaced, for men and women in the West were cut off from the center of life in Byzantium. Roman law was adopted, Latin became the language of scholarship, and the Greek spirit, including Plato's understanding of human experience, was lost.

Instead, the thinking of Aristotle, revived by the Arabs, was brought to the West soon after 1000 C.E. Thomas Aquinas became convinced of the truth of Aristotle's worldview, particularly that individuals receive direct knowledge only through sense experience and reason, not by divine inspiration. Thomas Aquinas concluded that Christians ought to accept this view, so he wrote the *Summa Theologica,* attempting to show that Aristotle's worldview was compatible with Christian tradition. Toward the end of his life Thomas Aquinas did have a powerful experience of God, but his writings from before this experience were instrumental in shaping the official doctrines of the church.

Thus the ideal of certainty based on logic rather than experience became the chief cornerstone of theology and the church. And it was this attitude of possessing final knowledge that could not tolerate priest-philosopher Copernicus's scientific inquiries.

Naturalistic Science and the Western Worldview

The eventual result of the scientific inquiry by Copernicus was the conclusion that the ultimate nature of the universe was materialistic and mechanistic. Johannes Kepler perfected Copernicus's theories, showing that heavenly bodies act as any physical thing acts and need no heavenly beings to account for their movements. Then Newton theorized that the entire universe acted as a machine working according to precise mechanical laws. Next, Darwin's evolutionary theory of natural selection seemed to indicate that humankind was simply the result of chance interaction of material atoms, and thus human life had no ultimate meaning or significance.

These theories were systematized by such thinkers as Karl Marx in Germany, August Comte in France, Herbert Spencer in England, and B. F. Skinner and other early behaviorists in the United States. The idea common to these systems was that human beings were only intricate combinations of physical atoms and thus the idea of a spiritual reality and of a divine-human encounter became absurd.

Because of the variance between the dogmas of the church and the theories of science, the average Christian has been caught in a terrible dilemma. He or she has had to maintain a divided mind with religion in one compartment and science in the other. This split makes it difficult to hold an integrated worldview and has led many Christians to turn to fundamentalist types of religion that ignore the reasoning of science. Many other modern people have dismissed the realm of the spirit as complete nonsense and adopted the hypothesis of science as the cornerstone of their belief system. It is interesting to note how few people have ever thought that this religious/scientific division could be solved with a new worldview, a new hypothesis of reality that allows belief in both a material and a nonmaterial reality, room for sense experience and logic on one hand, and an encounter with the numinous on the other.

Unable to ignore the impact that scientific discovery made upon human thinking, the church eventually attempted to update its thinking. This attempt, however, resulted in merely trying to fit the Christian faith into the rationalistic framework provided by the secular world. Such Protestant theologians as Rudolf Bultmann, Dietrich Bonhoeffer, and Karl Barth believed that God does not break into the modern world in a personal way, and Catholic philosophers like Karl Rahner, Jean Daniélou, and Bernard J. F. Lonergan hedge on the subject of a direct encounter with God.

The Solution of Philosophical Idealism and Eastern Thought

For thousands of years religious thinkers in India have provided a quite different view of reality. In both Hinduism and Buddhism there are powerful schools of religious thought that perceive the physical world as illusion and the spiritual world as real. Faced with the rampant materialism developing in the West and with the agnostic thinking of Kant, Western philosophers developed a Western version of the idea that the mind alone is real. Bishop George Berkeley proposed the view that physical objects were real only because they were ideas in the mind of God. They had no independent physical reality. Hegel, rebelling against Kant's agnosticism, developed this point of view to its logical conclusions in *The Phenomenology of Mind*. Baron von Hügel was raised within this framework, the philosophical and theological atmosphere of the late nineteenth century. This point of view had many problems. It offered no solution for the problem of evil; it offered only an intellectual experience of God and little place for the discrete, direct encounter with the Holy; it did not often provide the impulse to go out into the world to serve those suffering there.

Von Hügel's Solution

At mid-life Friedrich von Hügel came to a crisis of meaninglessness. He was rescued from this abyss through the guidance, care, concern, and spiritual wisdom of Abbé Huvelin. Von Hügel experienced a transformation that kept him loyal to the Catholic church and led him to study the life of one of the less well known saint-mystics of the church. He selected Catherine of Genoa because she lived before the Reformation divided the church, because she was a married woman, and because no serious study had been made of her astonishing experiences and her devotion to the sick and the poor. After ten years of study and research he was convinced of the genuine nature of her direct experience of God. He also realized that the philosophy of German Idealism in which he was reared did not provide an adequate framework for understanding the power of her life and her experiences of the Divine Lover. He came to the conclusion that neither idealism nor materialism was adequate, and he formulated a view of reality that Douglas Steere calls "existential realism" and I would call "critical realism". He maintained that both the physical and spiritual realms of existence were real and that they had been created by the Holy Creator who was immanent within both worlds but was also transcendent over and beyond them and wished to relate directly with human beings.[5] It could be diagramed in the following way.

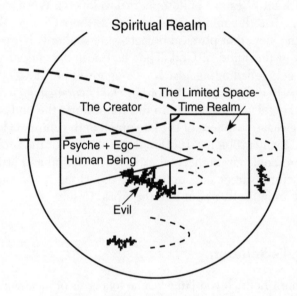

Von Hügel also thought that true Christian mysticism involved several quite different elements: one needed to be a practicing member of a historical religious tradition; one needed to be open to and experience the Holy One; one must use the critical capacities of one's mind to provide an adequate view of total reality; one's response to God's love was to go out to others, particularly those with the greatest need; the full use of these elements would enable one to live to full spiritual potential. The importance of these elements is discussed not only in the books we have mentioned, but also in *Eternal Life: A Study of Its Implications and Applications, Selected Letters, Letters from Baron Friedrich von Hügel to a Niece,* and a posthumous volume edited by Edmund Gardner, *The Reality of God and Religion and Agnosticism.*

The Institution

First, there can be no development of real Christian spirituality without being rooted in the traditional practices, beliefs, and morality of the church. People who try to "go it alone" without belonging to the institutional church are deprived, for they lack the nurture and guidance the body of Christ can provide. One cannot fulfill one's religious potential without support, encouragement, and teaching. The church can provide guidelines to the experience of the inner world while keeping its members rooted in the stability of rituals and extraverted practices.

The idea that each person's religious opinion is of the same value is nonsense, for there is a body of knowledge that is tested by time that can be transmitted by the church to believers.

The danger in limiting one's religion only to the institution is very real, however. Religious belief can degenerate to mere superstition if a ready-made dogma with a set of hand-me-down beliefs is accepted without question or study. An obsession with detail, organization, and blind obedience to the church's authority can cause sterility, which drives people away from the church and causes the institution itself to lose its vitality. The symbols and rituals of the church lose their richness and mystic qualities, and the church becomes a set of rules and regulations.

Mystical Experience

The second element essential to mature religion is mystical experience, or the direct apprehension of God by human beings. Many Christians believe that mysticism is merely a flight from reality and responsibility and would thus subscribe to the remark of Joseph Fletcher, author of *Situation Ethics*, that mysticism begins in mist and ends in schism.

But religion that consists entirely of institutional practices and intellectual knowledge is dead indeed. A direct, vital encounter with God can be experienced, and it can occur in three main ways— through sacraments, through contemplation, and through an inner perception of the divine in images.

These experiences of the Divine can be sought or they may come spontaneously. They may be heeded or ignored. Catherine of Genoa's devotion was kindled by a spontaneous experience. One day in church she was suddenly presented with a vision of the blood of Christ filling the church and washing her clean. As a result of this vision, Catherine started attending mass daily, fasting, and ministering to the sick, some of whom were healed by her touch. In *Companions on the Inner Way* I have detailed over thirty ways in which such experiences can touch us.

Just as we run into danger if we try to base our lives only on the religious institution and its rites and laws, so can we court disaster if we concentrate solely on mystical experience, which has no guidelines. Sole reliance on mysticism can, on the one hand, lead people to do the most absurd things, as exemplified by the Münster Anabaptists. On the other hand, it can cause them to withdraw from the world and become passive, inert, even schizoid. It also short-circuits God's love, for Christianity must be practiced in community, in the hard realities of honest encounter, if it is to be as God intended. We are, after all, called to "make connections between the human story and the divine story," as Henri J. M. Nouwen says in *The Living Reminder*.

Critical Thinking

As we noted earlier, von Hügel was much impressed with the *genuine* scientific method by which the physical sciences had made such great strides. He believed we need to learn to deal with *facts*. The theories of the physical sciences change as new facts are discovered. He believed that religious facts and experiences were the data of genuine philosophy of religion. Von Hügel himself was a universal scholar. He felt that we should keep up with the latest developments in science, history, and psychology. Learning the theory and practice of one of the hard sciences could help us in learning to deal with religious facts. Were he living today he would, I am sure, suggest that we know something of the mathematical discoveries of Kurt Gödel, the physics that Werner Heisenberg described in his *Physics and Philosophy*, the psychology of Jung, the biology of Robert M. Augros and George Stanciu in their book *The New Biology*, the sociological studies that Andrew Greeley describes in his study *The Sociology of the Paranormal*, and the scientific theory outlined by T. S. Kuhn in *The Structure of Scientific Revolutions*.

Some Christians are fearful that if they exercise their critical thinking capacity, they will lose or weaken their faith. On the contrary, honest searching and openness to secular disciplines can lead us back to our faith. After all, modern-day scientists and psychologists such as those mentioned above have pointed out truths about spiritual reality that most theologians and clergy have never thought about.

Our minds are God given and reasoning is important, but intellectual thinking about God can be the driest and dullest of attempts to know God. Without the institution and mystical experience theology can become deadly twaddle. However, these other two elements without a well-developed thinking can easily slip into deadly legalism or mere emotional sentimentality.

Relationships with Other Human Beings

Christians who experience the unconditional love of God make other people feel more loved or cared for; Christian religion that does not have this result is a stillbirth. One of von Hügel's most insistent emphases was that we reach out to the poor, the broken, the lost, the hungry, and those in prison. When Evelyn Underhill first came to von Hügel for spiritual guidance one of his suggestions was that she visit the poor in the London slums twice a week.

We cannot love unless we listen. We cannot know anyone until we listen to them, and we cannot truly love another who has not disclosed his or her life to us. The practice of listening to other people, as Douglas Steere demonstrates so dramatically in *Gleanings*, opens us to listening to God. Listening to the God of love who is always waiting for us gives us an example of how to listen to one another. This is love in action. In *Eternal Life*, von Hügel says that the dealing with one another can be aided if we know something of the newly understood dynamics of psychology, but he wrote that this knowledge was not within his competence to describe at length.

Certainly familiarity with the human psyche and reaching out to others do not by themselves constitute mature religion. The logical extension of too much outward relationship with too little critical

thinking, institutionalism, or inner experience is the free-love com-
mune where everyone lets it all "hang out" and ends up by hating
everyone else. The mature Christian life needs all four elements we
have discussed.

Von Hügel wrote that the genuine Christian life is alternation
between inward turning in detachment and outward turning in
attachment:

> the movement of the specifically Christian life and conviction is not
> a circle round a single centre,—detachment; but an ellipse round
> two centres,—detachment and attachment. And precisely in this
> difficult, but immensely fruitful oscillation and rhythm between, as
> it were, the two poles of the spiritual life; in this fleeing and seeking,
> in the recollection back and away from the visible (so as to allay the
> dust and fever of growing distraction, and to reharmonize the soul
> and its new gains according to the intrinsic requirements and ideals
> of the spirit), and in the subsequent, renewed immersion in the
> visible (in view both of gaining fresh concrete stimulation and
> content for the spiritual life, and of gradually shaping and permeat-
> ing the visible according to and with spiritual ends and forces); in
> this combination, and not in either of these two movements taken
> alone, consists the completeness and culmination of Christianity.[6]

Conclusion

The best way to show the wisdom of von Hügel is to quote from
Steere himself in an essay on von Hügel as spiritual guide for Evelyn
Underhill. These two students of mysticism had known each other
since her book *Mysticism* had been published ten years before. Steere
writes:

> He had written her of his appreciation for her great book but had, in
> his inimitable way, after expressing appreciative things about the
> book, gone on to share his uneasiness about her desire to have the
> mystics without the church and her failure to realize that "the
> Church came first and the mystics afterwards." He also was not
> satisfied at the way she had leaned on naturalistic Bergsonian
> intuitionism and on the Vital Thrust (Elan Vital) without any real

weight being given to the historical revelation that had come in Judaism and in the figure of Jesus Christ as the setting in which Christian mysticism could alone be interpreted. Over these intervening years, she had been facing in von Hügel's great book *The Mystical Element of Religion* his own powerful interpretation of mysticism as one element in a living religion, but as being fruitful only when it stood in creative tension to the historical and traditional element and to the intellectual and critical element. There grew up in her a strong suspicion that she needed to rethink her relationship both to Jesus Christ and to the church.[7]

In her mid-life crisis she appealed to von Hügel for spiritual guidance and Steere describes the transforming process that followed:

From the very outset she had made it clear that she felt no call to move toward entry into the Roman Catholic church and that she had in the last months and years been drawn to renew her roots in the Anglican (Episcopal) church where she believed she belonged. Von Hügel, with her as with all whom he touched, believed that persons should never move from their own religious connections unless compelled to do so in a way that they could not resist. The result of this was that in the next few years, from 1921 to the very time of his death in 1925, von Hügel served as Evelyn Underhill's spiritual director and did much to encourage her in a way of thought and a way of life that would release her to interpret the Christian interior life in all of its richness. I have described this process in documented detail in an essay that I wrote, *Baron von Hügel as a Spiritual Director*, that introduced an anthology that I published, *The Spiritual Counsels and Letters of Baron von Hügel*, where I turned to Evelyn Underhill as a case study. I will say here only that in these nearly four years of guiding her, von Hügel helped draw Evelyn Underhill into a Christian accent in which the figure of Jesus Christ became more central to her own prayer life and her world view. Christ became for her the expression of the infinite caring for each soul that pours continuously from the ground of being that is the living God. This might be gathered up in saying, "In Jesus Christ, God came all the way downstairs" to the creation.

God's poulticelike attraction, this continuous siege of each soul and
perhaps of each call by God's transforming love that is so dramatically expressed in the historical appearance of Jesus Christ, is the
ultimate frame in which all Christian devotional life and spiritual
growth can be adequately expressed. Why do I pray? Because God
first loved me into this most suitable response to the divine caring.
What happens when I pray? I become aware of what is already
going on in the universe and I join in its operative redemptive
action.

About 1927 Evelyn Underhill wrote:

Until about five years ago I had never had any personal experience
of our Lord. I didn't know what it meant. I was a convinced
Theocentric, and thought Christocentric language and practice
sentimental and superstitious. . . . I had from time to time what
seemed to be vivid experiences of God, from the time of my
conversion from agnosticism (about twenty years ago now). This
position I thought to be that of a broad-minded intelligent Christian, but when I went to the Baron he said I wasn't much better
than a Unitarian. Somehow by his prayers or something, he
compelled me to experience Christ. He never said anything more
about it—but I know humanly speaking he did it. It took about four
months—it was like watching the sun rise very slowly—and then
suddenly one knew what it was. . . . The New Testament, which
once I couldn't make much of, or meditate on . . . all gets more and
more alive and compellingly beautiful.[8]

The historical, the mystical, the intellectual, and the deep caring
elements in her life merged and she became the magnificently
whole and vital person who helped so many others on their religious
way.

Notes

1. Douglas V. Steere, *Gleanings: A Random Harvest* (Nashville: Upper
Room, 1986), 17–18.
2. Ibid., 16.

3. Ibid., 16.

4. Thomas Kelly, *A Testament of Devotion* (New York: Harper & Row, 1941), 19.

5. Strong and sophisticated support for this point of view has recently been provided by John Polkinghorne in his many books and particularly in chapter 5 of his 1988 *Science and Creation*. Polkinghorne, president of Queen's College, Cambridge, England, is a former professor of nuclear particle physics and an Anglican priest and theologian.

6. Friedrich von Hügel, *The Mystical Element of Religion* (London: J. M. Dent & Sons, 1927), II, 127.

7. Steere, *Gleanings*, 63.

8. Ibid., 64–65.

3

Listening in the Rule of Saint Benedict

DORIS DONNELLY

If you want the truth,
I will tell you the truth:
Friend, listen:
The God whom I love is inside.
—*Kabir, fifteenth-century; version by Robert Bly*

In the beginning was the Word that was the Son, and all the rest is listening the Word into being.

Saint Benedict sensed that the key to human wholeness lay in listening to the Word. Centuries before Paul Ricoeur pointed out the connection between the German words *hören* and *zugehören* ("listen" and "belong to"),[1] Benedict knew that to belong to God meant to listen to God. One who failed to listen, or one who listened to voices other than God's, established an identity elsewhere and could not claim discipleship.

The decisive injunction to "listen" (*ausculta*) opens Benedict's *The Rule*[2] (Prol. 1), and the theme of "listening" threads its way throughout this classic. To read *The Rule* attentively is to sift through wisdom about the need for silence, ways of listening, the ways God speaks, and obstacles to listening that Benedict identifies with characteristic candor and simplicity. We will take a look at each of these areas in this chapter, probing a subject of perennial interest to Douglas Steere. Professor Steere's often reprinted essay "On Listening to Another"[3] has become the centerpiece for any serious study of the phenomenology of listening, and his exposition of listening in the Quaker tradition[4] has provided a legacy that writers and theologians repeatedly mine for insight. Steere has also enjoyed a kinship with the Benedictine tradition and is friend to many (including some contributors to this volume) who have been formed by Benedict's Rule. Choosing to write of listening and *The Rule* seemed to combine the best of two worlds close to Douglas Steere's heart.

Silence

Silence comes first. When the American novelist Tillie Olsen sought a metaphor to describe the depth of women's experiences, she chose as her title *Silences*.[5] The poet Adrienne Rich called one of her collections *On Lies, Secrets and Silence*[6] to tell the same truth as Olsen, namely, that certain important discoveries are made only when there is silence. Isak Dinesen reminds us that "where the story-teller is loyal, eternally and unswervingly loyal to the story, . . . silence will speak."[7] If Dinesen is correct, and Benedict would hold that she is, we can be relieved and grateful that God's story can be heard again and again by each of us, if there is but silence.

Not all silences are the same, of course, and the distinctions established in Leslie Kane's *The Language of Silence* are revealing:

> The dumb silence of apathy, the sober silence of solemnity, the fertile silence of awareness, the active silence of perception, the baffled silence of confusion, the uneasy silence of impasse, the muzzled silence of outrage, the expectant silence of waiting, the reproachful silence of censure, the tacit silence of approval, the vituperative silence of accusation, the eloquent silence of awe, the unnerving silence of menace, the peaceful silence of communion, and the irrevocable silence of death illustrate by their unspoken response to speech that experiences exist for which we lack the word.[8]

Silence in its many forms, some more vital than others, is the place where all effective listening happens. The most important silence in the Benedictine tradition is the inner kind; it kindles the peace that characterizes the monastery* (*RB* 34.5). But inner silence usually presumes an outer silence, and both inner and outer silence is the sine qua non for the life of listeners, whether they be in or out of the abbey. T. S. Eliot's raw caution reflects the Benedictine spirit to its core:

> Where shall the word be found, where will the word
> Resound? Not here, there is not enough silence
> . . . .
> The right time and the right place are not here
> No place of grace for those who avoid the face
> No time to rejoice for those who walk among noise and deny the voice[9]

The Rule would have us believe that the corollary is true: silence invites the word/Word; it forms the "place of grace"; it is without the noise that disables attentive listening; it welcomes the sometimes muffled, inchoate, and/or crystal clear voice of God.

Silence for Benedict provides for Eliot's "right time and the right place." It roots the contemplative life by offering a rhythm that slows things down on the outside so that the inside can come alive. The fluidity of silence gives us access to the depths of the psyche and to what the Symbolists termed *l'état d'âme*.[10] Silence is not a "tuning out" for passive receivers; it is rather a "tuning in," a place to take notice and attend, gradually, to ourselves, to others, and to the Other (*RB* 38.5, 6.6). It is supremely active, exhausting, and demanding in its concentration, yet at the same time, noncoercive and freeing. The peace at the heart of Benedictine silence is not achieved by our own efforts. It is always grace. Silence does not make one holy, but it prepares the ground, as no other resource does, for the path of dying to self which is the *conversatio morum*, the heart of the Benedictine paschal mystery.

The discovery of the self which conversion entails happens only in silence because silence removes props and hiding places. Silence itself hunts us down until we come clean and discover who we are and who this God is who refuses to abandon us when we love ourselves least. Silence plunges us into a severe awareness of our

---

*Note: In this and subsequent chapters, references to monastery and monk include both men and women, as in early Christian usage. Benedict, however, addressed only men, although women's monasteries followed the same Rule with minor adaptations.

naked selves, without defenses and masks.[11] "Speech," on the other hand, according to British playwright Harold Pinter, "is a constant stratagem to cover nakedness."[12] The silence of the monastic tradition enables the struggle of the false self and the true self to happen in a fully relational setting by pledging the support of a community (*RB* 1.4) to strengthen us to face the deceit we camouflage as part of our existence,[13] and by reinforcing confidence that God is always at our side. When we surrender, our capacity to listen expands; the narrow way, after all is said and done, is the right way (Matt. 7:14; *RB* Prol. 48; *RB* 5.10).

In the peaceful stillness of silence, our energy is focused and a power is released to let us move away from our personal agendas and interests and to attend to the call of God. Some call this process "centering," and the word seems particularly appropriate to describe the urgent need we have to find the God within our heart of hearts, at the still point and center of our beings.

Many have spoken of a form of centering in their lives; John-Eudes Bamberger, Thomas Keating, and M. Basil Pennington are especially articulate spokespersons from within the tradition.[14] Even outside the Benedictine (or even Christian) tradition, however, centering is a helpful metaphor. Writing of her experience of solitude and silence in a cabin at the Maine seashore, Anne Morrow Lindbergh describes her life as messy, fragmented, and without a core holding it all together. She uses the image of spokes flailing about wildly without the hub of a wheel to center them as descriptive of the chaos in her life. There is no English word equivalent to what she is living through, she explains, but the German word *Zerrissenheit* comes closest. Literally, it means "torn-to-piecehood," and its antidote is the inner, inviolable core, the single eye that effects balance, no matter what centrifugal forces tend to pull us off center.[15]

In the Christian tradition, the still point is Christ. For Bamberger, centering is "the hidden place of the heart, at the center of our being, the place of encounter between heaven and earth, between God and the human person."[16] The centering process focuses on God in Christ, who becomes a person's emotional equilibrium, reordering things until balance is restored (or achieved for the first time). Centering is also the ability to listen in prayer without resistance because our being has space and silence and is open to discover the

God within. The balancing act is always a process, never accomplished once and for all. Yet, as Bamberger points out: "Unless men and women attain to this center they cannot achieve their full humanity; life is diminished when there is no relation to it, for it is the heart of reality; in fact, it is associated with Paradise."[17]

Ways of Listening

Like silence, listening is done by the outer and the inner ear, and *The Rule* clearly favors the inner one (*RB* Prol. 1). For Benedict, the term "inner ear" signifies the whole person paying attention to what it is that God says. For the contemporary person, it might encompass listening to body language, to the language of gestures, facial expressions, movements of the eye. One is urged to watch, as the contemplative does, and to survey the whole scene. The listening done is by a friend who gives total undivided attention to the other. Ricoeur's comment that "to listen means not founding oneself"[18] comes to mind to reinforce the truth that listening is not a self-serving exercise. Listeners willingly move from center stage and allow the spotlight to fall on someone else.

When the whole person listens, *The Rule* exerts no pressure about what is to be found. God is in charge and will disclose on God's terms and in God's time. The listener's responsibility is to wait in silence and expectation. Vigilance is the virtue. When God speaks, it is just as likely to happen in the quiet bushes as in the earthquake or the tornado. A person must be ready, come what may.

It often happens that listeners hear something for which they were unprepared, and even things they would rather not hear.[19] Lewis Thomas, the prize-winning author, physician, and chancellor of Memorial Sloan-Kettering Cancer Center in New York City, recounts his experience of listening to Mahler's Ninth Symphony late at night. He explains that there was a time he could listen to this music, which evokes thoughts of death, yet remain reassured and at peace. Lately, though, he listens to Mahler not as a solitary, private listener contemplating a single death but rather as an informed adult contemplating the potential nuclear destruction of all humankind. He wonders how the young can bear listening to the music and the news and their messages of possible annihilation. "If I were sixteen or seventeen years old and had to listen to that, or read things like that, I would want to give up listening and reading."[20]

The Rule is prepared for this. It anticipates discoveries we would rather not make and invites us to a depth of listening that must not lead to despair but to hope. Confidently, *The Rule* encourages the monk, and by extension, all of us, to face the truth, to embrace an attitude of humility, and to grow in solidarity with the rest of humanity.[21] "Silence does not pull us away from human beings but instead makes real fellowship possible."[22] In other words, the shared quiet of the community moves us into a rhythm that strikes a balance between acting and solitude. The identification of the monastery as a "school of service" (*RB* Prol. 45) invites the mature monk not only to long for a new world fully enlivened by the spirit of Jesus Christ but also to help that world to come into being. Action and contemplation are two sides of the same coin. Always.

Where God Speaks

While *The Rule* respects a God of surprises who speaks wherever God chooses to do so, it also suggests that once silence is effected in a praying community, it is likely that God will speak through the abbot and through *lectio*, devotional reading.

Listening Through the Abbot

The obvious linguistic connection between *oboedire* (to obey) and *audire* (to hear/to listen to) needs clarification.[23] Like all authoritative guides in the spiritual life, Benedict is aware that obedience is due only to God, but he delineates the role of the abbot carefully so that the abbot is positioned as one who "holds the place of Christ" who "must not teach, or establish or command anything outside the precept of the Lord." In this context, obedience is appropriate because Benedict has carved out an awesome responsibility for the abbot as one who must preach nothing but the gospel to the monks. The monks know that a heavy responsibility rests on the abbot's shoulders; the abbot will be held accountable by *The Rule*, and more important, by God, for how well he discharges his office (*RB* 2.6–7, 2.37, 3.11).

Two of the images Benedict uses to describe who the abbot is and what the abbot does are "shepherd" and "physician/healer." Presumably, in the context of each image an individual monk grows to trust the teaching, direction, admonishment, and/or encouragement of the abbot in his life. And trust is central to listening; one cannot be fully engaged in the process of listening to the message unless one has confidence in the messenger.

What is it that these images do to increase a trust level? From the image of shepherd, the monk learns that the abbot will be held responsible for being a *good* shepherd (*RB* 2.7–10; 32, 39; 27.8, 9; 63.2). It is not axiomatic that every abbot is one. In fact, *The Rule* spells out the difference between good and bad shepherd behavior (*RB* 27.7; Ezek. 34:3, 4), and cautions the abbot in very clear and precise terms about his duty to follow the path of one and eschew the path of the other. That means that the abbot must provide for, protect, care for, and be held accountable for the salvation of those entrusted to him . . . or else (*RB* 64.18; Gen. 33:13). The abbot needs (and is given) a wide berth in responding to many needs and many different kinds of persons, but even with such latitude, the task is daunting. The abbot is hardly excused from the humility expected of all monks; in fact, if he does not lead the way in this area (and this does not overstate the case) there is little hope for the community. Yet it is difficult to imagine that any reasonably integrated adult in charge of a monastery, with all its problems, concerns, and responsibilities would *not* be humble!

The abbot is also asked by *The Rule* to model good listening to others in the community. The writer/composer Paul Williams once wrote on one of his albums, "There are those who listen, and those who wait to talk. This album is dedicated to the listeners."[24] The monastery is so dedicated as well. Thus, the abbot's consultations with the community (*RB* 3.1; compare note in Fry), including its youngest members, need to be genuinely broad based, and these must be experienced by the community as open, honest, truth-seeking, not as proforma occasions with decisions made beforehand or arrived at by a small inner circle.

The abbot who expects to be listened to must be a listener too. And an above-average one at that.

The abbot is also a healer (*RB* 27.2–3, 27.6, 28.2–6).[25] The healing

he effects often flows from the silence, balance, and listening he helps
to encourage in the monastery. Peace is the essence of a therapeutic
environment. Silence and listening serve that peace.

Many years after the first appearance of *The Rule,* Dr. James
Lynch, codirector of the Psychophysiological Clinic and Laboratories
of the University of Maryland, claimed that he had data to support the
therapeutic effects of listening. He reached this conclusion by
studying closely a sample of hypertensive people who used words to
keep people at a distance, who listened defensively, and who acted as
though they were engaged in a contest or a fight rather than in a
comfortable dialogue. Occasionally, when the conversation was dete-
riorating into argument, Lynch tried to show his own vulnerability by
revealing some personal history that caused him uneasiness. He
noticed when he did so that patients, with some consistency, were
able to forget themselves and to listen, even if momentarily, and their
blood pressure invariably fell to levels far lower than they had known
in years.

A group of people was invited to participate in an experiment to
explore this idea further. For twenty minutes, each person was asked
to stare at a blank wall in a relaxed mode. For the next twenty
minutes, each was asked to watch a tank of tropical fish. Blood
pressure was monitored by a computer, which showed that blood
pressure lowered while people stared at the blank wall, but it lowered
even more when people attended to the fish. In other words, involved
attention or active listening was more therapeutic than passive
relaxation.

These studies led Dr. Lynch to conclude that there is an elevation
in blood pressure when speaking and a decrease in blood pressure
when one listens. According to Lynch: "Gradually, we began to see
that when one listens to someone else, one's blood pressure goes
down, sometimes even below its baseline level."[26] Genuine healing of
the cardiovascular system takes place in listening.

The hypertensive patients, however, had a problem. Rather than
listening, these patients appeared to be preoccupied with what they
wanted to say next, and so they were trapped in a vicious circle.
Instead of listening, which would allow a see-saw effect in blood
pressure, the hypertensive did not allow his or her pressure to fall
back to a baseline level, so "that person's blood pressure was

inadvertently set to rise all the higher the next time he or she spoke."[27] For the nonlistener, then, no healing could happen.

The Rule may be unaware of such sophisticated connections, but it certainly recognizes the therapeutic effect of listening. The insistence on silence as central to monastic living and community existence and as conducive to listening, the identification of the monastery as a place of peace, and the significant number of allusions connecting the abbot with healing coalesce to suggest that in his own way, Benedict knew this all along.

Listening Through the Word of God

Benedict also proposes in *The Rule* a total immersion in God's holy and living word (Prol. 9, 16, 24, 39; 64.21). Just as a person learns a foreign language by direct exposure to it, preferably in a country where it is spoken and among people who speak it familiarly as well as by exercising it regularly, so does constant exposure to scripture form the monk. The Word of God, of course, is not a "foreign" language but rather a language that speaks with unerring conviction about who we are as human persons in a created universe. About four hours a day,[28] depending on the season, are devoted to *lectio divina,* a prayerful reading of the scripture, which often in the experience of Benedict led to a transformation.

Listening is the key to transformation—listening very closely, because what one waits to hear is not a collection of words but a call and invitation. Even more than that, one waits to hear the voice; one waits for nothing but hearing the voice of the living God.

The reading to which one listens may be done in silence or aloud; in Benedict's time it most often was done audibly. In those instances, one listened to the "voices of the pages," in what Dom Leclerq refers to as a "real acoustical reading."[29] The connection between *legere* and *audire* is symbiotic. Just as the current colloquial expression "Do you read me?" means "Do you understand me?" or "Do you comprehend me?" so too, for the Rule, the whole person was called to be attentive to the reading so that he or she would "get it," and in the getting be steeped in it and formed by it.

Lectio is a process of growing in a relationship with the God who speaks the word to which we listen. The relationship begins with the actual reading (*lectio*), apparently designed to get our attention focused. Lectio introduces us to the salvation story and tradition into which we will become immersed. We read words—or words are read to us—and we seek to personalize them in the second stage, *meditatio*. This is the occasion for us to mull over the word, to let it soak in and become part of us. The friendship with God is no longer detached; as the word takes root in our beings, we become more attached to that which absorbs us. The friendship deepens. The third developmental stage in the relationship involves a call to respond in prayer (*oratio*) of awe and praise at what we love. The connections between lover and beloved are forged and cemented. Now and in the next stage, we are moved by God's sheer grace into a contemplative (*contemplatio*) stance vis-à-vis the one we love. In our beholding, the detail of the other is revealed, and our heart is penetrated with a depth of love that satisfies our longings as nothing else has been able to do.

The formula of lectio is deceptively simple: read, meditate, pray, contemplate. But it assumes first and foremost a listening heart so that the routing is ensured and so that our journey to contemplation is not detoured. The sign that genuine listening takes place is that we bear fruit by being "words" or sacraments or signs to others, speaking the word to a noisy world in need of experiencing the power of the living word of God.

Obstacles to Listening: "Motion Words" in *The Rule*

When Gregory the Great identified "discretion" as critical to *The Rule,* he related that quality to balance and order in the monastery.[30] When balance and order are disrupted, and the abbot's discretion is eroded, these events can be traced to four behaviors among the monks that are clearly named in the *The Rule*. Each of these behaviors is identified by a particular, descriptive motion word, sometimes onomatopoeic, which destroys the shared quiet of the monastery. The motion words are *gyrating, grumbling, laughing,* and *talking*. Benedict firmly censures these behaviors as injurious to silence, listening, community, prayer, and peace. At the same time, it is true that when the heart is centered, motion is useful. In fact, there is concern in *The Rule* about laziness and immobility (*RB* 4.38). The following comments pertain to "motion words" in a very restricted sense when the heart is derailed and unpeaceful.[31]

1. *Gyrating.* The *Rule*'s brief sketch of "the monks called gyrovagues" (1.10–12) would be even more amusing if it were not for the severe reprimands Benedict issues to those people who jump around from place to place. It is true that the Rule of the Master from which Benedict drew much of his material spends sixty-two verses criticizing these monks compared to two verses in *The Rule.* Nevertheless, the spirit of the gyrovagues in its varied manifestations was intolerable to Benedict.

A look at *Roget's Thesaurus* under the entry that includes *gyrate* contextualizes *The Rule*'s concern for the negative influence of gyrovagues in the monastery. Synonyms for *gyrate* and words associated with it include whir, whirl, swirl, vortex, whirlpool, turbination, dizzy round, cyclonic, tornado, flywheel, rolling stone, teetotum, merry-go-round, wheel of fortune. It would be difficult to miss the point. Any one of these words related to the gyrovague conveys a lack of concentration and an inability to be present to the here and now. Those caught up in such frenzy show no inclination to reinforce a spirit of contemplative love. They do not stay put long enough for the Word of God to sink deeply into their hearts. Simply put, the gyrovague keeps neither exterior nor interior silence and does not possess, even minimally, the disposition to be an effective listener.

The gyrovague also contradicts the principle of stability, which governs Benedictine monasticism (*RB* 7.8, 65; 7.49; 58.9, 17). The stability in question is both of the heart and of the place. In both instances, it is violated by the instability of the gyrovague who moves, haphazardly or intentionally, from the center.[32]

Stability is fundamental to monastic life since it is a statement about commitment, fidelity, steadfastness, and a graced awareness that God is here and now and need not be sought elsewhere. "The man or woman who voluntarily limits himself or herself to one building or a few acres of ground for the rest of life," comments Esther de Waal, "is saying that contentment and fulfillment do not consist in constant change, that true happiness cannot necessarily be found anywhere other than in this place and this time."[33] Gyrovagues contradict these values with impunity.

2. *Grumbling.* Like the gyrovagues, grumblers or murmurers also

trouble the peace of the monastery (5.14, 17, 18; 23.1; 34.6; 35.13; 40.8, 9; 53.18). Characteristically, grumblers do not bear wrongs patiently and they do not tolerate the foibles of humankind with any indulgence. What disables grumblers' ability to listen is that they carry on a perpetual conversion within themselves, which disturbs inner peace with a spillover effect that impedes the peace of the monastery. Unwilling to extricate themselves from their private, selfish negativity, grumblers thrive on creating upset in others and in causing dissension in the ranks. With polished skill, grumblers agitate others to be faultfinders too. Once again, the thesaurus comes in handy: associated with *grumbler* we find: malcontent, croaker, grouser, growler, censurer, complainer, murmurer, faultfinder, scowler, whiner, whimperer.

Would a day ever pass in any Benedictine house when the community is not grateful to their founder for doing his best to reform grumblers or to redirect them to do their complaining elsewhere? When *The Rule* identifies the grumbler as a source of trouble, it exercises an unerring sense of wisdom about the human condition and human interaction. The grumbler sows seeds of discord that undermine the foundation of silence that undergirds the ability to listen.

Those who murmur critically are not seasoned in the virtue of humility, in regarding themselves as unworthy servants, and in allowing another's needs to take precedence. Furthermore, they have not attended to the injunction to be empty of pride and self-will (*RB* 7.5; 7.31–35; 7.51). Grumblers believe intractably that their judgments, opinions, determinations, and views of the world are the correct ones. Nor do grumblers give evidence of a spirit of obedience; they remain stubbornly rooted in their ego-centered preoccupations, chipping away at the foundation of community life.

3. *Laughing*. The third behavior that Benedict finds inconsistent with monastic life is identified by the word *laughter*. Laughter shakes up the physiological and emotional systems and renders a spirit of stillness impossible.

Keep in mind that *The Rule* appears to recognize a distinction between laughter and a sense of humor. A sense of humor has to do primarily with balance, with not taking ourselves too seriously, and with an ability to deal gracefully with the incongruities of life. In principle, *The Rule* is committed to all of these things. Often enough, laughter and a sense of humor go together, but they are not synonymous. This is a wise distinction indeed, for it has been established that many persons who tell jokes, and laugh, and otherwise chortle at funny stories, do not have a sense of humor. Reinhold Niebuhr points out that laughter can (and often does) lead to despair. For Benedict, laughter breaks silence; for Niebuhr laughter breaks hope.[34]

Benedict seems to be aware of laughter that exists apart from a sense of humor and is disruptive of inner peace and the collective quiet of the monastery. According to the thesaurus the word *laughter* is associated with ridiculousness, farce, comedy, buffoonery, frippery, Irish bull, joke, horseplay, snigger, jollity. When Benedict admonishes against laughter, what he has in mind ought not to be confused with the healthy joy of a sense of humor. "Humor is characteristic of the spiritual person," Dom Leclerq commented. "It supposes detachment, levity—in the Gregorian sense of the word—joy."[35]

Joy is a sign of the spirit of God, plain and simple. What Benedict has in mind most explicitly is the one who is given to frivolity, joke telling, laughter at others' expense. None of these activities support monastic communal living.

4. *Talking.* The fourth motion word that concerns Benedict is *talking.* Obviously, nothing contradicts silence more than verbal communication. Talking violates the stillness and the quiet of the monastery. While it is true that one can speak and yet retain an interior stillness, and that sometimes talking is necessary, *The Rule* is working with a law of averages, and that law maintains that the monk who talks will eventually succumb to gossip, slander, idle conversation, and detraction.[36] The simple counsel of *The Rule* is to avoid speech in order to avoid sin. And in order to help temper the desire to talk, Benedict noted that there are times when even "good words are to be left unsaid out of respect for silence" (*RB* 6.2–3). Like many of the entries in *Roget's Thesaurus, The Rule* usually presents talking in a pejorative way: chat, chit-chat, small talk, confabulation, interlocution, conversation, oral communication, discourse, dialogue, tittle-tattle, prittle-prattle, gossip.

It may be helpful to note that when Christian meets Mr. Talkative in John Bunyan's allegory, *Pilgrim's Progress,* he confronts Benedict's greatest fear: a person who knows a great deal *about* God but does not know God. Bunyan confesses in his autobiography, *Grace Abounding to the Chief of Sinners,* that he himself was once a "brisk talker." Perhaps that is why he draws so compelling a character in Talkative, who cajoles any who would hear: "[To] talk of . . . things is most profitable, for by so doing, a man may get knowledge of many things . . . and the benefits of things above." But Faithful sees through the sham and in effect raises the larger question: "Do you *experience* that about which you speak?"[37]

It seems that much talk about God is not the answer concerning how we can better hear God's voice. Instead, both Bunyan and Benedict believe that the way is through silence. Experience has taught them that chatter gets in the way, and they pass their wisdom on to us.

Conclusion

Benedict recognized the inextricable connection between silence and listening. Silence is not merely an absence of noise but also a receptive posture that waits with patience. To that end, *The Rule* encouraged both silence and listening as the preconditions for inner peace and fruitful monastic living. Peace, humility, stability, love, service, and prayer were all wrapped up in attentive listening of the whole person to the living God.

Benedict's wisdom is echoed in the writings of Douglas Steere. The legacies of Saint Benedict and Professor Steere are vital to spiritual growth, to community, and to discipleship. Their insights about listening are basic and wear well as the foundation stone of the spiritual journey.

Notes

1. Paul Ricoeur, *The Conflict of Interpretations* (Evanston, Ill.: Northwestern University Press, 1974), 451.

2. The edition and English used is Timothy Fry, O.S.B., ed., *RB 1980: The Rule of Saint Benedict in Latin and English with Notes* (Collegeville, Minn.: Liturgical Press, 1981).

3. Douglas Steere, "On Listening to Another," in *The Doubleday Devotional Classics,* vol. 3, ed. E. Glenn Hinson (Garden City, N.Y.: Doubleday & Co., 1978), 205–57.

4. Douglas Steere, "Introduction," in *Quaker Spirituality: Selected Writings,* The Classics of Western Spirituality series (Mahwah, N.J.: Paulist Press, 1984), 3–53. This excellent overview of Quaker spirituality provides many insights on the value of listening in the Quaker tradition.

5. Tillie Olsen, *Silences* (New York: Delacorte Press/S. Lawrence, 1978).

6. Adrienne Rich, *On Lies, Secrets and Silence: Selected Prose* (New York: W. W. Norton & Co., 1979).

7. Isak Dinesen, "The Blank Page," in *Last Tales* (Chicago: University of Chicago Press, 1967), 100. She comments further: "Who then tells a finer tale than any of us? Silence does."

8. Leslie Kane, *The Language of Silence: On the Unspoken and the Unspeakable in Modern Drama* (London: Associated University Presses, 1984), from the "Introduction," unpaged.

9. T. S. Eliot, "Ash Wednesday," in *The Complete Poems and Plays* (New York: Harcourt, Brace & Co., 1952), 65.

10. For this insight, which is the basis for Kane's study, see Kane's *Language of Silence,* "Introduction," unpaged.

11. Gordon Rupp's insightful and ecumenical analysis of this condition: "Benedict went away not only to be alone with God, but to learn to live with himself, to listen to the voices of that soul which, as Turgenev said, is as full of murmurs as a dark forest. He not only looked up to a God whose glory is beyond the light of setting suns, but down into his own heart, into that conscience which Augustine says is an unsearchable abyss: not to stare placidly as a man might find his face mirrored in the still waters of a lake, but like Wrestling Jacob of old, in the sweat and agony of that grim fight for which Luther gave the special name 'Anfechtung'." See his article, "St. Benedict: Patron of Europe," in *Church Quarterly Review* 1, no. 1 (July 1968): 16.

12. Harold Pinter, "Between the Lines," speech to the Seventh National Student Drama Festival in Bristol, *Sunday Times* (London), March 4, 1962, 25.

13. Michael Casey connects this to compunction of the heart, effective at "shattering one's deluded complacency . . . [which] is more than disgust at one's personal failure. It also includes an insight into one's heavenly vocation and a desire to be with God." See his "St. Benedict's Approach to Prayer," *Cistercian Studies* 15 (1980): 341.

14. See John-Eudes Bamberger, O.C.S.O., "Defining the Center: A Monastic Point of View," *Cistercian Studies* 15 (1980): 370–88; Thomas Keating, O.C.S.O., *Open Mind, Open Heart: The Contemplative Dimension to the Gospel* (Amity, N.Y.: Amity House, 1986), ch. 3 in particular; M. Basil Pennington, O.C.S.O., *Centering Prayer* (Garden City, N.Y.: Doubleday & Co., Anchor Books, 1980).

15. Anne Morrow Lindbergh, *Gift from the Sea* (New York: Pantheon Books, 1975), 56, 28–29.

16. Bamberger, "Defining the Center," 388.

17. Ibid., 382.

18. Paul Ricoeur, "Naming God," *Union Seminary Quarterly Review* 34 (1979): 219.

19. A related approach to this theme is found in Robin Stratton, "The Ministry of Listening," *Spiritual Life* 31, no. 4 (Winter 1985): 224: "If we truly listen, we will sometimes be asked to absorb more pain than we ever thought possible."

20. Lewis Thomas, *Late Night Thoughts on Listening to Mahler's Ninth Symphony* (New York: Bantam Books, 1984), 166. A point that will be established later in this chapter invokes Jean Leclercq's observation concerning the allied enterprise of "listening" and "reading" *The Rule*. Thomas makes a similar observation here.

21. An intrinsic connection between humility and solidarity is established by Antoine Vergote, "A Psychological Approach to Humility in The Rule of St. Benedict," *American Benedictine Review* 39, no. 4 (1988): 404–29. See esp. p. 413.

22. Henri J. M. Nouwen, *Reaching Out: The Three Movements of the Spiritual Life* (Garden City, N.Y.: Doubleday & Co., 1975), 28.

23. The thoughtful comments by Sandra Schneiders were helpful. See "Religious Obedience: Journey from Law to Love," in *New Wineskins: Re-Imagining Religious Life Today* (Mahwah, N.J.: Paulist Press, 1986), 293, n. 9. The translation that follows on the abbot's role is Schneiders'.

24. Quoted in Robert J. Wicks, *Helping Others* (New York: Gardner Press, 1982), 13.

25. Mildred Murray-Sinclair, O.S.B., in "The Concept of Healing in the RSB," *Cistercian Studies* 15, no. 3 (1980), makes some interesting points. She refers to the abbots' flexibility in prescribing remedies as "Differential Diagnosis" (p. 274) and proposes in addition to the abbot that healing takes place through the Holy Spirit, through the community, and through liturgy.

26. James J. Lynch, *The Language of the Heart: The Human Body in Dialogue* (New York: Basic Books, 1985), 160.

27. Ibid., 161.

28. Jerome Theisen, O.S.B., points out that in the *horaria*, "prime time" is apportioned to *lectio*. See "Personal Prayer in The Rule of Benedict," *American Benedictine Review* 40, no. 3 (1989): 299.

29. Jean Leclercq, O.S.B., *The Love of Learning and the Desire for God* (New York: Fordham University Press, 1960), 19. See also F. di Capua, "Osservazioni sulla lettura e sulla preghiera ad alta voce presso gli antichi,"

Rendiconti della Accademia di archeologia, lettere e belle arti di Napoli, n.s. 28 (1953): 59–62.

30. A fine edition of the work in question is by A. de Vogue (P. Antin, French translator), *Gregoire le Grand: Dialogues* (Paris: Les Editions du Cerf, 1978, 1979, 1980). While scholars maintain that some ambiguity surrounds the phrase *discretione praecipuam,* there is general agreement that it pertains to the order of the monastery, maintained through the gift of discernment, proportion and moderation (see *RB* 64.1719; 70.6). See also Harald Schutzeichel, "The Rule of Benedict as a Guide for Christian Living: II" in *The American Benedictine Review* 39, no. 3 (September 1988): 241–42.

31. While it could be argued that I have taken some liberty here with the connection between "gyrating" and the "gyrovagues," Fry's notes in the *RB* point to similar etymological roots. "Gyrovagues" is a hybrid formation from the Greek *gyros* (circle) and the Latin *vagari* (to wander). See Fry, *RB* 1:12.

32. Ambrose G. Wathen, O.S.B., *Silence: The Meaning of Silence in the Rule of St. Benedict* (Washington, D.C.: Cistercian Publications, Consortium Press, 1973), 36–37.

33. Esther de Waal, *Seeking God: The Way of St. Benedict* (Collegeville, Minn.: Liturgical Press, 1984), 57.

34. "The sense of humor remains healthy only when it deals with immediate issues and faces the obvious and surface irrationalities. It must move toward faith or sink into despair when the ultimate issues are raised. That is why . . . there is only faith and prayer, and no laughter, in the holy of holies." See Reinhold Niebuhr, "Humor and Faith," in *Discerning the Signs of the Times* (New York: Charles Scribner's Sons, 1946), 130–31.

35. Leclerq, *Love of Learning,* 173.

36. The *RB* (6) quotes Prov. 10:19: "In a flood of words, you will not avoid sinning" and Ps. 14 [15]:2–3: "Do not listen to slanders against one's neighbor" (Vulgate) to reinforce this insight.

37. John Bunyan, *Pilgrim's Progress* (New York: Pocket Books, 1957), 74, 81.

4
Spirituality in the Dialogue of Religions

MARY LOU VAN BUREN

It has long been my belief that if we want to know and understand a people, we should join them in their worship, in their liturgies, in their rites and rituals. Tune in as you would to the voices of the natural world. Walk gently through the unfamiliar. Watch and listen. At one or more points it is possible that we may "see" that reality common to us all.

Points of Meeting

Spirit is the first point of meeting. The mystics of every tradition recognize their home in the depths of the spirit and together bask with joy in the oneness found here. Going down, they come to that common source knowing that this is that from which all things spring. Their attempts to describe such an experience may finally result in systems of theological and philosophical thought, in symbols and art. But for the mystic these are always secondary to the reality and are powerful only in so far as they are themselves transparent in pointing to that reality.

Henry P. Van Dusen, a well-known ecumenist in his day, tackles in his book *Spirit, Son and Father* a theological understanding of the Christian faith in the light of the Holy Spirit. Seldom, if ever, do Christian theologians begin with the third Person of the Trinity. Van Dusen has said that "the Holy Spirit is not only the point of contact between Christianity and other faiths" but within Christianity it is the crucial issue.[1]

Today *spirit, spirituality,* and *spiritual* are words commonly used in a variety of contexts. Here *spirit* is used specifically in relation to that which is holy. Rabbi Abraham Heschel has brought us back again and again to the realization of the holy. I have heard it said that Judaism will never let us forget the holiness of God. When we know the holy, we know that everything can be or become holy.

In an ecumenical prayer service of Christians at the Cathedral Church of St. John the Divine in New York City, Bishop Paul Moore greeted Brother Roger Schutz, prior of the Taizé Community in France. In the course of doing so, he shared the observation that holy moments make holy places and that that was one of those moments. Sanctifying takes place when the holy fills a time, a place, a thought, a deed. It is precious indeed when this happens. Light and life flood our being and all things become possible.

In all religious traditions attempts have been made through rites and rituals to sanctify places and times and deeds in recognition of holy moments. From tradition and culture these take different forms. It is my conviction that they are diverse expressions of a common reality. This does not necessarily mean they are all understood or are perhaps even compatible. It may be that expressions of different traditions and cultures seem contradictory. We need not back off, however, for the very differences may indeed reveal another facet of truth. Who is to say definitively how God lives and moves? In Christianity we hear the admonition to welcome the stranger lest perchance God is sending us a message. The "strange" is not a priori "bad." It may have possibilities of revealing a truth.

A second point of meeting is our *common humanity*. Many groups and movements are formed of very diverse people around common human concerns. These movements at their best lift up cares, concerns, rights for the least and marginalized among us, for these cares, concerns and rights are not for a few but for all. We are one in our humanity—for better or for worse.

Communities of people have organized their common life usually but not always around systems of religious values. I should like to focus at this point on what the Dalai Lama of Tibetan Buddhism shared with us in an address he gave at Cornell University in the spring of 1991:

> We are born with compassion and love. This is a human quality, not religious, and comes before religion. There is gentleness in basic human nature. Human affection comes from a good heart. And so there is universal responsibility not only for human beings but for all sentient beings. Mental attitude is key to calmness of mind which creates peace and a friendly atmosphere. Anger is an enemy within us, for, when we are angry, that anger finally is destructive to us. Genuine tranquillity is the foundation of genuine peace.

And what about evil? There is much evidence to indicate there is evil as well as goodness in our common humanity. It is important however, to identify the struggle between good and evil as a battle in spiritual life. There is a saying that we become what we give our attention to. I should think that attending to the depths of the spirit and embracing the holy would tip the scales toward the stirring up of the compassion, love, and goodness within us.

Our common humanity is a point of meeting, whether we come together out of desperation to confront the evil rampant among us and to re-create a global community or to savor the communion we know when we are at one with one another in compassion and love.

A third point of meeting is our *connection with nature*. Human beings are made of the "stuff" of the earth, stardust, and we are connected to and dependent upon other forms of life on this planet as well as to the planet itself. We are a part of one another. A distortion within Christianity occurred when humanity separated itself from the rest of creation. "Dominion" became "dominant" and manipulative. I think the dualism comes through thought and will, not from experience. Within the Judeo-Christian tradition is a wide stream that gives expression to the wholeness of creation, indeed the cosmos. While human beings can and do create and are creators, they remain creatures.

Many groups are coming together in these times when concerns for the earth and every bit of life in and on it have reached a crisis. Save the Earth, Save the Planet, Save the Rain Forests, Have You Hugged Your Dog Lately? are samples of bumper sticker messages that regularly cross our vision. The pollution of waters and air are pushing us to survival tasks.

The dimension of spirituality at this meeting point embraces, yet brings a fullness to the specific concerns as such. Abraham Heschel's "A Song for God" points to this fullness.

> He who chooses a life of utmost striving for the utmost stake, the vital, matchless stake of God, feels at times as though the spirit of God rested upon his eyelids—close to his eyes and yet never seen.
>
> He who has realized that sun and stars and souls do not ramble in a vacuum will keep his heart in readiness for the hour when the world is entranced.
>
> For things are not mute:
> the stillness is full of demands, awaiting a soul to breathe in the mystery that all things exhale in their craving for communion.
>
> Out of the world comes a behest to instill into the air a rapturous song for God, to incarnate in stones a message of humble beauty, and to instill a prayer for goodness in the hearts of all men.[2]

This leads us to a fourth point of meeting, that of *conscience*. There is a sense of knowledge of good and evil, right and wrong, that which leads to life and the sublime, and that which leads to destruction and death. Religious traditions "line out" what makes for good and evil, for life and for death. Obedience or disobedience to the rules of thought and behavior bring about particular consequences. Nothing is lost in God's economy. As individuals and as communities and nations we contribute to that which brings forth life or to that which brings forth death.

Recently I was rereading the words of God to the prophet Amos, "See, I am setting a plumb line in the midst of my people Israel; I will never again pass them by" (Amos 7:8b, NRSV). There is a "plumb line" in all religious traditions that is a reminder to "true up" to that which *really is*, to the way life was set out to be, to the way it can be lived in harmony and communion. It is we whose depths are plumbed and tested.

The contribution of spirituality to the dialogue/conversation of religions is to draw forth the holy of each tradition, lift up our common humanity and our connection with all of creation, and point to the "plumb line" quickening our collective conscience.

Points of Struggle

Together with points of meeting there are points of struggle. These are the greater challenge. Some are negative and some are positive.

Exclusiveness and exclusion are the downside of uniqueness and particularity. The "ins" and the "outs," the we-they syndrome, drawing the lines and parameters in terms of what "we have and you don't," need to be overcome if there is to be any mutual sharing and mutual enlightenment. There is a fear of syncretism or watering down. Then comes the tendency to think either that we are all heading toward the same place anyway or our way is *the* way, take it or leave it, and so live and let live. There is a fine line between being nourished in a tradition and believing it is the one and only way for everyone. Some traditions lean in this latter direction more than others, and some people by personality lean in this direction more than others.

It is difficult not to feel insecure. In our *insecurity* there is a grasping for what can be counted upon, the unchangeable, "firm ground." Sometimes heads leave hearts and hearts leave heads, and thinking and feeling are not integrated but separated. When we have, however, plumbed the depths and reached the deep underground spring through our own tradition there is a security that surpasses all securities. Elusive though it sometimes may be, if it has been known, it will never be forgotten. Sometimes it is meeting others of different paths that enables us to touch this wellspring more deeply. We can say with the Christian mystic of the fourteenth century Julian of Norwich: "All is well. And all shall be very well."

Coupled with insecurity is *ego need*. The need for continued affirmation and/or to "lord it over" everybody intimidates and blocks an easy flow of give and take. Egos need searching and tending, so that each can grow toward health rather than illness.

The will to power is related to the foregoing barriers. There can be a great need to "be in charge" and to run everything. To be able to exercise one's will over others is a great temptation and, if given in to, results in the dominating of others in having one's way. The will to power is something to be monitored within oneself. The will to dominate and to gain power in an interreligious gathering is not only to ignore but to shut out the Presence that draws us together.

The interrelationship of the above barriers finally peaks in *idolatry*. I/we *know* and I/we know *best*. The place of God, Spirit, Creator has been usurped. My/our tradition, theology, philosophy, and way of doing things finally cuts us off from others, from the Mystery, Source, and creative possibilities of life and at last from ourselves, for we have lost all sense of who we are, whose we are, and where our place is. John of the Cross of the sixteenth century, another Christian mystic, reminds us that if we think we know the Way, surely we do not.

These difficult barriers, which are points of struggle, can be watched, kept in check, and worked through by parties to the engagement beforehand and during encounters with people different from ourselves. The following points of struggle can keep the above in check and bring a positive influence to bear on the kind of sharing that issues in mutual enlightenment.

We come with our *integrity* when approaching the Mystery. We stand with integrity in the Presence. In our integrity we share with others. Singleness of heart is the key to breakthroughs. "A good heart, human affection, compassion and love," says the Dalai Lama. "Love the Lord your God with all your heart, mind, soul and strength and your neighbor as yourself," says the Torah. "Love one another as I have loved you," says Jesus the Christ. And from the nineteenth-century Christian Søren Kierkegaard, "Purity of heart is to will one thing." Here is integrity, and it is recognized when one is present to another.

There is a need to bring *fresh insights from one's own tradition to current times*. Conflicts continue to be discovered between what we experience and what tradition says. These conflicts surface in intellectual thought and verbal expressions, in practices and institutionalizations. Some years ago while he was at the University of Chicago, Ross Snyder spoke of the necessity of being grasped by the "pulse of tradition." Spirituality lifts into bold relief the pulse, the heartbeat. Even though the outward body of theological, philosophical thought and religious practices may gradually be renewed through the course of history, the life-sustaining heartbeat continues.

The *courage really to listen* is indeed a point of struggle, particularly for most people affected by present Western values. The importance of communication is focused on the communicator, with not much concern for the receiver, except as that receiver may be convinced. This classical problem of missionary-minded religions must be overcome if respectful dialogue is to occur. So experience and tutoring in the art of listening, for its own sake and not for manipulative purposes, is hard to come by, except in the spiritual paths of religious traditions. To still the mouth, body, mind, and heart in order to be attentive and expectant is a necessity or the point is missed. Douglas Steere's "On Listening to Another"[3] and *On Being Present Where You Are*[4] are jewels luring the reader to want to listen and to learn to be present to another.

Hand in hand with the courage to listen is the *hospitality of mind and heart,* the willingness to create the space to welcome new or different thoughts and a variety of human experiences. Henri Nouwen has spoken helpfully on this in his book *Reaching Out*.[5] Hospitality is a readiness, a welcome and provision for the needs of the guest, known friend, or perfect stranger. Simplicity, fearing no loss, and offering what one is and has, spiritually and materially, are marks of genuine hospitality. There is a hospitality among many of the poor of the world that surpasses imagination. I dare say they are within or influenced by the "pulse" of the great religions of the world.

Humility probably sums up these positive influences at points of struggle. Freedom from pride and arrogance puts us in the stance of receptivity. Tenderness and mercy soften our brittleness. We can bend without breaking. Knowing my place and where I stand, I can be open and resilient to hearing you share with me how things are and look from where you stand. And without arrogance I have a responsibility to share from my view what will be helpful to others or contribute pieces to the puzzle. To sort out the needed key points to enrich the dialogue or conversation requires some preparation ahead of time and discernment on the spot. Douglas Steere's *On Speaking Out of the Silence*[6] gives good counsel here. While this was written for the vocal ministry in the unprogrammed Meeting for worship in the Society of Friends, this guidance and the learnings from it can be transferred to other occasions.

So we have to struggle against negative influences and for positive influences to make fruitful any dialogue of religions. The knowledge, practice, and experience of these struggles are good "work outs" for the muscles of spirituality.

Meeting at the Crossroads

Greeting one another comes to mind at once. When Mother Teresa arrived in Taizé to meet with Brother Roger, they went first to the church to pray. They greeted each other by entering into silence and were together before the holy and eternal Presence. To know we are standing in and before the Presence when we greet one another is a contribution of spirituality to the dialogue of religions. In *To Meet at the Source, Hindus and Quakers*, Martha Dart has quoted Gerald Kenway Hibbert, who in 1924 said, "The mystics of the world everywhere join hands."[7] The people of prayer who have touched the deeps of their own traditions seem to be the "glue" that keeps us from completely breaking away from one another.

I have heard the story told of a Christian minister preaching on "Love your neighbor as yourself." He developed his points around the idea of the need to love ourselves before we can love our neighbor. At the close Rabbi Heschel approached him and commented that he found his sermon interesting, but he had always understood the text to mean my neighbor *is* myself.

Hindus expect God to come to them in others. Mother Teresa sees the face of Christ in the face of each person. Howard Thurman concluded a lecture on Meister Eckhart with the point that there is within every person a *core* (not unlike the Quaker view, "There is that of God in everyone") and that it is the business of human beings for "core to salute core." This is the greeting of which I am speaking when we meet at the crossroads.

Greeting with *affection* is a qualitative dimension. It is as if we were greeting a relative. Close or distant, there is a family connection among relatives and we are glad to see one another. Sometimes this affection is more spontaneous at the outset and cools as we get to know one another better. On the other side of tough times, having gone through deep waters together, hammering out, better yet clearing the way, to Truth and discovering together what is really *real* . . . affection deepens.

We meet with an *appreciation* for one another. Within this appreciation there is a spark of anticipation. What are the surprises in store? What will come of our meeting? What new possibilities will be let loose? What will surface in this fabric of life which until now has not been brought forth? Will we be diminished or will we be enhanced? Will we see Truth or will we cherish our opinions? Will there be a "hardening of the categories," a Steere expression, or will they be opened up to reveal the Light?

Exchange and acceptance of another's gifts is kin to *sharing as offering*. Spirituality brings this quality to the meeting. Sharing as offering is giving and receiving from the whole of one's being. The mite and the riches are received equally. It is the totality of the giving and receiving that makes it more than it first appears. It is in the spirit of giving what one can and will and the fullness of receiving with thankful hearts that the gifts flower and are multiplied. And we are not the same, not what we were. We are quickened, renewed, re-created. We know again that the Spirit that moved across the face of the earth, the Spirit known by Christians in the person of Jesus Christ, who revealed that God loves the world, is still moving universally.

Meeting at the crossroads can be a collision with casualties or a careful greeting of "core saluting core." Greeting with affection and appreciation and sharing as offering are signs of a genuine meeting.

A Call for Help and Signs of Hope

The times are calling for meaning. Many routes in the search for meaning lead to dead-ends or distortions that cut off, separate, divide, and hurt the body of God's creation. Religion can be and has been made into the worship of evil and the demonic. There is no holiness there, and this discussion is not referring to that kind of religion. Only the Creator of all that is, the One who does not leave us without illumination or revelation is worthy of our devotion, worship, and loyalty.

There is one God and his name is Allah, says Islam. There is one God who is revealed in Jesus Christ, says Christianity. The Lord our God is one Lord, says the Shema of Judaism. The Way of the Buddha, the Enlightened One, is the way to Nirvana. The Pure Mind, the pure spirit within, breaks forth in comprehensive Presence in Hinduism. The Great Spirit of Native American spirituality is the One to whom all gratitude and thanksgiving belong. The concreteness of African spirituality reveals dependency upon the Source of the beauty and fecundity of their lands.

There are variations and diverse religious expressions within each of these great traditions. There is no question, however, that at their core the intent and focus is upon the Source, the Creator, the life and death of creation, particularly human life and death, and eternity. Time and space are held within eternity, and therefore to discount this larger context is to cut ourselves off from life.

To speak of spirituality in the dialogue of religions without relating it to the times in which we live would be incomplete. So much of what we know tempts us to despair of any possible breakthrough from this larger context into our present reality.

Hope is a way out of despair. When things get so bad that the only way is "up," then hope is a reality. Human destruction of one another has not been enough for us. Our greed and willfulness and selfishness have reached to the life that sustains us. Mother Earth, her soil, water, and air, are rumbling to get our attention. A sickness permeates us. Perhaps it takes all this for us to grasp the situation and to see where the responsibility lies. Imperatives for not only human survival but survival of many other forms of life confront us.

Some have seen and are giving us signs of hope: the re-recognition of Spirit within and pulsing through all of life; the quickening of conscience; the growing concern and care for the whole of humanity; the coming together around ecological and planetary crises and concerns. There is a breaking out of tradition's restraints, on the one hand, and the need for limits, meaning, and direction on the other. Individuals, small groups, and large groups are taking initiative to express in concrete ways care and concern for one another, the earth, and a new way of living in spite of human greed for power and possessions. There is the discovery of joy in simplicity, in the ordinary newly perceived; there is growing appreciation and respect for the rhythm of life; and there is the imperative to take responsibility and focus resources of every kind on the task at hand.

One major initiative is a forum of parliamentarians and religious leaders from across the world that began in 1985 in Oxford, England. At the meeting held in January of 1990 in Moscow, James Morton, Dean of the Cathedral of St. John the Divine in New York City, said in the opening address, "As long as we believe we are met here only as humans, set apart from the rest of Creation, we are part of the problem. A solution begins only when we invite nature herself into our hearts, minds, souls, even our words this week. . . . We are met here as Creation reflecting upon itself, its glory and its needs. That's who we are. Not humans in a conference room."

Scientist Carl Sagan and twenty-two mostly American colleagues said environmental problems "must be recognized from the outset as having a religious as well as a scientific dimension. . . . Efforts to safeguard the planet and cherish the environment need to be infused with a vision of the sacred."

The premises of "The Moscow Declaration" were plainly stated. "The environment that sustains life on Earth is in peril. Human actions are responsible. . . . Poverty and environmental destruction are insidious partners. . . . Our loyalties must go beyond narrow frontiers to all life. . . . We must find a new spiritual and ethical basis for human activities on Earth."

There is a call to the religions of the world to bring their contributions of spirituality to the planetary life we share. It is a responsibility not to be ignored.

Into the Future—A Life of Thanksgiving

The Spirit brings new life on the wings of thanksgiving. Gratitude for truth as it is shared in the living out of the depths and core of each tradition will enrich, inform, mutually illumine, and animate the global community that is in the making. The dimension of spirituality in the dialogue of religions will bring openness, gentleness, and an eagerness for harmony, community, integrity, justice, and peace.

The way jazz musicians play together is instructive. They play with and to each other, bringing their artistry to the improvising moment. Each takes a turn while the others watch and listen, and then at the right moment they slip into playing together. The delight of the creative moment, the laughter and the applauding of one another spills over into the audience. I have been in an audience that itself rose to its feet while increasing its appreciative applause and then sat while its applause subsided, over and over again, as part of the musical dialogue. Each builds on the other. Each is unique. In solo and in company they make music.

I was a student at Union Theological Seminary in New York at a time when the Robert Shaw Chorale rehearsed at the seminary. The seminary community had the opportunity to sing Bach's B Minor Mass under Robert Shaw's direction, the first half one year, the second half the next. For two full evenings each time about three hundred singers and an orchestra of Juilliard School of Music students were immersed in this great sacred music. As the musicians played the opening measures of the *Et Incarnatus Est* the baton beat them to a halt. The words of the director rang out, "You're playing as if you can put your finger on God! You can't! You can only aspire . . . !"

In our aspiring in the dialogue of religions let us make music together to delight, to heal, and to let loose the life that is waiting to be born.

Notes

1. Henry P. Van Dusen, *Spirit, Son and Father* (New York: Charles Scribner's Sons, 1958), 84.

2. Abraham Joshua Heschel, "A Song for God," in *I Asked for Wonder, A Spiritual Anthology*, ed. Samuel H. Dresner (New York: Crossroad, 1983), 4.

3. Douglas V. Steere, "On Listening to Another," in *The Doubleday Devotional Classics*, vol. 3, ed. E. Glenn Hinson (Garden City, N.Y.: Doubleday & Co., 1978).

4. Douglas V. Steere, *On Being Present Where You Are*, Pendle Hill Pamphlet 181 (Wallingford, Pa.: Pendle Hill Publications, 1967).

5. Henri J. M. Nouwen, *Reaching Out: The Three Movements of the Spiritual Life* (Garden City, N.Y.: Doubleday & Co., 1975).

6. Douglas V. Steere, *On Speaking Out of the Silence* (Wallingford, Pa.: Pendle Hill Publications, 1972).

7. Martha Dart, *To Meet at the Source, Hindus and Quakers* (Wallingford, Pa.: Pendle Hill Publications, 1989).

5

Action and Contemplation: Two Ways Toward the Ultimate Reality

JEAN LECLERCQ, O.S.B.

From its very beginnings, Western Christianity has experienced an intimate tension between the temporary condition of each and every human being in this world and humankind's final state, the realization of which, at the end of a long progression, is epitomized in the word *eschatology*. Within this tension, contemplation represents the ultimate goal, while action often signifies the means of reaching it. Because this condition has always been intertwined within a history, however, we may not speak of it abstractly, by merely alluding to the past. The range of issues involved here results from a long and rich tradition.

The evolution of that tense relationship between contemplation and action was complex and paradoxical: more often than not, great men and women of action wrote the most persuasive treatises about the contemplative life, and, vice versa, the people who chose the contemplative way of life accomplished the most far-reaching deeds. The history of this meandering rapport is a rather long one to recount: over twenty centuries of happenings in the institutions and the spiritual world of the West. One may attempt, however, to trace it back to its roots by concentrating on a few periods endowed with symbolic significance; these periods, moreover, became normative for the present-day Christian outlook upon the contemplative and the active life-styles.

In the philosophical and religious traditions of the Greco-Latin West, contemplation, from the literal significance of gazing upon or *theoria,* came quickly to signify a whole spiritual attitude: the state of peace in the total human being that enabled, furthered, and sustained this gaze. Action, in its turn, primarily signified not the outward movement of making or causing to happen anything exterior to us but an interior movement: a training of the mental capacities—that is, of understanding, reason, and of creative love—and hence of the highest human power destined to produce changes in the human environment. In the Christian tradition, it meant particularly such action as would unite humankind to God, liberating thus their whole capacity for love, including their contemplative powers.

Ancient World

In the Greek philosophical tradition, continued by the Latin, the dilemma "contemplation-action" has been expressed in a series of words of which the most typical, by a play of assonance, is that which in Latin opposes the terms signifying leisure, *otium,* and its antonym, *negotium,* consisting of the negation of the first, *neg-otium.* We might venture translating these terms as "busiless" and "business." The word *leisure,* like every other word, is ambivalent: it may evoke a state of freedom, free time, but also inaction, laziness, and the facile, licentious pleasure used to while away time without filling it, leaving it void. This is the lowest meaning. The highest suggests freedom for a useful purpose. This very busy leisure led to the construction of a paradoxical expression: *negotiosum otium.* This sort of leisure lies halfway between inertia and undue haste; it is a fruitful leisure consisting in a certain relaxation of the mind as it refuses to be entirely taken up with immediate worries, with business; it is an open, disinterested time that leaves scope for an interest in truth, for ideas, and for humankind.

On the level of the organization of society, these various elements were reflected in early ancient Greece by a traditional contemplative distinction between three states of life: the "theoretical" or contemplative life, the "practical" or active life, and the "luxurious," the latter in fact a distortion of the contemplative, or misused leisure. Each person, more or less consciously, chose one of these three forms of life, adopting its values and its specific occupations. The theme appeared among the ancient lyricists, the pre-Socratic schools of thought, and in Pythagoreanism; Plato, Aristotle, and then the Stoics elaborated what we might call a sociology and psychology of these states, situating them in the city life, connecting them with the different faculties of the soul, the different professions or crafts, and even with different political institutions. The dilemma gradually came to be expressed in terms of an alternative: contemplation versus politics; or, Which is preferable, the search for wisdom and knowledge or the exercise of authority?

With these sociopolitical overtones and their ensuing implications for everyday human life, the question was passed on to the Latin philosophers—Cicero, Seneca, and Pliny. Cicero gave preeminent place to leisure without entirely denying the value of involvement in public affairs. It was he who coined the formula *otium cum dignitate,* denoting leisure truly worthy of humankind. Seneca endowed it further with subtle moral and psychological overtones: inner pacification, detachment from the pleasures of the flesh or futile occupations. In the next generation, Pliny allied concepts inherited from Cicero and Seneca and conceived of leisure as mainly the study of letters, a noble endeavor, if anything, but unfortunately a privilege of only a few wealthy persons; this preference betrayed the general scorn for manual work typical of the economy of slavery.

Concurrently, a biblical notion—the Sabbath—joined and mingled with these philosophical ideas; it was considered not merely as the day when people rested from all save strictly necessary labor but also as a propitious time for activities pertaining to worship.

Christianity emerged from and grew within a cultural and religious milieu influenced by the trends inherited from Greek and Latin philosophers and from Jewish tradition. But very early on, we notice a real "conversion" of terms and ideas: words that had served to convey Greco-Latin or Jewish wisdom—for Judaism itself had been partly hellenized, at least in its terminology—came henceforth to signify realities of a quite different order. Profane facts came to be translated into sacred ones, conforming to the new religion that had as master and model Jesus Christ and to which an uninterrupted lineage of writers and thinkers were to assure continuity and expansion.

The Gospels propose the perfect model of this conversion of meanings—Jesus of Nazareth. Preceded by John the Baptist—himself a contemplative, for it is in the solitude of the desert that he receives his message—Jesus spends only three years of his earthly existence in public life; all the rest is private, hidden, unknown. But even during these three years, the Gospels tell us, he often adopted the attitude of religious leisure, symbolized by evocative expressions: withdrawing, going up to that lonely retreat on the mountain for prayer, sitting, worshiping.

The Virgin Mary is saluted as a "contemplative of the eternal sun" (aeternis soli contemplatrix). Mary embodies the prototype of the contemplative Church, ecclesia theoretica, she who "is constantly hearing the words of Christ," gazing up constantly at him, guessing at his mystery.

One may ask from our modern perspective whether Jesus might have been under stress because of the delicate balance between contemplation and action to be found in his life. The writings are nonequivocal: Jesus of Nazareth was strained, tempted, anguished, but never on account of an oscillation between the two sorts of activity—one exterior, the other interior. Quite to the contrary, he was able to reconcile them. Toward the end of the third century the monks and the fathers of the church built all this into a whole corpus of doctrine. A single name will serve here to illustrate this double evolution, that of a man of genius tributary to two traditions, Augustine. Saturated with the philosophical doctrines of Greece and Rome, he had a lofty idea of leisure, which, for him, consisted in a search after wisdom beginning with self-mastery. From 389 onward, having arrived back in Africa from Italy, he had gathered round him, at Thagaste, a community whose aim he defined in the formula deificari in otio, "to become similar to God through leisure." In a series of writings he circumscribed the sense of these words: to carry out that activity that consists of knowing God, being united to God, and serving God.

But the historical circumstances of his existence also led him to lay emphasis on the active aspect of Christian conduct. He was soon to become a bishop at Hippo, in charge of a community that he not only had to govern but also to instruct. Furthermore, he noticed the existence of marginal, eccentric groups that, though truly fervent, were clearly dissident and that one would be almost tempted to call the "hippies" of the fourth century. Among other manifestations of that "counter culture" was the refusal to work under the pretext that monks had chosen that particular state in order to give themselves to prayer. Confronted with these "deviations," Augustine composed part of his ethical work to point out that the search for contemplation should exclude neither work for a living nor the service of others. On this condition alone could there be any enjoyment of sanctifying leisure.

Augustine's work opened up new vistas in connection with this reconciliation of work and leisure. He was the first to show that the notion of active leisure had its model in God himself, in whom there is no alternation between action and rest, but the two coincide in a creative and tireless eternity. In humankind, there may be succession between action and contemplation, and each of these aspects may become realized to a greater or lesser extent according to the capacity of each person. The supreme exercise of the highest and most intensive of all activities coincides with the instant of the resurrection of Christ when he passed over from the total gift of himself to all persons into the beatifying contemplation from which he continues to be at work in the world through the Spirit whom he sends. The faithful are called to this state of the glorified Christ, and they must already attempt to anticipate it here below, as far as within them lies. A leisure filled with works that lead to God—such is this program, the doctrine of which Augustine had worked out—this is what the monks endeavor to live and in view of which they legislate. This leisure is the enemy of any laziness; a new pair of Latin antonyms is introduced in the Rule of Saint Benedict: *otium* (leisure) versus *otiositas* (laziness). This is a contemplative leisure that can and must be accompanied by the hard labor of ascesis and work, both manual and intellectual. For this fruitful state of vacancy, devoid of any uselessness and vanity, to engender peace, it must be ordered, organized. Therefore, all legislation in ancient monasticism aims at determining the proportion and the rhythm of alternation between contemplation and action, service to others. The lofty mystical ideal gave rise to a realistic and strictly adequate code of morals according to which any evasion from concrete circumstances in the life of individuals and groups is to be shunned; one must resign oneself to this form of pregnant tension that will only be dissolved in the life to come. It is, then, a state of imperfect calm, one that is relative albeit totally oriented toward a full participation in God's eternally active rest.

The Monastic Middle Ages

Of the two "Middle Ages," the first, which extends from the sixth to the twelfth century, was particularly marked by monasticism; the second, stretching from the twelfth century to the sixteenth-century Renaissance, saw the development of a highly differentiated and subtle speculative thinking, but, from the viewpoint that concerns us here, did no more than clothe in theoretical garb what had been lived practically in the preceding era. These periods may be symbolized by the names of two eminent theologians, Bernard of Clairvaux and Thomas Aquinas.

At the opening of the Middle Ages, a mastermind had drawn up the synthesis of everything received from antiquity, and particularly the doctrine of Augustine. This man was Gregory the Great. He excelled at transmitting the Christian tradition to the younger peoples who had invaded and conquered the West in the fifth and sixth centuries. He had led successively the active life of a high lay functionary in Rome and a contemplative life that lasted five years in a monastery he had founded. Called back to the active life by the church, he reached the highest ecclesiastical office at a time when the Goths were still besieging Rome. Ever after, he was to be torn between his own need for contemplation and his government duties. Many a time he gave vent, in his writings, to the sufferings caused by this unsatisfied aspiration. Overcoming this tension, however, he was able to acquire a serenity, transparent in his style, that allowed him to unite his whole being—over and beyond self—in God. He contributed greatly to the clarification in Christian terms of the distinction between the two types of life which, even with Augustine, had retained something of a speculative character. He shows them both to be manifestations of the same *love*. In both instances, it is a matter of working at salvation: one's own, through ascetical and contemplative activities, and the salvation of others, by having them share in the inner peace and the knowledge of God thus acquired. He illustrates his view by means of biblical symbols that were to have a definitive influence on medieval imagination and even on that of modern times. It was a clear and simple doctrine, flexible at that, one that could be easily translated into life by the monks° during these first centuries of the Middle Ages, called "the monastic centuries of the West." But contemplatives were not the only ones to put it into practice. Their writings, the network of organizations they set up everywhere in Western Europe, and the architectural gems that lasted longer than all other buildings accounted for their all-pervading influence.

Monastic life was contemplative in the sense that it gave the first place to the acquiring of the knowledge of God through reading, meditation, and study, as well as prayer, both private and collective. But it was also rich in activities pertaining to ascesis, claustral observances, and in particular work of all sorts—manual, artistic, and intellectual—in every field of culture, from agriculture and medicine to doctrinal reflection and teaching. Monks carried out any job that no one else did, and especially the more difficult ones, those which implied the greatest risks and to which so many contemplatives fell victim. The human requirement for work, and the Christian demand of service to one's neighbor, led them to invent an entirely paradoxical type of economy, which did not aim at production, profit, or accumulation of wealth, but rather tended toward sharing, giving, creating for all an environment where spirituality could blossom.

The evidence of that reconciliation which contemplatives brought about in their lives between action and contemplation is to be seen in the type of economy they promoted not only within their own monasteries and in their immediate neighborhoods but even far abroad. In this connection, one can really speak of a "contemplative economy," a phenomenon that is common to Christian and non-Christian—for example, Buddhist and Hindu—monastic centers.

In a "contemplative economy" the organization of work has to be harmonized with the leisure required for the undisturbed practice of worship and of contemplation, which is to say, it has to be restricted.

° In early and medieval periods the term monk included both men and women. The order of virgins or nuns was attached to churches and was not the same as women monks.

In monasteries, neither work per se nor its end products have an absolute value. There is no profit motive; therefore, work is disinterested. Even more, since contemplation requires a certain distance from society, it restrains the possibilities for exchange and commerce. It also necessitates the invention of other means for the sake of produce. There is need, too, for the organization of those who do not yet possess the aptitude for spiritual leisure; it happened that, around the monasteries, villages and towns sprang up where families could live in the spiritual reverberation of those who, in the cloister, gave themselves up to prayer. It even happened—and this holds true today for some developing countries in the world—that when the contemplatives, for various reasons, had to move, the whole population in the neighborhood also packed up their tents and followed them. Again, monks had to organize communications between the centers of spiritual and economical culture; this led them to build roads, canals, bridges, and hostels and to invent new means of transport and communication.

Numerous monks unwittingly realized the sort of social archetype common to many philosophical and religious traditions and became itinerant preachers. In those places where they took up abode in stable groups, they gathered round them what were known as "societies," "families," "friendships." This whole program, put into words by the founders, the legislators, and the spiritual writers, was not lived flawlessly: there were failings which many a reformer attempted to remedy. But at least the great business was always charity; the constant preoccupation of these groups was to reconcile their solitude with a sense of solidarity and a solicitude that enabled them to go into action for the benefit of other persons. The outcome was the rise of a contemplative type of culture, entirely oriented toward something other than immediate results. What is termed the apostolate of the missionary monastics, or the civilizing work of monks, is in a sense nothing but the overflow of their contemplative life.

Hence a whole new series of paradoxes came to express this astonishing reconciliation. For it was something that was not always easily obtained and maintained; one could say there was even a struggle for this leisure, that one had to take time off for tranquillity, calm, peace, in order to fight a bigger battle. Action and contemplation are always ordered in conjunction with one another, and since effective action is always easier and more encouraging than disinterested contemplation, this last is proposed as being the trophy of a combat; it has to be conquered and its possession is always precarious. As such, it becomes compatible with itinerant, ever peaceful stability; a leisure free from inertia, full of a dynamism preparatory to the salutary activity in works or words.

But from the start of the twelfth century the increasing complexity of economic and social organization favoring the development of urban civilization and the appearance of new forms of work, exchange, and circulation of persons and goods, gradually led to the realization that a group could not do everything, nor reply to every demand. This led to an increasing specialization in the performing of monastic tasks. Some groups devoted themselves more intensely to contemplation; others took a growing interest in the apostolate of good works. At this point we must bring in the great name that symbolizes all this evolution, Bernard of Clairvaux. He was a disconcerting man, all the more paradoxical in that he was head and shoulders above his contemporaries in human and religious culture. He would describe himself as "the chimera of his day," and yet it was he who, in that century, combined the greatest mastery of contemplation with the greatest gifts for action.

For him the function of meditation unfolds in the space between memory and imitation. ("Memor ero . . . recordabor.") Memory is trained in an assiduous reading of the Bible, accompanied by prayer and reflection within the liturgical atmosphere. Liturgical prayer requires absolute concentration, but even outside the liturgy, during secret prayer and during work, the soul must rest in loving contemplation. Upon it, when and if it shall please the Word, it will grant us one of those ineffable visitations that are the summit of Christian experience, the highest act in contemplation, the most sublime nourishment of love.

But Bernard was a member of the Cistercian order, which places much emphasis on work, including manual. He himself was very soon involved in the service of both the church and society: the foundation and animation of numerous monasteries and the reformation of several others; the establishment of an enormous "peace corps" made up of thousands of young knights whom he turned away from

ceaseless local wars whose victims were the poor; the solving of
conflicts between princes, lords, and bishops; the dissolution of a
long-standing schism in the Roman church, opposing an antipope to
the pope; the taking in hand of a badly organized crusade, which in
fact ended up as a failure; the composition in literary style of
numerous writings destined for every possible sort of public; distant
and exhausting journeys. His work is, nonetheless, one long defense
and illustration of the primacy of contemplation. In his last writing
addressed to the pope, a most active person in the society of that time,
Bernard traces a program of "Consideration," that is, of contemplation of God and divine mysteries, that would allow the pope to remain
peaceful and unified in the midst of the responsibilities and worries
that harried him on all sides.

Bernard had solved the conflict by fixing an alternation in his own
life between contemplation and action, as he advised others to do. But
this success might well have provoked just another form of division
had not, in the deepest depths of being, the two manifestations of the
same personality been reconciled by an inner disposition. This
synthesizing catalyst is the ordering of love. Love alone, coming from
God, could moderate and regulate the spontaneous, anarchic drives
of a personality of such richness and strength. The last word is for
unity, a theme Bernard sublimely developed in the "Consideration":
a person no longer divided, torn, strained, but free, open, supremely
available. The person who forgets himself or herself and empties of
self is able to attract, console, enlighten, elevate in every way; the
person who prays reveals the presence of God. His or her action
comes neither from pretensions to influence, nor from any formal
will; it results from a deep conviction within, an abiding interest for
the salvation of the whole world.

This reconciliation between action and contemplation has been
presented by the monastic mystics of the Middle Ages less as the
object of theory than as the fruit of an experience. God is at once the
most active and the most calm being: in God activity and repose
coincide. God is at work in us, and by that fact unifies us, simplifies
and pacifies us. For that reason the contemplation that consists of
resting in God is the highest of all activities, that from which all others
emanate as from some ever-flowing source. The perfect reconciliation of leisure and activity, which was always the ambition of the

ancient philosophers, was seen by Christians to be realized to a maximum in God and in the Christ; a partial realization that was no less real was in all those who shared in Christ's life. This constant progress in faith and the awareness of its content led them to an increasingly precise definition of ideas, symbols, vocabulary; they thus came to distinguish more clearly the activity of contemplation, not only from exterior activity but also from interior agitation. Christian action is an intense and calm activity, similar to the activity that exists in God, of whom Bernard of Clairvaux wrote: *tranquillus Deus tranquillat omnia* (a tranquil God tranquilizes everything).

At the close of this long and decisive period of six centuries, throughout which many Christians had lived in the radiance of monastic example and influence, certain of these Christians accomplished existentially the ideal that philosophers and theologians had previously formulated—the primacy of contemplation over action. Ideally, contemplation was the condition for all action, the source from which it flowed: action, in its turn, was the fruit and the blossom of it. Ideally, they were not separated, but intermingled, in various proportions and degrees, beyond duality or multiplicity. In all simplicity, contemplation was to manifest itself in relationships of *sharing, exchange,* and *welcome:* many acts but one thought; many occupations but one preoccupation: God—contemplated upon and communicated.

The problem with an ideal, of course, is that it is never perfectly attained. Nevertheless, at least in part, little by little, institutions grew up whose sole end was to further the possibility for individuals and for groups to live forms of life more or less specifically inspired by this ideal. And within each group, even if certain members were more contemplative, others more active, all were trying to contribute to the spiritual equilibrium of all the others. Neither in practice nor in theory was there any opposition or clash of identities; there was an attempt at synthesis of the two activities of prayer and service. In the literary field this central attitude was expressed in a symbolism common to many non-Christian and Christian traditions, and in Christianity especially in the hesychastic traditions of both East and West. Let it be said in passing that the expression "Western hesychasm" is quite appropriate, as will easily be grasped if we bear in mind the frequent use of the verb *sedere* (to sit), evocative of the Buddhist *zazen* as well as of the Eastern Christian *hesychia*.

After the Twelfth Century

A great medievalist, M. D. Chenu, has summarized in two sentences the evolution that followed immediately: "The twelfth century had been one of creativity," he writes; "the thirteenth century was to be one of order."[1] And it is true that what had been lived as an experience during the monastic centuries was now to be systematically analyzed by the scholastics—in Paris and elsewhere. What Bernard of Clairvaux and other commentators on the Song of Songs had sung in poetic strains throughout the twelfth century was now to become the subject matter of the various *Summa theologiae*. But underlying this increasingly complex and technical teaching there continued to exist the mysterious tension and reconciliation between the aspiration for pure contemplation and for serving humankind, especially considered under the aspect of service through the spoken and the written word. The preeminence of contemplation was best and most abundantly formulated by the great mystics and thinkers belonging to institutions (specially created for preaching, teaching, and apologetics). Particular mention must be made of the Franciscan Bonaventure and of the Dominican Thomas Aquinas. The latter merits privileged attention both because of the immense influence that was to be his and because his teaching is an astounding synthesis of the whole preceding monastic tradition and the new possibilities for reflective thought introduced into the West by the theories of Aristotle, which had filtered through by way of the Moors in Spain. The final form he gave to his teaching on this point, at the end of Part II of the *Summa Theologica,* is especially worth summarizing. It is hardly possible to grasp the nature of this work, at once traditional and original, without setting it within a personal evolution, for it is the mature fruit of a personal history.

Thomas Aquinas was an alumnus of the Benedictine monks of Monte Cassino, and he died in a foundation of St. Bernard at Fossa Nova. In between times, he never ceased feeding his mind on all that he could find in the way of ancient texts, including those of the Greek Fathers and the Eastern monks. When he wrote of contemplation, he spoke of tradition that he himself had deeply lived before learning and teaching the theory of it. He never sacrificed realities to ideas, or experience to abstraction, even though he did adopt the schema of scholastic discussion and borrowed quite a few expressions from Aristotle. Actually, when Thomas Aquinas drafted the disputed *Questions*, another of his famous works, he was dealing with two series of facts, divergent not only in their origins but also in the conceptual category to which they belonged; it was a discrepancy that he had to reconcile in his own life before doing so in his teaching. He had received from the Bible, the fathers of the church, and monasticism the rich and complex conception, more practical than speculative, that has been sketched in the preceding pages. Along with that, he was also more than familiar with the philosophical thought of Aristotle. This mode of thought allowed particularly subtle distinctions that, though well-defined, risked reducing the religious to something purely rational. Finally, a keen altercation, not without some verbal violence, was opposing the masters in theology of the secular clergy to those who belonged to the orders that had appeared in the thirteenth century, and in particular the Dominicans and the Franciscans, whose members attempted to exercise certain forms of evangelizing activity while maintaining a style of life predominantly contemplative. Thomas set out to justify the latter without, however, condemning the former. He maintained an admirable serenity in the midst of intellectual violence.

The essence of his teaching was drawn from the great witnesses of the monastic tradition. The "authorities" whom he most frequently quoted are, besides the biblical texts, Augustine, the desert fathers, Cassian, Bernard, and, above all, Gregory the Great. By means of different terms and symbols he illustrated the notion of spiritual leisure; the philosophy of Aristotle, though by no means theological, gave him the tools to arrange in an orderly way facts and ideas accumulated before his times.

The most original contribution he made to the interpretation of the contemplative life seems to have been that he defined it by its primary and habitual orientation toward contemplation as an act—which was precisely the way that Aristotle viewed the life of a philosopher. The active life was equally defined by its primary and habitual *orientation* toward action, which molds, as it were, a person's existence and determines his or her manner of living down to the least detail. Thomas placed great stress on the *intention*, on what he called the "ordination" of an existence. He then restated the primacy of contemplation, which he compared to a hill with regard to a plain; both are equally necessary, but the former is more elevated. Contemplation is of higher dignity because it is a limited anticipation of the future human state, of the final and beatific union with God.

What distinguished the teaching of Thomas Aquinas from preceding tradition was that he generalized what previously had been considered as a personal solution and made it into the characteristic of an organized group; he drew up a theory of what hitherto had been a merely practical solution; he institutionalized something that in the past had always been the fruit of personal charisma; he introduced logic into what had so far been mainly a question of intuition. This enabled him to set tradition in a powerfully metaphysical framework, yet he was ever careful to remain faithful to this tradition and to its specific language.

Thomas Aquinas and his followers attempted to institutionalize what had traditionally been individual experience; it was, if anything, a risky undertaking. An evolution followed on this attempt: institutions laid stress on one of these aspects, made it into a life project, and tried to justify the practice in theory. The most perfect synthesis—perfect because at once lived and explained in theory—was to be found at the end of the thirteenth century and the beginning of the fourteenth in one of the greatest philosophical and literary men of genius, Dante Alighieri. In him converged the wisdom of ancient Greece and Rome, the ideals of the gospel, the teachings of the Fathers, and medieval experience. Though involved in politics, he freely proclaimed the primacy of contemplation. In his *Convivio* (II, 4; IV, 17) he showed that the contemplative life, in its most divine form, the one most beloved by God, is the "better part," similar to that chosen by Mary, as the Gospel relates. It allows one to transcend those transitory joys procured by the life of virtue, through ethical and intellectual endeavors. It is contemplation that sets us on the road to absolute bliss. Dante thus echoed the Greek thinkers Plato and Aristotle and then Thomas Aquinas. But toward the end of the *Divine Comedy*, in Song XXXIII of Paradise, we feel him to be in fellowship with Bonaventure and the Franciscan tradition. No wonder it is Bernard whom he chooses to lead him over the different stages from action to contemplation, and over and beyond this to peace and universal unification. Then contemplative knowledge becomes one with love, and love has the last say:

How weak are words, and how unfit to frame
   My concept—which lags after what was shown
   So far, 'twould flatter it to call it lame!

Eternal light, that in Thyself alone
   Dwelling, alone dost know Thyself, and smile
   On Thy self-love, so knowing and so known!

The sphering thus begot, perceptible
   In Thee like mirrored light, now to my view—
   When I had looked on it a little while—

Seemed in itself, and in its own self-hue,
   Limned with our image; for which cause mine eyes
   Were altogether drawn and held thereto.

As the geometer his mind applies
   To square the circle, nor for all his wit
   Finds the right formula, howe'er he tries,

So strove I with that wonder—how to fit
   The image to the sphere; so sought to see
   How it maintained the point of rest in it.

Thither my own wings could not carry me,
   But that a flash my understanding clove,
   Whence its desire came to it suddenly.

High phantasy lost power and here broke off;
   Yet, as a wheel moves smoothly, free from jars,
   My will and my desire were turned by love,

The love that moves the sun and the other stars.[2]

    The following centuries dealt with the rapport between contemplation and action mainly in terms handed down by the preceding tradition; there was, in this respect, little room for innovation. The Flemish and the Rhineland mystics of the fourteenth and the fifteenth centuries and the inventors of methods of prayer during the sixteenth century in Spain and elsewhere all proposed, in their own way, an equilibrium between the facts, whose pattern and perspectives were inherited from the past. In the sixteenth century, Ignatius of Loyola, a most practical man, proposed a formula that, because of its simplicity, acquired universal value. He taught how it is possible in daily life, in the midst of mundane occupations, to attain an attitude that should lead to what he calls *contemplatio ad amorem*. He was himself and he wanted all his disciples to be "contemplatives in action," as his well-known expression put it. But after him, especially among the Spanish masters and then in seventeenth-century France, contemplation came to be identified more and more with high mystical states, sometimes accompanied by somatic manifestations or visions rooted in fantasy; these latter, moreover, inspired a certain amount of distrust. The greatest minds, Teresa of Avila, for instance, gave proof of a magnificent balance, both in their lives and in their teaching. This balance is seen in the way they went about things, a way that is at once actualizing, efficient, and yet spiritualized: a mode of existence that, though demanding in its aspirations, is extremely human. Francis de Sales in the seventeenth century reintroduced the contemplative life into the world of ordinary men and women, while yet letting them take into account the obligations of family and profession. Former mystics had insisted a great deal on "nights" and purifications, on all that was extraordinarily hard and painful in the contemplative effort, but Francis de Sales stressed gentleness, sweetness, even the pleasantness to be found in such an effort. After him many other writers on the subject gave attention either to one or to the other aspect that had been highlighted in the tradition. It was only in the twentieth century that authors began to take an original step toward synthesis, trying to achieve what Allan Watts terms the "incarnation of contemplation."

On the Eve of the Twenty-first Century

The most strenuous effort was put out in the mid-century years by Thomas Merton, a North American who was to give the answer to so many questions raised by his contemporaries before he died accidentally and prematurely in 1968 at the age of fifty-three. Merton was one of those authors who attempted to reply to the two complementary questions: the need for contemplation and the necessity of involvement with the concrete movements of modernity.

To start with, let us mention the stress he put on the *experiential* nature of contemplation and of the contemplative life, and their reconciliation with action:

> Should not the contemplative life be seen in terms of *event* and *encounter* rather than simply as "viewing" and "tasting" of essential love: Is love an *object* or is it a *happening?*[3]

> Is contemplation an objective static "thing," like a building, for which there is a key? Do you hunt for this key, find it, then unlock the door and enter? Well, that is a valid image from a certain point of view, but it isn't the only image.[4]

> The contemplative experience originates from this totally new kind of awareness of the fact that we are most truly ourselves when we lose ourselves. We become ourselves when we find ourselves in Christ.[5]

Modern interpreters postulate even nowadays the necessity for certain persons who devote themselves exclusively to contemplation, though by no means consider them to have the monopoly on it. There is a necessary complementarity in life-style between them and the purely and intensely active personalities. What counts is that each category realize it is not the unique model of existence but only part of the whole complemented by the other part, an interdependence working for the perfect, harmonious development of the whole toward its full stature and function. On each side there must be mutual understanding and an attitude of welcome, solidarity, and help so that every person in both categories can become authentically himself or herself in his or her own right.

The word "contemplation" has come to be applied more and more frequently to every sort of poetic, artistic, aesthetic activity, and even to scientific research. The term evokes any reality that has something enigmatic about it, of a mystery bound up with the very nature of the object of research and with the mode of knowledge that leads to its discovery.

The increase in leisure time resulting from automation offers new possibilities for the use of this free time, which could be time for contemplation in between intense periods of activity. Those whose "specialty" is the correct use of contemplative leisure are bound in duty to educate others toward this by sharing with them their own free time. This should and does happen in every monastic location— those in rural solitude but also more and more those near the towns and in city centers. Where activity is at its highest there should be, within easy reach, contemplative time to spare.

Every normal psychosomatic function, the racing pulse of one's life rhythm, one's thought mechanisms, and, in fact, every form of activity now raises hitherto unimagined problems of psychology and philosophy, but there seems to be a general consensus that a contemplative attitude has proved to be quite compatible with rapid and efficient mental and spiritual activity. Contemplation is not synonymous with slowness, no more than action is with speed.

Concerning this new reconciliation, Western contemplative traditions join hands with other traditions both in Eastern Christianity and non-Christian religions or spiritual heritages. Possibly the dichotomy between action and contemplation that was denounced in the West for the period between our own and that which ended with the seventeenth century is a typically Western problem, as sometimes has been said in Asia. Possibly the poetic sense and its accompanying potential for synthesis is stronger in civilizations that pay less heed to rational distinctions, speculatively clear in themselves but threatening irretrievably to divide reality.

It is useful now to quote from the book *Contemplation in a World of Action,* by Thomas Merton, for in it we find mentioned every aspect of the question, the dilemma, as outlined above.

Aware as he may be of the psychological and social roots of this dilemma, Merton is affirming the continuity of the tradition in deriving the one from the other:

> I am talking about a special dimension of inner discipline and experience, a certain integrity and fullness of personal development, which are not compatible with a purely external, alienated, busy-busy existence. This does not mean that they are incompatible with action, with creative work, with dedicated love. . . . Traditionally, the ideas of prayer, meditation and contemplation have been associated with this deepening of one's personal life and this expansion of the capacity to understand and serve others.[6]

He is really addressing the younger generations and warning of the dangers of immature immersion into a spiritual passivity:

> The mystique of humility and contemplation is good only for those who have an identity which they are capable of surrendering as though it were a nothing, in exchange for the "all" of God, in which they too are found and recovered, with all the world besides. To the immature man for whom the accession to full identity is too difficult a step, a role of passivity and anonymity, a laudable and highly respectable "nothingness" can become a very convenient evasion.[7]

More than anyone else he was aware of the necessity for sharing this particular mystical experience with that of other traditions:

> Nevertheless the classics of monasticism and contemplation are there to be reinterpreted for modern readers, and above all the Greek and Russian (hesychast) tradition can infuse a new life into our rationalist Western minds. Oriental ways of contemplation (Zen, Yoga, Taoism) can no longer be completely neglected by us. Sufism and Hassidism have a great deal to say to monks because of their explicit or implicit Biblical content, and because they are so closely related to a monastic type of spirituality. (Hassidic and Sufi communities are not strictly monastic in our sense, but very interestingly provide a monasticism for people "in the world but not of it.") Modern psychoanalysis, social anthropology, comparative religion, some schools of philosophy, also have much to contribute to rethinking monastic discipline. Contact and communication of monastic communities among themselves, dialogue with one another and with other groups, scholars, psychoanalysts, Zen People, hippies, etc., can be of great importance for monks today.[8]

In the final analysis, it behooves love to unify the two antithetical aspects, that Christian love which is personal and intersubjective, rather than diffuse and pantheistic. The source of any sanctified activity in the world resides in this free openness of love (and this last quote rejoins the truly Augustinian "motto"):

> If contemplative love is some*thing* which one acquires or receives

in secret and jealously preserves from contamination, then one can build walls around it for safekeeping. But if contemplative love is a response to some*one* who is supremely free and whose "thoughts are not our thoughts, whose ways are not our ways," then we cannot really pin Him down to purely predictable relationships. We have to be "open" in the sense that we are ready and available in all possible situations, including those of human encounter and exchange. Christian love, including contemplative love, starts from the basic realization that those who are unable to relate to others in a valid human encounter are also handicapped in their relations to the encounter with God.[9]

Notes

1. M. D. Chenu, *2000 ans de christianisme* (Paris: Les Editions du Cerf, 1975), 64.

2. Dante, *The Divine Comedy*, trans. Dorothy Sayers (Harmondsworth and Baltimore: Penguin Books, 1950).

3. Thomas Merton, *Contemplation in a World of Action* (Garden City, N.Y.: Doubleday & Co., 1971), 133.

4. Ibid., 340.

5. Ibid.

6. Ibid., 157f.

7. Ibid., 53.

8. Ibid., 113.

9. Ibid., 133.

6
Contemplation and Work

RICHARD LUECKE

In a poem called "Muckers" about workers stabbing yellow clay and pulling their boots out of suckholes to lay gas mains in old Chicago, Carl Sandburg set down three lines that say a lot.

> Of the twenty looking on
> Ten murmur, "O, it's a hell of a job,"
> Ten others, "Jesus, I wish I had the job."[1]

This gives poetic and, we may note, religious expression to a first ambiguity about work. It is painful to work and it is painful to be without work. Most of us cannot be happy until we find a job; once on the job, we start thinking about Friday.

Much hard work, like mucking, has been partly relieved by machinery—an indisputable step forward. But today it has also become clear that heavy industries are no longer in the business of creating many net new jobs; the numbers and percentage of employment in agriculture, manufacturing, and construction have sharply declined. Goods-producing work has not only mechanized and merged but has also moved from the land to the cities, from cities to

suburbs, from northern suburbs to the sunbelt, and overseas—
often leaving unemployed workers and disinvested communities
behind.

We Americans like to think of ourselves as hard, productive
workers, yet most of us by far (two out of three and the gap
is widening) are now performing softer services. Sandburg's most
famous poem described an earlier Chicago as "Hog Butcher of
the World" and "City of the Big Shoulders." On a Sandburg birthday
fifty years later, newspaper columnist Mike Royko composed an
update.

> Hi-rise for the World,
> Party-goer, Stacker of Stereo Tapes,
> Player with Home Pool Tables and the Nation's Jets;
> Dapper, slender, filter-tipped,
> City of the Big Credit Card . . .[2]

This new work may be easier but it raises questions of its own.
Even though laying gas mains was hard work, it nonetheless seemed
necessary for livelihood in the city—in a way that stacking stereo
tapes does not. This vast shift in the nature of work has taken place,
moreover, without ever absorbing a pool of unemployed laborers
who are not likely to turn to softer and lower-paying jobs and who
are, moreover, woefully compacted in terms of race—and this bears
worrisome consequences for future households and children in
the city. The rising costs of services now enter threateningly into
the prices that must be charged for goods, making it harder for
producers to compete with imports in steel, automobiles, and tex-
tiles. (General Motors complains that the cost of health insur-
ance now exceeds that of steel in its cars.) But even if service
employment could be expanded indefinitely, some critics say that
would raise the specter of a "clientele society," one which needs
nothing so much as an expansion of "needs" and therefore of
deficiencies and dependencies in people—which could "turn citizens
into clients."[3]

Thus both productive work and services are developing at present in ways that may portend diminished capacities and functions on
the part of families and communities, especially those of the poor.
Many present efforts in education appear to serve these trends.

Elements of Work

In 1959 Douglas Steere wrote a treatise titled *Work and Contemplation* to show how these two terms, or what they signify, depend on each other. Contemplation discovers a frame of reality and meaning for work, thereby buoying it, sustaining it, and informing a sense of responsibility. Work, however, especially when its methods or effects threaten to dissolve old frames of meaning, drives us back to contemplation—thus keeping contemplation from becoming escapist, individualistic, or precious. *All* workers want to see the worth of what they are doing not only by reference to pay, hours, and amenities but by a sense that they are exercising their own agency and skills toward achieving genuine ends. This entails, to fill out the picture, using appropriate materials and tools, functioning in socially cooperative ways, and doing all this in ways that accord with larger purposes.

Early in *Work and Contemplation,* Steere unforgettably described an experience of wood cutting with an eye to all these elements— agent and need, materials and tools, operation, social cooperation, and larger purposes—which interact and alter one another along the way. Thirty years later, for most of us, wood cutting has become at most recreational, and those who do it for a living are confronted by new questions from soil conservationists and those concerned about spotted owls. It is a time for contemplation. Contemplation without work is empty, and work without contemplation is blind.

Informational or intellectual work, at least in its manual aspects, is also involved in such a struggle. Here Steere took sides in an old controversy, for many contemplatives have seen no valid release from ordinary labor by virtue of study. But scholars and writers need in their own way to pose a significant problem, assemble evidence and manage materials, devise and improve methods, struggle with vehicles of expression while giving attention to other minds, and actually produce something—to the point of moving paper off the desk. Descriptions by Charles Darwin of the psychic toll exacted in scholarly labors, or by William James of the manifold devices by which one postpones such labors, or by writers who reveal their travails in interviews, might help us to agree—that's work. Such work, too, can be buoyed and (as we shall see) moderated through contemplation.

Because jobs and careers of both a back-straining and a sedentary sort have become increasingly specialized and problematic, Steere saw a continuing role for intentional communities in renewing human responsibility in work.[4]

Worlds of Work

It is no surprise that religious communities through the centuries have felt compelled to come to terms with the worlds of work in which they were set down. We may begin with those encountered by biblical peoples. The Pentateuch can be read as the story of a people going out from slavery to find work that is rightly related to land and community, and then adopting legal provisions against anyone's becoming or remaining trapped in heteronomous labor.[5]

At the other end of the Bible we find the First Letter of Peter addressed to "resident aliens" (i.e., displaced workers) called *paroikoi* (people without homes) in a Roman world that was dispossessing people. They cannot claim the patrimony by which property was secured and transmitted in the empire, but neither are they on the streets. They have come together in intentional communities or working households of faith (*oikoi tou theou*), where they are called, surprisingly, "a chosen generation, a royal priesthood, a holy nation"—a new race, a new humankind, a new Adam, and (by some accounts) a new Eve. What is more, these homeless workers are inviting established residents to join *them*, and some people are doing so—this man's wife, that mother's son. For all these reasons they are, understandably, enduring "fiery trials," but they are told in this letter to rejoice because a touch of the spirit and glory of Christ rests on them.[6]

In between these bookend worlds of work are not only other work settings but very ambiguous counsels that serve to open the question and prompt reflection. Work is both blessed and cursed; it is vanity like everything else under the sun *and* it is collaboration with the creator; it shares the groaning of the whole creation *and* the sighing of the spirit in hope. Prophets and disciples are told to leave their ordinary work and follow, or they are told to work but not for a living, like the birds of the air (Matt. 4:18–22; 6:26). Later, when people started to take this too literally, an epistle repeats another scriptural injunction that those who do not work should not eat (Prov. 6:6–11; 2 Thess. 3:10).

During the years that followed, sharp opposition was taken by Alexandrian Jewish communities as well as by the Apostolic Fathers, apologists, and monastics East and West to the classical Greek, Hellenist, and Roman ideal of leisure, in accordance with which manual labor was relegated to slaves. They pointed to the God of the Bible who, unlike the languorous and merely contemplative gods of Hesiod and Lucretius, both worked and rested and who commanded humans to work before as well as after the Fall. One of the first teaching handbooks to come to general use in the churches, the *Didache*, made clear that the clergy were not to be excused from labor, and this rule was repeated in the *Statuta ecclesiae antiqua* of the fifth and sixth centuries: "A cleric, no matter how learned in the word of God, should earn his living by handiwork." In this way a new brotherhood of labor became firmly enough established to allow slaves to become popes (Pius I, 140–155, and Callistus I, c. 223) and allow a bishop to sell himself into slavery to purchase the freedom of a widow's son (Paulinus of Nola, c. 425). Moreover, this early countercultural teaching about work included some listings of jobs that appeared incompatible with a vision of life together before God.[7]

From the outset of the Middle Ages work was conceived in terms of an ordered relationship between labor, activity, and contemplation. This stood codified in the influential and periodically renewed Rule of Benedict, which appointed fixed daily periods of labor, sacred reading, and contemplation (Rule 48). Labor here meant *manual* labor and exceptions were such as proved the rule (e.g., Jerome's concentrated translation against time). Manual labor was the beginning of charity, for by it one took care of one's own needs and was able to minister to unmet needs of others, while at the same time avoiding idleness and acedia, subduing the flesh, honoring the way of the apostles, and reflecting the image of God. A monk* who felt exempted from labor by virtue of spirituality was "trading on the name of Christ" (*Christemporos*) or was at least "pusillanimous." Douglas Steere repeats a story from the desert fathers about a monk who said he wanted to be like Mary and not like Martha. The abbot put him to reading in his cell while others went to work. When the monk showed up at mealtime, the abbot reminded him that he had

---

* Monk in this chapter refers to both male and female contemplatives.

chosen that good part and could have no wish for carnal food. "The point," comments Rembert Sorg on this story, "is that the abbot who went to work was the true contemplative and the Mary-monk was a quack."[8]

Brother Rembert makes an essential point that the Benedictine Rule was understood as communal. Only in community could you combine work, poverty, and charity. It was preferable, since this was the goal, to achieve self-sufficiency within the closure. Benedict could then specify, for example, harvesting by the brotherhood for a famine in the town. Asceticism goes astray, on this view, unless it is understood as removing obstacles to life together and as a means to "conviviality" (a term used by Ivan Illich to explain "austerity"). Such a community is not only a result but also a subject of contemplation. To this vision of a working community townsfolk paid their respects by coming to join the monks for a time in their fields or shops.

The Reformation of the sixteenth century, in the phrase of Max Weber, sought to bring the disciplines of the monastery to the streets. Martin Luther's polemic against religious "works" (among which he named "contemplation")—that is, works viewed as salvific that therefore compromised the saving grace of God—led him to speak glowingly of ordinary "callings." If work in a monastery or religious order was a divine calling, so was the work of the craftsman, the housewife, the teacher, the magistrate, or the citizen, whose roles could be described as "masks" for the providential work of God in the world. Nevertheless, Luther's use of the word "calling" to refer to daily work amounted to a linguistic cultural innovation, and neither the church nor the world has ever been the same.[9]

The point to remember is that for Luther the primary calling remained the calling by the gospel, made visible and effective in baptism. Neither Luther nor Calvin ever taught that we find our chief "identity" in our daily work. Thus we may take exception to cultural historians who see in the teachings of these Reformers a hinge to the modern world of work.[10] A much-valued treatise by Einar Billing titled *Our Calling* shows Luther making two points: (1) Since the calling by the gospel is primary, we should never become totally identified with our daily work, and (2) in so far as God is also in our daily work, we should never be bored with it.[11]

It was Luther's point that we are saved by "grace" and not by "works"—of any kind. But such a confession may be seen to contain, in its own way, a liberating significance for daily labors: it can lead one to say, "God has taken care of my salvation, now I will take care of those things that God entrusts to me." Some find here an echo of Meister Eckhart, whose reference to "God beyond God" implied a return to full engagement in the world. It was a further suggestion by Luther that bringing disciplines from the monastery to the town could result in something like a cross within worldly engagements. An older Luther complained that fat burghers had heard the first part about going to work in the world but not the other part about the cross.

Something more like a "gospel of work" did come to expression in later Calvinists, especially the Puritans. Like previous Reformers, Cotton Mather spoke in America of two callings: a first calling of all Christians by God and a second calling "by which one's Usefulness in [one's] neighborhood is distinguished." But R. H. Tawney cites Puritan self-help books in which spiritual fervor appropriate to the first calling was clearly slipping over to the second: *Navigation Spiritualized, Husbandry Spiritualized, The Heavenly Use of Earthly Things, The Religious Weaver.* A Puritan pamphlet of 1654 found cash value in a passage from the New Testament: "Godliness is *profitable* unto all things" (1 Tim. 4:8, KJV, italics added). Puritan godliness did indeed prove profitable in many things, combining, as it did, hard work on a commercially untapped continent with delayed gratification, such that the only thing you could do with the proceeds was reinvest them. Where profitability was taken, moreover, as a sign of divine favor—not, to be sure, as salvational but as a proof of divine election—there was additional reason to be industrious. Poverty, by the same reasoning, could seem a sign of the reprobate. A tract of 1771 said, "Everyone knows that the lower classes must be kept poor, or they will never be industrious."[12]

Once again we must not oversimplify. Wealth accruing to the Puritans from hard work was, strictly speaking, incidental to their efforts. They were conscientiously opposed to consumerism and committed to stewardship. They preserved the town meeting as an instrument of citizenship and usefulness in the neighborhood. They observed the Sabbath, which placed a limit on work and on commerce in view of further ends in life. They spoke not of individualism but of "covenant." The writers of *Habits of the Heart* point to other cultural influences that took hold on the American scene along the way to Benjamin Franklin, by whose time, they say, "work was defined in secular terms rather than as calling and society was viewed in individualistic rather than covenantal terms."[13] Only then could it be said that the Rule of Benedict, "To work *and* to pray" was becoming the dictum of Thomas Carlyle, "To work *is* to pray." The transition from Puritanism to Yankeeism was made. The work ethic had lost former moorings and was floating by itself.

The story of that floating is told, with the wisdom of hindsight, by historian Daniel Rodgers, who describes a series of nervous religious and ethical responses made in the course of a steady retreat before the success of industrial engines.[14] First (to summarize), critics questioned, *Was it right?* Divines early compared the new assembly lines with slave labor. The answer was always that such jobs were only temporary stepping-stones, but fewer and fewer hirelings labored their way to ownership. Near the end of the nineteenth century, with new products flooding the markets and labor agitating at Haymarket and in the Pullman Strike for an eight-hour day, the question changed to, *Could it last?* At the Republican Convention of 1900 Chauncey Depew thanked God that in opening the Cuban and Philippine markets the administration had averted that impending crisis— though labor remained unconvinced. After the Great Depression and two world wars the word became "industrial democracy"— employers, workers, and government should cooperate in a system of production and rewards sufficient to compete and win in world markets. Near the end of the twentieth century there came a third response, which may be capsulized, *If we don't, somebody else will!* This brings us up to date.

Modes of Contemplation

In classical descriptions contemplation is the very opposite of work. It is "rest"—though not "resting up." One does not contemplate for the sake of returning with renewed vigor to one's work or for any other ulterior motive. One does this, if one does it truly, for no reason at all. Contemplation is, as Romano Guardini put it, "a waste of time for God." We do not ask when raising a glass or singing a song, "What are we doing this *for?*" Much less do we seek an end beyond enjoyment in the presence of God.

Yet it is exactly in this way, they said, that an uncustomary light comes to be shed over us and all our work. We who have been examining things, making things, buying and selling things—talking all the time—are now made to stand, or more likely sit, in silence beside things and other people. This passivity and receptivity suggest a different mode of coexistence, attentiveness, and response. Aristotle described knowledge in terms of a power of the soul to "become all things." Thomas Aquinas spoke similarly of "a simple, unimpeded and penetrating gaze on truth." Others have spoken in terms of "listening" rather than "gazing," but they are after the same thing. Steere, who loves the phrase "He maketh me to lie down," called this restful attention "the stub of contemplation."

This "stub" can grow to illumine the activity we undertake with other creatures. Even for those of us who find it hard to speak of a vision of God or a knowledge of essences, this "rest" can have a twofold effect: it can lift the horizon for all our work, while at the same time setting limits on what may be attempted through work. Here let's try to sketch the importance of such a "goal" and "limit" for all our busy efforts to know things, to do things, and to make things.[15]

Knowing. We have agreed with Steere to let scholarly activity count as work. Not the least intellectual work, and one which requires perpetual redoing, is that of clarifying the goals and limits of intellect itself. Contemplatives point in both directions. Through contemplation "knowing" becomes something more than learning how to measure and manipulate things; it includes giving attention to them as "subjects" (a term appropriately used in school) and as members of a larger whole. But by this very intuition limits come to be set because "subjects" and "wholes," even where they are affirmed, are seldom if ever fully perceived, described, written up, or published.

Intellectual work becomes diminished by ignoring this horizon. It may also become dangerous by ignoring this limit. In contemplative days from Augustine to Scotus, people shared an understanding that they were contingent beings along with all the matters they studied, that no tracing of causes within nature could reduce this codependency, that every cause was "equidistant from eternity." But who will say that our modern search for ultimate particles or for the origins of biological life is still accompanied by such a sense? Without it, "knowing" can affect "doing" in ways that would have brought horror to our forebears.

Doing. Work has expanded in the past century through enlargement of jobs in services and therapies that focus new needs, introduce new techniques, and certify new cures. Medical procedures now extend to in vitro fertilization at one end of life and organ harvesting at the other. Even though every procedure, now as ever, is "equidistant from the eternal" (Kierkegaard), new techniques have brought us to the very brink of speaking about "life" itself as an entity or a thing to be managed.

We now speak in many fields—ecological, medical, legal, social—in ways that suggest new human tasks with respect to "life," scarcely remembering how this was formerly regarded as a direct gift and even a presence of God. This opens a way to replacing the traditional understanding of inviolate "persons," which has ennobled and moderated Western individualism, with a supposition of manageable "life." It appears to warrant the expansion of professional and institutional prerogatives that were unthinkable when we spoke about a "person" rather than a "life." Ivan Illich, who presses this theme, cites Jacques Maritain in response to a question about management techniques or "manpower planning": "Is not [such] planning a sin, a new species within the vices which grow out of presumption?"[16]

This presumption seems not far from the entrepreneurialism now at work in social services. In Cicero's *De natura deorum* (I.26.71), the leading character, Cotta, remarked that he did not see how social experts of that day could meet in the street without doubling over with laughter. In our own day it would seem a much greater strain for them to keep a straight face.

In contemplation the straight face is no longer necessary. To stand beside fellow humans, as we do in contemplation, is to stand not simply with "patients" or "clients" but with persons and responsible agents. It sets a limit to "caring" activities by imposing a respectful hands-off discipline. If therapeutic and social services have tended to turn fellow citizens into clients, contemplation turns clients into fellow citizens again.

At the same time a goal is set for social and public activity: that is, to foster conditions in which humans can exercise personal and common responsibility. A space opens for reform and reorganization of professions and services. Such "doing" bears a large import for "making," including the development and deployment of tools.

Making. The engines of production seem prone today to run on mindlessly, or to proceed by a rationality and efficiency of their own, in ways which ignore or postpone dealing with the most basic needs of many people or with the approaching limits of certain natural resources. Jacques Ellul has described such productive work as "dissociated," as implying "an absence rather than a presence" in the workers.

In contemplation, things and materials are no longer merely useful, they *are*. Steere repeats lines from a letter written by G. K. Chesterton about "taking a fierce pleasure in things being themselves. . . . The startling wetness of water excites and intoxicates me; the fieriness of fire, the steeliness of steel, the unutterable muddiness of mud." He cites a Chesterton poem that ends: "And stones still shine along the road / That are and cannot be."[17]

Today not only a "shine" stands to be lost from stones, basic and wondrous as that is, but entire species stand to be lost from the earth. What is recovered through contemplation is not an overweening determination to save "the life of the biosphere," but something more modest—respect. Respect must be paid to the spotted owl, the snail darter, and the furbish lousewort as fellow creatures, just as the voice from the whirlwind relished the "useless" crocodile in the book of Job.

"We are working well," writes Wendell Berry in *The Unsettling of America*, "when we use ourselves as fellow-creatures of the plants, animals, materials, and other people we are working with." In so far as we consume other creatures in order to live, we do so with a heightened sense of sacrifice required for all organic existence and a readiness ourselves to be recycled when the time arrives. What looms as required at present is some reorganization of work so that people in communities can address their basic needs while respecting other life and a larger scheme of things. Far from being antitechnological, this entails a recovery of the *logos* of *techne*, of reason (both larger and more modest) in our making.

Herein lies renewed appreciation for the "making" that goes into the fine arts. The artist calls attention to the intrinsic qualities of objects and materials, and to their enjoyment rather than to their consumption (except in occasional "eat your art out" exhibits where objects are eaten to make this very point). For this reason objects of art and artful performances are drawn into occasions of contemplation and worship, though long and sometimes violent controversies have taken place about this.[18] Anthony Burgess referred to this rightful treatment of materials in *Writers at Work:* "Art is, so to speak, the church triumphant; the rest of life is the church militant."[19]

All of the above takes place, of course, not only through solitary contemplation but in corporate worship. It may even become clearer in settings that are not private and in communities that are not closed, in what Parker Palmer calls "the company of strangers." For there rest and vision are shared, manifestly and not merely intentionally, by both rich and poor, employers and employees, workers and unemployed alike. It was a point (and a scandal) of the Sabbath, as it was of the eight-hour workday, that leisure belonged equally to all.

The democratic character of contemplation is not only signaled but enacted and realized in common song and common confession, in common scripture lessons and creeds that bring up past companions, in an offertory where all are free to offer their gifts to a future no one fully plans for all the others, in intercessions for all sorts and conditions of people during the course of which (as Bonhoeffer said) previously intolerable faces become transformed, in the Our Father that we pray with and for all people (Luther), and eminently in the supper—where, as Paul said, if some are full and some are empty, it is better to do our eating and drinking at home.

At such a supper we would commit, said Paul, the very crime that those people committed who slew the Lord of glory, not discerning the Lord's body, and we would know ourselves as belonging to a sick and dying world (1 Cor. 11). Where, however, the Lord's body *is* discerned in such a way as to reject hurtful social divisions, there comes a fresh recognition of what is always the case: the real presence of a paschal, betrayed, denied, crucified, but risen and community-creating Lord.

This was early called *leiturgia,* "the work of the people"—not nonwork but a special form of work on which all ordinary work depends. What the people wish for one another is something very like the condition of contemplation: "The peace of the Lord be with you always!" "And also with you!"

Work and Contemplation Together

It is in community, the Benedictines said, that poverty and charity can be combined and vision can take place. Of an earlier congregation we are told "there was not a needy person among them" (Acts 4:34, NRSV). The modern world assumes "scarcity" and makes it into an organizing principle: scarce things, scarce intelligence, scarce services, even scarce religion—this justifies gatekeepers, accreditors, and presumptuous services. For people who accept such "scarcity," human existence becomes a constricted and competitive thing. For poor people who accept it, life becomes a virtually closed thing. What if we began instead with that early discernment of "no needs"? If we not only ended the week with the Sabbath rest but began it with this Sunday vision?[20]

"Everything begins in mysticism and everything ends in politics," said Charles Péguy. Religious bodies have moved from their vision and social teachings to form public advocacies, including advocacies for work.[21] In most major religious traditions there is at this time a search for ways to combine what David Tracy calls "the mystical and prophetic trajectories," and this is likely to increase as interreligious "dialogue" affects each tradition's self-understanding.[22] Such attention to "prophetic mysticism" might help answer questions: Why aren't contemplative people more subversive and reforming? Why aren't social activists more imaginative and innovative?

This search has become at once more necessary and more complicated by the new plurality of religions and cultures in American cities. In 1993, unlike 1893, it seems possible to get up a "parliament of the world's religions" in virtually any major metropolitan area of the United States without sending invitations overseas. During the 1990s, moreover, 80 percent of new people entering the work force will be members of minority groups or women—requiring many-partied revisions and reforms for success in workplaces.

Contemplative claims and espousals are complicated today not only by this plurality but by arguments of postmodern literary and philosophical critics who show there is no getting beyond words or interpretations in our communications—that there is no finding any words that simply mirror what is. In this twofold bind or aporia, we may find a way forward through "prophetic mysticism." If there is no looking above or beneath words to get at what is real today, we do nonetheless look forward together. Moreover, in any practical conversation or argument about the future that is more than an expression of wishes, a trade-off of interests, or a prediction from trends—within any conversation that struggles to say what the future should be like and what is to be done—there is "a tacit sense of relevance" (Richard Bernstein).[23] That silent assumption within the course of ordinary social communications—that is, that talk about the future is *about* something, that there *is* something to be discovered and pursued together—seems close to what many contemplatives have said or have pointed to in the past. To rest on this assumption may be seen, in its own way, as a "practice of the presence of God," who alone can lend a kind of facticity to discussions of the future. It is in this way that communications about the future, about what is to be studied and done and made, become required, warranted, and disciplined, and a basis is laid for imagination that is more than fantasy, even though no one can expect to have the only or the last word.[24] It remains only to give a reason for the hope that is in us (in us all) exactly while we converse about the future or about the city that is to come—a city that was biblically depicted as comprising "every nation and kindred and people and tongue."

Voices we've cited were aware of pitfalls whenever we speak of work or of contemplation all by itself or try to prioritize them. The enemy of work, we say (especially to the young or the unemployed), is laziness. But when medieval Christians spoke of the deadly sin of "sloth"—deadly in the sense that it destroyed the soul—they did not mean simply the avoidance of labor. *Acedia* was a lassitude of the spirit that could be present in the midst of physical motion. It could, in fact, account for a lot of unnecessary motion, overbusyness, and restlessness. It was a sin against the spirit if not the letter of the Sabbath, a rejection of the peace of God, a fall into idolatry. It amounted to despair, a "sickness unto death." The deadly sin of sloth lay in neglect of contemplation.

This was the theme of a classic essay by Josef Pieper, *Leisure: The Basis of Culture*, in which "leisure" was treated as something akin to contemplation. Steere paid his respects to this cultural landmark but took issue with what here seemed a pitting of leisure *against* labor, whereas the dampening of compulsive busyness was only preliminary to something more. For this he cited English mystics who spoke not of rest in place of busyness, nor of busyness in place of rest, but of "the rest most busyee." He quoted Thomas Merton on "a silence that is the fountain of action and joy."[25]

We would be misled, finally, to think of contemplation or spirituality as the one "work" that makes all our other work come out right. That too could become a slothful busyness. Against this last deception we have the testimony of Reformers who warned against reliance on religious works and spoke instead of Word and grace, who spoke of themselves as living by the forgiveness of sins, as both sinners and saints, as sinning boldly, as knowing joy over seventy thousand fathoms. We have the testimony of all who pointed to Martha instead of Mary.

What is to be done is to stay at the table, to continue the conversation, to sing a song and go out into the night.

Notes

1. Carl Sandburg, *Chicago Poems* (New York: Henry Holt Co., 1916), 21.

2. Mike Royko, "San-Fran-York on the Lake," in *I May Be Wrong but I Doubt It* (Chicago: Henry Regnery Co., 1968), 3–6.

3. See John McKnight, "Professionalized Services and Disabling Help" and "Good Works and Good Work," both available through Center for Urban Affairs and Policy Research, Northwestern University, Evanston, Illinois. Also available from this center is a study, "Public Spending on Low Income People in Cook County," showing that total funds directed toward poverty in the county during 1989 amounted to $6,200 per person under the poverty line, or more than $24,000 per family of four—this exceeds the median family income. Yet only 37 percent reached poor families in cash, 12 percent as commodities (food, housing); 51 percent went to services over which they exercise no control. The 37 percent figure exactly matches findings in New York.

4. Douglas Steere, *Work and Contemplation* (New York: Harper & Brothers, 1959). Further testimonies by writers and poets are cited in "Contemplation and Leisure," *Humanitas* 8, no. 3 (November 1972). Cf. a long series of *Paris Review* interviews edited by George Plimpton in *Writers*

at Work, 5 vols. (New York: Viking Press, 1981). Exemplary work is found in a professional sport by George Will, *Men at Work: The Craft of Baseball* (New York: Macmillan Publishing Co., 1990).

5. On the intent and historicity of provisions summarized in Lev. 25 see, for example, Robert North, *The Sociology of the Jubilee Year* (Rome: Pontifical Biblical Institute, 1954). For those who are doubtful of the Egyptian context, the significance of these provisions is not diminished. Norman Gottwald notes that the word used for the "horn" to be blown at the inauguration of a jubilee year is the very word that was used for the horn blown at the walls of Jericho, a city built with slave labor. This "liberation" is, if anything, heightened in the New Testament, which announces "the acceptable year of the Lord" (Luke 4:19, RSV).

6. See this sociological interpretation by John Elliott in his now reissued *A Home for the Homeless* (Minneapolis: Fortress Press, 1990).

7. Painting that included decoration of idols, merchandising that required a use of false weights in order to compete, and (in Augustine) work at the spectacles in the stadium where people "came only to grieve not to relieve." All this is documented in Arthur T. Geoghegan, *The Attitude Towards Labor in Early Christianity and Ancient Culture* (Washington, D.C.: Catholic University of America Press, 1945), 22, 229f.

8. *Towards a Benedictine Theology of Manual Labor* (Lisle, Ill.: St. Procopius Abbey, 1951), 20. It may be noted that Meister Eckhart later read the Mary/Martha story in the same way. Both Augustine *(De opere monachorum)* and Thomas Aquinas *(Contra impugnantes dei cultum et religionem)* felt compelled by criticisms to deal with the question of whether working at books really counted as labor, though they adjudicated their specific cases somewhat differently. Thomas also found grounds for a more accommodating view of mendicancy than was allowed by the Benedictines.

9. Biblical writings use this term almost exclusively for spiritual callings— the calling of a prophet or disciple or of Israel or of people to the *ecclesia.* One passage is occasionally cited as referring to a secular "calling": "Let every man abide in the same calling *[klesis]* wherein he was called" (1 Cor. 7:20, KJV). But is it "wherein" or "wherewith"? Even in the former case it might be talking about circumcision or uncircumcision.

10. This is the famous interpretation by R. H. Tawney in *Religion and the Rise of Capitalism* (New York: Harcourt, Brace & Co., 1926), Max Weber, *The Protestant Ethic and the Spirit of Capitalism* (New York: Charles Scribner's Sons, 1950), and Adriano Tilgher, *Work: What It Has Meant Through the Ages* (New York: Harcourt, 1930). It then becomes necessary to treat Luther's commendation of crafts and agriculture over commerce, his objection to selling and lending for whatever the market will bear, and his

warning against working with money alone (which "buries the poor" and "opens every door and window to hell") as something left over from the Middle Ages.

11. Einar Billing, *Our Calling*, trans. Conrad Bergendoff (Rock Island, Ill.: Augustana, 1950). Thus Christian faith introduces an essential ambiguity into labor. Frequently noted differences between Roman Catholics and Protestants on work may be traceable in part to their coming down on different sides of a Christian duality that's always there.

12. This bears a seed of what John Kenneth Galbraith would call a conventional wisdom: namely, that the rich don't work because they get too little money and the poor don't work because they get too much money. For this sleuthing in Puritan tracts we are indebted not only to Tawney but to George Forell, "Work and the Christian Calling," *Lutheran Quarterly*, May 1956.

13. Robert Bellah et al., *Habits of the Heart: Individualism and Commitment in American Life* (Berkeley: University of California Press, 1985), 28–33.

14. *The Work Ethic in Industrial America 1850–1920* (Chicago: University of Chicago Press, 1978). We here draw on chs. 2, 3, 6. In *The Culture of Narcissism* (New York: W. W. Norton & Co., 1979) Christopher Lasch similarly traced a successive emptying of traditional understandings of work: from Cotton Mather (socially useful work) to Ben Franklin (development of virtue) to P. T. Barnum (virtue as a means of getting credit) to Dale Carnegie (winning images and interpersonal preferment) to T-groups and aggressiveness training that pay little attention to the objective import of human work. See chapter 3, "Changing Modes of Making It: From Horatio Alger to the Happy Hooker."

15. Notions of horizon and limit have been treated by theologians, especially Langdon Gilkey, *Naming the Whirlwind* (New York: Bobbs-Merrill Co., 1969), 305–414, and *Reaping the Whirlwind* (New York: Seabury Press, 1975), 36–69.

16. From a speech to the national staff of Evangelical Lutheran Church in America, March 29, 1989.

17. Steere, "Contemplation and Leisure," *Work and Contemplation*, 301.

18. Resolution of the most famous controversy over the possibility of idolatry in sacred images was made on theological grounds by reference to the incarnation. See Jaroslav Pelikan, *Imago Dei: The Byzantian Apologia for Icons* (Washington, D.C.: National Gallery of Art; Princeton, N.J.: Princeton University Press, 1990).

19. Plimpton, ed., *Writers at Work*, 4th series, 348.

20. This Sunday significance and much more is set down by Douglas

Meeks in a chapter titled "God and Needs" in *God the Economist: The Doctrine of God and Political Economy* (Minneapolis: Fortress Press, 1989). Ivan Illich treated this theme in *Toward a History of Needs* (New York: Pantheon Press, 1978). Parker Palmer treated it in a chapter called "Sources of Action: Scarcity or Abundance?" in *The Active Life: A Spirituality of Work, Creativity, and Caring* (New York: HarperCollins, 1990). An occasional paper by Parker Palmer on the theme "Scarcity, Abundance, and the Gift of Community" is available from Community Renewal Society in Chicago.

21. Roman Catholic utterances from *Rerum novarum* of Leo XIII (1891, the very decade during which "unemployment" became a public word) and *Quadragesimo anno* of Pius XII (1931) to *Laborem exercens* (1981) and *Centesimus annus* (1991) of John Paul II, as well as statements by the U.S. bishops, have reasserted personalism, pluralism, and subsidiarity, while warning against social exclusion and forms of development that destroy rather than preserve communities. Protestant bodies have issued similar statements and have joined in supporting, for example, labor mobilization or full employment legislation. At local levels, similarly, people have moved from worship to advocacy. A Committee on Unemployment and the Future of Work convened by Community Renewal Society in Chicago adopted the following policies. They would support such measures and initiatives as (1) got through to workers and communities in need and did not rely on a roundabout trickle-down, (2) had an investment character and served to give the people some stakes, (3) used comparatively little fossil energy and produced comparatively little unreusable waste, and (4) served to create and activate communities rather than to leave them passive and waiting.

22. David Tracy, *The Dialogue with the Other* (Grand Rapids: Wm. B. Eerdmans Publishing Co., 1991). See esp. the last chapter, "Dialogue and the Prophetic-Mystical Option."

23. See his book with an equally suggestive title: Richard Bernstein, *Beyond Objectivism and Relativism* (Philadelphia: University of Pennsylvania Press, 1983).

24. Coleridge insisted on this distinction between imagination and fantasy. This prophetic-mystical practice is enforced and clarified by theologians who speak of God not simply as transcendent upward or in the depths downward but as coming or as bringing the future.

25. Steere, "Contemplation and Leisure," 304.

7

Discernment:
An Ignatian Perspective on
John Woolman's Journal

THOMAS E. CLARKE, S.J.

Quaker and Jesuit spirituality would seem at first glance to be at opposite ends of the ecumenical spectrum. In the former we see reflected an outlook and life-style characterized by simplicity, inwardness, wariness of pomp and ritual, and a strong abhorrence for whatever smacks of hierarchy and centralized ecclesiastical control. In contrast, the sons of Ignatius, deservedly or not, own the dubious distinction of a dictionary entry all their own—jesuitical. One might go on to list, from the Ignatian side, other illustrative points of difference, beginning with the famous (or infamous) "Rules for Thinking with the Church" of Ignatius's *Spiritual Exercises,* particularly their endorsement of relics, indulgences, images, and rules of fast and abstinence; their exaltation of religious life over the married state; their requirement of total subservience of judgment to the hierarchical church, and the like. Features as diverse as Jesuit patronage of baroque ecclesiastical art and their special vow of obedience to the pope might also be invoked.

Acknowledging such strong differences, which have a great deal to do with history and culture, it is all the more important not to miss some interesting points of similarity. Both groups own a tradition of compassion for the oppressed.[1] Students of both have manifested interest in the respective approaches to decision making, especially of a communal kind. And, happily, the paths of Quakers like Douglas Steere and Jesuits like Gustave Weigel have increasingly crossed in the present century, in circles where spiritual, social, or ecumenical concerns are being addressed.

What initially struck me was the presence in both traditions of the journal or diary as a form of Christian witness, particularly in the context of missionary journey. Ignatius of Loyola was himself author of two very different kinds of personal records. The one he wrote himself was a terse daily account of his prayer and discernment in Rome as he labored to formulate the *Constitutions* of the Society of Jesus (Ganss 229–70).[2] The other was a kind of autobiography that he dictated to his secretary, in which he refers to himself simply as "the pilgrim" (Ganss 66–111).

From their founder's accounts on, Jesuits have often had recourse to written descriptions of their apostolic journeys. A notable example, not yet translated into English, is the *Memoriale* of Pierre Favre, the first Jesuit priest, which describes his journeys in Italy, Spain, and northern Europe in the early years of what has come to be known as the Counter-Reformation or Catholic Reform. As Jesuits traveled to the newly "discovered" lands of the Americas and the Orient, their fidelity to Ignatius's insistence that they should keep in touch yielded a whole body of apostolic travel literature, which has become of major interest to religious and secular historians in the form of the *Jesuit Relations*. In our own times many Jesuits have continued this tradition. A few examples: the account of a foot pilgrimage to Rome by Gerard Hughes, an autobiography by Daniel Berrigan, and reflections on his imprisonment in the Soviet Union by Walter Ciszek.

On the Quaker side, Howard Brinton has traced the history of journaling in early periods of Quaker history. Both in the mother country and in America the journals of individuals became perhaps the most characteristic form of the literature of Friends. Members like Samuel Bownas, Thomas Chalkley, Thomas Story, John Smith, and John Richardson, among many others, have provided rich accounts of this aspect of early Quaker history in the colonies. Their aim, someone has said, was to provide "edifying entertainment." These books differed from the autobiographies more familiar to us in several respects. They tended to neglect the purely personal. One would look in vain to Woolman's *Journal,* for example, for a description of life at home with his wife and children, or for an understanding of how the death of one of his children at an early age affected him. Quaker journals generally tended to fit themselves into certain edifying conventions. Woolman's account of his early religious experience, his minor deviations from piety and morality, and his later finding of a more consistent path to God, can be better understood within the context of this journaling tradition among Quakers of his era.

In the incipient stage of my musings toward this essay, I played with the idea of writing a comparison between the journals of John Woolman and Pierre Favre. Pragmatic considerations have led me to relinquish such a project. I propose instead simply to reflect on Woolman's *Journal* from an Ignatian perspective. Under several headings I will comment on some of the singular features of this American classic, indicating some points of comparison with my own Ignatian tradition. I will deal with the latter only cursorily, in order to identify the perspective from which I am viewing the *Journal.* Hopefully it will be for readers, whatever their acquaintance with one or both of these spiritual traditions, a stimulus to explore the wealth of the *Journal* from their own vantage points.

John Woolman's *Journal*

For those not familiar with John Woolman and his *Journal* (this, I regret to say, was my own situation till several years ago), a few words of introduction will be in order. The *Journal* describes Woolman's life and journeys from his birth in 1720 to devout Quaker parents in a small town in New Jersey until shortly before his death of smallpox at York in England in 1772. The first three chapters depict his life until the year 1756, when he began to respond to "a motion of love to leave some hints in writing of my experience of the goodness of God" (23). Despite some adolescent straying from the path of virtue and some vacillation in following a special call addressed to him during sickness, he came to adult life deeply aware of God. He "was early convinced in my mind that true religion consisted in an inward life, wherein the heart doth love and reverence God the Creator, and learn to exercise true justice and goodness, not only toward all men but also toward the brute creatures."(28).

At twenty-one he began to work for a shopkeeper in Mount Holly, near Philadelphia, and subsequently, when his employer withdrew from business, continued in the tailoring trade with a view to his own sustenance. The first of his many religious journeys began in September 1743. Though he had in late adolescence contemplated leading a single life, in 1749 he married Sarah Ellis, with whom he had two children. For almost three decades, the bulk of his adult life, he spent several months of each year in apostolic journeys to Quaker communities from New England to North Carolina. One notable trip, in 1763, brought him to visit Indians in the town of Wehaloosing, about two hundred miles from Philadelphia. Later, in 1769 and 1770, he agonized, partially during a serious illness, over the decision of going to the West Indies. Ultimately his exercise of discernment brought him to abandon the idea. But in 1772 he embarked for England where, after initial inhospitality by a Quaker meeting, he found welcome and continued his travels fruitfully till his death at York.

Woolman and Ignatius

The Quaker spirituality of the *Journal* resembles the Ignatian tradition first of all with respect to *the centrality of apostolic decision*. In contrast with more contemplative paths such as those portrayed by John of the Cross and other mystics of the monastic tradition, God is here sought principally through obedience to God's will as it directs the missionary journey. Whether Ignatius's *Spiritual Exercises* are ordered primarily toward a concrete decision or "election" or rather toward growth in the basic contemplative freedom required for all holy choices is not agreed upon. In any case the accent in Ignatian spirituality on action and mission is clear. Woolman's discernment, in turn, was congruous with the tradition of the Society of Friends, which, in its business meetings, had creatively enlisted silence and other spiritual disciplines in the service of decisions that were faithful to the inner light.

Though an extended study of the ecclesial aspects of the two traditions would doubtless reveal more differences than likenesses, they are alike in the affirmation of a *close link between personal holiness and apostolic fruitfulness*. In both Ignatius and Woolman we find an acute sense of how effective mission and ministry are contingent on that purity of heart by which the minister permits God to work the divine purpose through human agencies. Ignatius expressed this somewhat dialectically in his *Constitutions*, where he plays back and forth between the need to perfect the human instrument and the more imperative need for that instrument to be docile and free in God's hand (nn. 813–14; Ganss 317f.).

Woolman makes a similar point in a key passage:

> From an inward purifying, and steadfast abiding under it, springs a lively operative desire for the good of others. All people are not called to the public ministry, but whoever are, are called to minister of that which they have tasted and handled spiritually. The outward modes of worship are various, but whenever men are true ministers of Jesus Christ it is from the operation of his Spirit upon their hearts, first purifying them and thus giving them a feeling sense of the conditions of others. This truth was early fixed in my mind, and I was taught to watch the pure opening and to take heed lest while I was standing to speak, my own will should get uppermost and cause me to utter words from worldly wisdom and depart from the channel of the true gospel ministry. (31)

I have quoted this passage at length because it so richly conveys the spirit of what was described in the spiritual physiognomy of Ignatius as his being "at one and the same time contemplative in action." Both of these ministers of the gospel were deeply convinced of the words of Jesus regarding his own preaching, "The word you hear is not mine but the word of the One who sent me" (John 14:24, author's trans.). In this purity and freedom, whose growth occurred in patient and painful waiting for the Spirit of truth to move to action (and for Woolman speech and silence are the primary forms of apostolic action), lies the heart of these two spiritualities.

Both Woolman and Ignatius find the ultimate norm of discerning choice in *the will of God the Creator*. Ignatius's "Principle and Foundation" at the beginning of his *Spiritual Exercises* sets forth with succinctness and logical clarity the purpose of human existence (the praise, reverence, and service of God and the salvation of the soul), the purpose of all other creatures (to assist in the fulfillment of this purpose), together with the twin rules of *"tantum quantum"* (use and abstention governed by the norm) and *"indifferentia"* (a disposition of inner balance or freedom), which are to guide the actual choices made (n. 23; Ganss 130).

Woolman, for his part, early realized that "all the cravings of sense must be governed by a divine Principle," that "true religion consisted in inward life, wherein the heart doth love and reverence God the Creator," and that "as the mind was moved on an inward principle to love God as an invisible, incomprehensible being, on the same principle it was moved to love him in all his manifestations in the visible world" (28). The right use of creatures requires that we "apply all the gifts of divine providence to the purposes for which they were intended" (55).

The occurrence of smallpox in his town during the winter brought Woolman to a typical examination of his conduct from the standpoint of *"tantum quantum."* The presence of the dread disease in a house where he did business led him to question whether he was going there in the first place from duty, from custom, or from "too eager a pursuit after some outward treasure" (103). Likewise, he asked, "Do I use food and drink in no other sort and in no other degree than was designed by him who gave these creatures for our sustenance?" He further asked, "Do I never abuse my body by inordinate labour, striving to accomplish some end which I have unwisely proposed? . . . If I go on a visit to the widows and fatherless, do I go purely on a principle of charity, free from every selfish view?" (103). The emphasis here and in other passages on Woolman's sense of right order and his monitoring of inner motivation bears comparison with the concerns expressed in the Ignatian "Principle and Foundation."

Likewise clear is the affinity between Ignatius and Woolman with respect to *interiority* and *the discernment of inner movements* as the primary path of access to God's will. In both cases the laws of nature, the Ten Commandments, and the ecclesial community have their due place. But the principal recourse for both is to what Ignatius in his *Constitutions* calls "the interior law of charity and love which the Holy Spirit writes and engraves upon hearts" (n. 134; Ganss 288).

Though the majority of the *Spiritual Exercises* proposed by Ignatius are contemplations of the life of Jesus, these are essentially dispositive in character with a view to the "election," whose primary requisite is, negatively, that it not proceed from any "inordinate affection," and, positively, that it result from a movement of the good spirit (Ignatius rarely speaks in the *Spiritual Exercises* of the Holy Spirit).

Woolman's Quaker tradition strongly disposed him, of course, to seek God's will by recourse to an *inner* divine principle. Though he spoke less than George Fox and other Quakers of "the inner light," it is abundantly clear that the "pure wisdom" of which he writes is an equivalent. He speaks, for example, of "the immediate workings of the Spirit of Christ" (41), the "spirit of Truth" (42), "attending to the pure guidance of the Holy Spirit" (114), and "the springing up of pure love" (117).

For Woolman and Ignatius the inner Spirit whose movements they are to attend to and follow is above all a *spirit of truth*. The word "truth" occurs again and again in the *Journal*. "We were taught by renewed experience to . . . live in the spirit of Truth, and utter that to the people which Truth opened in us" (42). He speaks of those "who are single to the Truth, waiting daily to feel the life and virtue of it in their hearts" (49). In England, as he mourns the decline of the original Quaker commitment, he grieves that many "too much neglect the pure feeling of Truth" (184). "Nothing," he said once in a Yearly Meeting, "is more precious than the mind of Truth inwardly manifested" (92).

In this process of finding God's will through discerning the inner movements of the Spirit of truth, both Ignatius and Woolman accent *a contemplative waiting for the movement of the Spirit*. In his own life Ignatius manifested a remarkable capacity for detached waiting upon God. His conversion experience at Loyola and Manresa in 1521 and 1522 had filled him with zeal for promoting God's reign on earth. But almost two decades were to pass before the actual foundation of the Society of Jesus in 1540. At a key point in the corporate discernment of the companions, they agreed to leave the future—whether Jerusalem or Rome would be the site of their life and ministry—contingent on whether a ship was available for the Jerusalem voyage.

Woolman's *Journal* is rich in passages in which he describes his waiting upon the inner Truth. Most often his "election" has to do with what he is to say if the inner Wisdom draws him from silence. One early episode is illustrative of how he struggled for total purity in this regard:

> One day, being under a strong exercise of spirit, I stood up and said some words in a meeting, but not keeping close to the divine opening, I said more than was required of me; and being soon sensible of my error, I was afflicted in mind some weeks without any light or comfort, even to that degree that I could take satisfaction in nothing. I remembered God, and was troubled, and in the depth of my distress he had pity upon me, and sent the Comforter. I then felt forgiveness for my offense, and my mind became calm and quiet, being truly thankful to my gracious Redeemer for his mercies. And after this, feeling the spring of divine love opened and a concern to speak, I said a few words in a meeting, in which I found peace. This I believe was about six weeks from the first time, and as I was thus humbled and disciplined under the cross, my understanding became more strengthened to distinguish the language of the pure Spirit which inwardly moves upon the heart and taught [me] to wait in silence sometimes many weeks together, until I felt that rise which prepares the creature to stand like a trumpet, through which the Lord speaks to his flock. (31)

This remarkable passage brings out not only Woolman's learned ability to wait for the Spirit, but the importance for him of what is probably the principal Quaker contribution to the tradition of Christian discernment, namely *the role of inner and outer silence*. To "distinguish the language of the pure Spirit which inwardly moves upon the heart" is for both Ignatius and Woolman the very essence of holy decision. Ignatius would agree on the importance of solitude and silence for one making the *Spiritual Exercises* (n. 20; Ganss 127). Woolman speaks of how, in his first apostolic journey, "I was often silent through the meetings, and when I spoke it was with much care that I might speak only what Truth opened. My mind was often tender"—a favorite descriptive term for Woolman—"and I learned some profitable lessons" (34).

Later, in 1757, he describes his waiting in silence during a meeting for worship and then for business.

I was silent during the meeting for worship and when business came on, my mind was exercised concerning the poor slaves, but I did not feel my way to speak. And in this condition I was bowed down in spirit before the Lord and with tears and inward supplications besought him to so open my understanding that I might know his will concerning me, and at length my mind was settled in silence (70).

Shortly thereafter, at another meeting, "I . . . sat a considerable time in much weakness; then I felt Truth open the way to speak in much plainness and simplicity" (71). Again, during a series of meetings on Long Island in 1760, "It was my concern from day to day to say no more nor less than what the spirit of Truth opened in me, being jealous over myself, lest I should say anything to make my testimony look agreeable to that mind in people which is not in pure obedience to the cross of Christ" (106).

This mention of the cross of Christ leads to another affinity between these two mystics of the apostolic word. Both of them situate Christian decision within a *theologia crucis* which contains a *strong antiworldly commitment*. Despite—or perhaps together with—their accent on the primacy of God the Creator and the divine will as governing all, both of our spiritual guides offer a decidedly redemptional outlook.

For Ignatius, creational and redemptional perspectives both alternate and cross in the *Spiritual Exercises* and in the *Constitutions*. The "Principle and Foundation" and the "Contemplation for Gaining Divine Love" are couched in theistic rather than in christological or soteriological terms, while in the exercises on the "Kingdom of Christ," the "Two Standards," and the "Three Modes of Humility," the struggle with the principalities and powers and with the spirit of worldly ambition that they engender in humans comes to the fore. In this regard the *Spiritual Exercises* is far from being a neatly integrated spiritual theology, which was, of course, far from its purpose.

Woolman for his part is acutely conscious of the importance of the cross of Christ and of the need for himself and his companions to discern the allurements of worldliness. He wrote of being "humbled and disciplined under the cross" (31). He regrets that many of his contemporaries, "having their religion chiefly by education, and not being enough acquainted with that cross which crucifies to the world, do manifest a temper distinguishable from that of an entire trust in God" (84). Again, he speaks of "that spirit which crucifies to the greatness and showy grandeur of this world" (96).

For both Ignatius and Woolman a crucial ingredient in this crucifixion with Christ, and an essential condition for truly effective ministry, is *the spirit and practice of poverty.* In his *Spiritual Exercises,* Ignatius identifies the love of wealth as the root of vanity and pride (n. 142; Ganss 155). His spiritual diary testifies that he labored over the poverty of his Society more than over any other point in his writing of the Jesuit *Constitutions* (Ganss 238–70 passim). The core group of members of the Society, the "professed," were called to *evangelizare in paupertate*—to proclaim the gospel from a situation of literal and attitudinal poverty. Ignatius's understanding of poverty, drawing on but notably differing from the poverty of monks and mendicants in previous eras, had a twofold preoccupation: first, radical trust in God's power working through, beyond, and despite the fragile efforts of human instruments; second, the credibility of the proclamation in the eyes of people accustomed to worldly clerics. Only those who experienced in their own lives a felt need for reliance on God were capable of revitalizing the preaching and teaching ministries of the church.

Early in his life Woolman came to embrace a simple life-style as an essential ingredient of his personal call.

> I was learning to be content with real conveniences that were not costly, so that a way of life free from much entanglements appeared best for me. . . . I saw that a humble man, with the blessing of the Lord, might live on a little, and that where the heart was set on greatness, success in business did not satisfy the craving. (35)

But his more passionate sense of need for poverty came from his perception of the linkage between easy living and the oppression of the poor. During his southern journey in 1746, he recorded the effect on his own peace of mind of different life-styles in the communities he encountered. "Where the masters bore a good share of the burden, and lived frugal, so that their servants were well provided for, and their labour moderate, I felt more easy; but where they lived in a costly way and laid heavy burdens on their slaves, my exercise was often great" (38).

Woolman had an especially intense experience of the connection between material comfort and the oppression of the poor during his voyage to England in 1772. His decision to travel steerage rather than in the cabin was not lightly taken, particularly as he was to share the voyage with a beloved friend, Samuel Emlen, Junior. One of his scruples regarding cabin passage was that his money would be used to pay for "sundry sorts of carved work and imagery . . . superfluity of workmanship of several sorts," furnishings which aimed "to please the mind of such who give way to a conformity to this world" (164). He told the owner of the ship,

> having many times been engaged, in the fear and love of God, to labor with those under whom the oppressed have been borne down and afflicted, I have often perceived that with a view to get riches and to provide estates for children, to live comfortable to the customs which stand in that spirit wherein men have regard to the honours of this world—that in the pursuit of these things I have seen many entangled in the spirit of oppression, and the exercise of my soul has been such that I could not find peace in joining in anything which I saw was against that wisdom which is pure. (165)

He did not, as a matter of fact, spend all of his time in steerage: during a fierce storm, "I believed the poor wet toiling seamen had need of all the room in the crowded steerage" (169). That such compassion was genuine is attested by what he writes about the condition of seamen. He witnessed "that almost universal depravity among sailors" (170), stemming from their lack of proper education and the squalid conditions of their work. He embraced opportunities to listen in on their conversations, and so to learn firsthand the sordid conditions of the slave trade in which some of them had engaged (172). In this intense situation he experienced once again the incompatibility of the love of money and honor with a life that is focused on the coming of God's kingdom on earth (173).

As he brings this part of his account to a close, he dreams of the next generation, "that they may have an education different from the present education of lads at sea," that remembering "the lamentable corruptions which attend the conveyance of merchandise across the seas," we may "so abide in the love of Christ that being delivered from the love of money, from the entangling expenses of a curious, delicate and luxurious life—that we may learn contentment with a little and promote the seafaring life no further than that spirit which leads into all Truth attends us in our proceedings" (180).

Nowhere is Woolman's facility for finding God in all things more manifest than in his account of the lengthy voyage to England, which was to lead to his death. He kept his eyes and ears and heart open to what was happening about him. Both in booking passage and in the course of the journey, he waited for the inner Spirit to show him how he was to cope and minister. The experience of human misery and injustice brought him to embrace more deeply the cross of Christ and to bear witness against worldly attachments that oppress humans and hinder the work of the gospel.

Woolman and Modern Jesuit Perspectives

Three other striking and important aspects of the spirituality of the *Journal* will not be developed here, as they relate less closely to the Ignatian tradition than to concerns of Jesuits and others today. The most significant of these is Woolman's keen realization and expression, through a rudimentary social analysis, of the connections between personal behaviors on the one hand and social, political, and economic injustice on the other. In today's jargon, we would say that his was a deprivatized spirituality. He viewed such issues as slavery, war, and the oppression of Native Americans as needing to be dealt with through personal and communal conversion from worldliness. And he passionately witnessed to the incompatibility of prevailing ideologies regarding these issues with discipleship to Jesus Christ.

A more extended study might also describe the way in which Woolman anticipated the outlook of today's ecological spirituality. For him not only was God to be experienced contemplatively in nature, but humans were called to exercise an unworldly stewardship toward all of God's creatures.

The third aspect is the manifest nonviolence that is characteristic of Woolman in both word and example. His inner Spirit sanctions no form, personal or communal, of vengeance, retaliation, or affront to enemies.

It seems appropriate to close this reflection with a word about love in Woolman and Ignatius. The latter, who was rarely facile or emotional in speaking of love, nevertheless is insistent on its centrality. He names the culminating exercise of his *Spiritual Exercises* as a "Contemplation for Gaining Divine Love" (nn. 230–37; Ganss 176f.). Its language is cool and rational. It presents love as intimate communion resulting from total and mutual self-gift of the partners. The famous offering "Take, Lord, and receive all my liberty . . ." crystallizes the total response that needs to inform every "election" worthy of the name. Taken against the background of previous exercises on the reign of God and the opposing standards of Christ and Satan, the commitment is an unqualified acceptance of apostolic mission. The very first words of the *Constitutions* written by Ignatius for Jesuits identify, as an inner principle far more important than external laws, "the interior law of charity and love which the Holy Spirit writes and engraves upon hearts" (n. 134; Ganss 288).

The language could well be that of Woolman, for whom the divine Spirit dwelling within humans was always a spirit of love, whose movements evoked a return of love, manifested especially in a loving concern for all of God's creatures, particularly those in need. Like Ignatius, Woolman is relatively slow to speak the literal language of love. More frequently he speaks of the tender mercies of God, or of God as the Father of mercies. But the very first sentence of the *Journal* expresses the core of his spiritual endeavor. "I have often felt a motion of love . . ." (23), and he speaks immediately thereafter of his first acquaintance, before the age of seven, with the "operations of Divine love." He speaks without differentiation of the love of God and of Christ, "influencing our minds" (101), being "the first motion" (127) in his reflection, being experienced as an "opening of universal love" (154), so that "my heart was overcome with the love of Christ" (178).

One final passage shows how divine love, received by and in turn going forth from the heart, was viewed by Woolman as extending to the whole of creation. He was attentive, at various stages of the voyage to England, to the condition of the birds as the ship came down the Delaware, and again as it approached the English coast:

> I often remembered the Fountain of goodness, who gave being to
> all creatures, and whose love extends to that of caring for the

sparrows, and [I] believe where the love of God is verily perfected,
and the true spirit of government watchfully attended to, a tenderness toward all creatures made subject to us will be experienced,
and a care felt in us that we do not lessen the sweetness of life in the
animal creation, which the great Creator intends for them under
our government. (178f.)

Notes

1. As detached a critic as Voltaire somewhat grandiosely noted this
historical affinity: "The establishment in Paraguay by the Spanish Jesuits
appears alone, in some way, the triumph of humanity. It seems to expiate
the cruelty of the first conquerors. The Quakers in North America and the
Jesuits in South America gave a new spectacle to the world." Quoted in
C. J. McNaspy, *Lost Cities of Paraguay* (Chicago: Loyola University Press,
1982), 9.

2. References to the Ignatian writings will cite the paragraph numbers of
most standard editions, followed by the page numbers of the translations
found in George E. Ganss, S.J., ed., *Ignatius of Loyola: The Spiritual
Exercises and Selected Works* (New York: Paulist Press, 1991). References to
Woolman's *Journal* will be to the page numbers of the text found in Phillips
Moulton, ed., *Journal and Major Essays of John Woolman* (New York:
Oxford University Press, 1971).

8
Eucharist: Joy and the Beams of Love

EDWARD J. FARRELL

Is the Eucharist the source and the summit of the entire Christian life? This is certainly a common "declaration" and assumption or presumption among Roman Catholics. I would ask: How long does it take for the Eucharist to be the center of one's life or how easily does "it" fade to the edge of one's life as a "nice" Sunday habit? The Eucharist is not an option. It must be more than a habit. Paul's cry to "discern" the body and the blood of Christ is an imperative for all time. In an age of highest participation and most frequent communion, spiritual anorexia can so easily emerge. If one is not nourished by what one eats, one can lose the capacity to eat and not even recognize one's hunger.

Eucharist: A Catholic Perspective

How does one grow in celebrating the Eucharist, Christ's presence in our midst? In our food- and nutrition-centered culture, eating is not enough for good health, exercise is necessary. We all love to eat, few enjoy exercise. Yet without exercise our bodies lose their vitality and vibrancy, their tonality. So it is with the Eucharist—without the spiritual exercise of adoration, contemplation, and compassion the fruitfulness of the Eucharist as mystery, sacrifice, and sacrament can be diminished.

Eucharistic Worship Outside the Liturgy

Documents continue to come from Rome inviting all the faithful to deeper understanding and fuller exercise of the gift of the Eucharist. The following is what struck me from *Holy Communion and Worship of the Eucharist Outside Mass:*[1]

> Pastors should see that . . . churches . . . are opened every day for at least several hours at a convenient time, so that the faithful may easily pray in the presence of the Blessed Sacrament. (No. 8)
>
> When the faithful adore Christ present in the Sacrament, they should remember that this presence derives from the sacrifice and has as its purpose both sacramental and spiritual communion. Therefore, the devotion prompting the faithful to visit the Blessed Sacrament draws them into an ever deeper share in the Pascal mystery and leads them to respond gratefully to the gift of Him who through His humanity constantly pours divine life into members of His Body. Abiding with Christ the Lord, they enjoy His intimate friendship and pour out their hearts before Him for themselves and for those dear to them and they pray for the peace and salvation of the world. (No. 80)
>
> Prayer before Christ the Lord sacramentally present extends the union with Christ that the faithful have reached in communion. (No. 81)
>
> Exposition of the Holy Eucharist . . . leads us to acknowledge Christ's marvelous presence in the Sacrament and invites us to the spiritual union with Him that culminates in sacramental communion.
>
> . . . Christ's intention of instituting the Eucharist [is] above all to be near us, to feed, heal, and to comfort us. (No. 82)
>
> . . . the celebration of the Eucharistic mystery includes in a higher way that inner communion to which exposition is meant to lead the faithful. (No. 83)

The Eucharist and "Amorization"

Eucharistic spirituality is incarnational spirituality. It is the spirituality of Jesus present in the most ordinary and the most extraordinary of our everyday. Through the Eucharist Jesus extends his presence in history, a presence that is constantly deepening, always intensifying, and continuously drawing all things and everyone unto himself. We are united to Christ and in Christ we are united to the Trinity. The Eucharist is the door by which the Trinity comes to us. God is the One, the only One, who can give everything and can share totally. Everything passes into and through the Eucharist. All things are gathered together. Like a cornucopia funnel, everything that is good flows out of the Eucharist to us and all things enter through the Eucharist as through a "white hole." Everything coming down and going up! The Eucharist is always happening. Christ is always transforming us and all things more and more into himself. Everything passes through the Eucharist and is taken into him and becomes the body of Christ. As metabolism is always going on in us, so is "amorization." Everything is being turned into love.

If we could only believe the truth! If we could only remember! "Do this in memory of me." Two kinds of remembrance are required: a remembrance by liturgical action and a remembrance by an attitude of service. "If I who am Master and Lord wash your feet, so you are to wash each other's feet." If we find it difficult to serve others, so often it is because we ourselves have not adequately experienced the service Jesus renders to us. We ask, "Are you running with me, Jesus?" And Jesus' response is, "Are you resting with me?" "Come to me. Come apart and rest awhile." "I will refresh you." "Unload all your worries on me because I care for you." "I am always with you." Jesus is in us as in his own bed. Jesus has grown up with each of us like our own body, our mind, our heart. Jesus has always been with us, knowing us, loving us, leading us, guiding us.

Jesus is the twin of each of us, our other self. Each of us has a double consciousness. Jesus is the teacher. We are not doing this. He is doing it in us. We do not know anything. He is the known, the understander. Each day Jesus calls us, connects us, relates us. He is our communication with one another. He is our understanding of each person. We cannot relate to anyone. He is the relationship. He opens the door. He draws people to us! He leads us, introduces us to others, attracts us to them and them to us. We are permitted to see his truth in every person, to experience something of his hidden light and joy in each individual, in each particle of creation. We are pierced by darts, arrows, beams of beauty and goodness from so many people and places. Wave upon wave of loveliness comes over us, a constant current almost throwing us backward. Christ is with us, all's right with the world. "Do not be afraid." "Go to sleep. Enjoy your rest and peace." Jesus is with us, always with us. Always he draws us deeper, higher, giving us more and more gifts, more and more love, more and more possibility. Jesus gives us of himself totally. He holds nothing back. He is willing to suffer, to make up for anything that we lack. Jesus lives in us more than we live in ourselves. Without Jesus there would be only nothingness in us.

Contemplation, Absorption, Recognition

These beams of love, peace, and joy are the gift and fruit of the Eucharist. Recognition dawns only slowly. It is an accumulated grace of his presence in us, of his constant coming to us, of his forever breathing into us the person of his Spirit. Eucharist is given to us because our hearts so quickly become empty and hungry. We are always running out of his Spirit. So Jesus comes to fill our hearts with himself. Jesus invites himself and brings the food, himself. He creates in us a hunger that can never be satisfied but with himself. The more we eat, the more there is; the more we understand, the more there is to know; the more we listen, the more there is to hear. Jesus is always speaking, always revealing himself, always loving us. Eucharist always increases our appetite and capacity for him, for joy, for life.

How do we receive the look of Jesus? How do we experience Jesus looking on us with love? How do we accept the compassion and understanding of the Word of God? We do not dare to dream our deepest desires, to hope for an answer to our greatest yearnings. How do we allow Jesus to manifest himself? How do we absorb, like solar panels, his love each day, the beams of his Word? "Look, I am standing at the door and knocking!" "Taste and see." How important it is for us to take the contemplative pause, the "Jesus" break. We cannot stay centered without it. "Live in me. Let me live in you." How do we practice the presence of God in each day, in each moment? There is the moment of sacramental communion of each day. There are the many moments of spiritual communion, communion by desire, our hearts hungering again to be with him. There is the inward drawing to find him dwelling within us and there is likewise the welling up of his presence within us. He teaches us. He bubbles up into consciousness, reminding us, "I am with you always."

How many of us live below a spiritual poverty level, unaware and inattentive to his presence, his love, his gentleness, his peace. Accumulative consciousness of the indwelling presence of Jesus results in a kind of meltdown. He increases. We decrease. We are commanded to do Eucharist not only that Jesus may be always present to human beings but that we too might be present to one another. We each tend to stand on our own island. We do not recognize our common shore. The cultic way, while continuing to be at the center of Christian life, is not the only way by which Christ continues his presence in the midst of his disciples; love and service are likewise a privileged way. So often we can be comfortable at the Last Supper but evade Good Friday. The mystery of the Eucharist is not a static mystery of Jesus' presence. It is not an inanimate wafer that we receive. The mystery of the Eucharist is the dynamic mystery of Christ drawing all things into his death and resurrection. It is the mystery of love drawing all suffering into himself. It is the mystery of the transformation of the earth. It is the mystery of our own life entering into and caught up by the incarnation, death, and resurrection of Jesus, and it is through us that Jesus thus continues his redeeming transformation in the human heart.

The Ministry of the Eucharist

The ultimate purpose of the Eucharist is to intensify in this world the familial world of love that is divine. The sacramental communion with the Son of God makes us grow in love. It is the school of active love for our neighbor. The more we are enabled to adore and contemplate Jesus in the eucharistic sacrament, the more we are called to recognize and contemplate him in our brothers and sisters. To contemplate is to look at someone with love. To contemplate Christ is to experience him looking at us with love, and unavoidably we then pass his look of love on to others. We develop a new kind of presence to ourselves and to others. "Let us learn, respectfully, to discover with respect the truth about the interior man, for it is this inner self that becomes the dwelling of the God who is present in the Eucharist."[2] We are to have an active participation in the ministry of the Eucharist. "I am the vine, you are the branches." Through the Eucharist we are connected to him, even the littlest, the tenderest of branches. Through the Eucharist the Father's love flows into us; Jesus' life is transplanted into us and the Spirit's breath becomes our own. Cumulatively and progressively we are sacrament! Together with the Trinity we work for the littlest branch, the smallest shoot, the most fragile bud. "The smoking flax I will not quench; the bruised reed, I will not break." At the Last Supper, Jesus took hold of his own destiny. His death became the sacrifice of communion. Through the Eucharist, we are enabled to take hold of our own destiny. The practice of justice, of holiness in everyday life, demands our sacrifice. "Everyday we experience something of the death of Jesus in these bodies of ours that we may also know the power of Jesus' resurrection." The very existence of the community of the church is dependent upon the words of eucharistic institution: "This is my body given for you." "This is the cup of the new covenant poured out for you." In Jesus the divinely given covenant with the created universe is fully renewed and this universe can now mediate his presence. The covenant celebrated in the Eucharist is God's, the Trinity's, covenant with us sealed in Jesus' blood and in Jesus' body. It is the Son given for the salvation of the world. This existential love of Christ is the only "reality" by which the church truly draws its life. Jesus sends forth his Spirit, his laser beam, into the hearts of all people. The church becomes the network of the Eucharist throughout the city, the country, the world. The church becomes a eucharistic satellite orbiting, encircling the world broadcasting his love. In and through the Eucharist we live at the level of the universal church in intercommunion with the whole human race. The words of institution not only render an alteration of the elements of bread and wine but likewise create a communion of persons, a communion of the most intense kind possible. The Risen Christ by his real presence takes believers into himself and thus plunges them into a mystical identification with the Divinity and with one another. The Eucharist is a wedding, a spousal union! Like a bride and groom and the mystery of one in another, the Eucharist is embedded in the universe; the universe is embedded in Christ. Jesus yearns to know his fullness in us. "I have come that they may have life and have it to the fullest!"

Eucharistic Joy

"That my joy may be in you and in you reach its fullness." Joy is the inflowing of Jesus' presence in us. It is the absorption of his radiance in us and it is born out of being consciously connected to him. Every sacrament is a sacrament of joy, but how long it takes to recognize the sacramentals of everyday life. How good God is! How good it is to be alive, to have been created, to be continually renewed! What joy there is in seeing, hearing, tasting, touching, smelling the goodness of creation. "How good it is for us to be here!" Yet there is even greater joy in experiencing the goodness of God's people. "He gives marvelous comrades to me!"

There are so many things to be joyful about even on a purely human level: the joy of human achievement in science, art, music, medicine, community, commitment; the joy of rest and recreation, of ministry and work, of reading and writing, of movies and poetry, of city and country, of friendships and family, of the newborn and of the aged; the joy of the seasons, of winter turning into spring and spring into summer; the joy of basking in another's goodness, grace, love; the joy of solitude, of one's own inner being; the joy of remembrance and the joy of anticipation; the joy of scripture, of prayer, of his indwelling presence, of the Eucharist.

Now with the Eucharist, there is nothing that remains just purely human. "Joy to the world! The Lord has come!" Everything is taken into Jesus each day. All of life—our joys, our fears, our hopes, and our dreams. Jesus takes all the people and friends who we carry in our hearts, our minds, our bodies. Jesus takes them and pours out on everything and everyone that touches us his forgiveness, healing, mercy, kindness, compassion, strength, love. Jesus' love within us passes through us into the world, and as it passes through us it transforms us and transforms the world. He wipes away every tear from our eyes and rejoices over us.

Jesus was filled with joy by the Holy Spirit and it is that same Spirit with which he fills us. We are given a new mind and a new heart to know the truth of creation united to the Son of man, and God disposes the mind and heart of his creature to meet joy at the same time as it meets truth. We are disposed toward a certain inner light, to experience something of the joy of God. Human joy will always be incomplete, fragile, threatened, vulnerable, but the joy that comes from the Spirit can never be taken away.

God is holy. God is love. God is joy. God has made us in God's own image. God has made us to be joy-filled. To be like God is to know and to touch God's holiness, love, joy within ourselves. Over each of us God announces as God announced to the Virgin Mary: "Rejoice, O highly favored son or daughter. The Lord is with you. Blessed are you among all people and blessed is the fruit of your heart in which dwells the Savior of the world." And, like Mary, we ponder these things in our hearts, and through the accumulative grace given to us in the Eucharist we are able to sing out with her our response to God: "My soul proclaims the greatness of the Lord and my spirit finds joy in God my Savior, for God who is mighty has done great things for me and Holy is God's name!"

Catholic Eucharistic Spirituality Complemented by the Quaker Spirituality of Presence

> . . . and we are put on earth a little space that we may learn to bear the beams of love.—William Blake

Joy and Beams of Love

On August 31, 1991, my friend Douglas Steere celebrated his ninetieth birthday. I have known him since 1980, when I was invited to become a member of the Ecumenical Institute for Spirituality, of which he was the cofounder in 1965. He is the foremost authority on *Quaker Spirituality* in the world today, the author of that volume in The Classics of Western Spirituality. He was an official observer at Vatican II. Few could rival him as a world person, an international ecumenical initiator of dialogue in depth. Douglas Steere seems to have learned so early in life, and so deeply, how to "give to the faith of another the amplitude of love. . . . We must learn how to create an inter-religious space and in such a space, God's Spirit can blow."[3]

My experience of Douglas Steere is one of eucharist, of thanksgiving and gratitude for the joy and beams of love that he has shared with me. He is my "vieux frère," my older brother, reared and educated in our native Detroit. How much he has been a "sacrament" for me, an outer sign of the inner reality of what is called in the Catholic tradition the "Real Presence and the Divine Indwelling." In his writings he rarely uses the word "eucharist," but in them he has given me a much needed contemporary spirituality in approaching the Eucharist . . . an approach through presence, solitude, listening, attention, and silence.

To live joy and radiate beams of love is more important than being able to describe it, yet Douglas Steere has also been given the gift of interpreting the tradition.

> The pan-sacramental sense of the holiness of every life relationship is also intimately connected with this inward experience of communion. The Quaker's reluctance to acknowledge the necessity of the outward sacraments of water-baptism and of the Eucharist cannot be understood without keeping his [or her] inward experience of communion in mind. The inward baptism and the experience of participation in the ever present life and spirit of the inward Christ to which these outward, symbolic practices of baptism and Eucharist point are both at the very center of the Quaker experience.[4]

For Eucharist is always an invitation to adoration . . . contemplation . . . to an inward experience of communion. Documents continue to come from Rome that encourage people to pray in the presence of the Blessed Sacrament that they might discover in these times of adoration a deeper spiritual communion and a more profound share in the Pascal mystery. Thus they come to enjoy an intimate friendship with Christ and are led to pour out their hearts for the peace and healing of the world. In coming to a fuller appreciation of Eucharist, people will come to experience Christ's companioning presence as close as their own breath, healing and comforting and guiding them as they inhale and exhale Christ's love. The celebration of the eucharistic mystery is meant to lead one to that inner communion of unity, peace, harmony, joy, and love that Quaker lives so beautifully exemplify.

The following is my collage of what Douglas Steere has imprinted in me from his writings, especially *On Being Present Where You Are, Together in Solitude, On Listening to Another, On the Power of Sustained Attention,* and *On Speaking Out of the Silence.*

Presence

Have we lost our capacity for worship and adoration? Or have we not yet discovered it? Do our liturgies take people where they are and draw them into an experience and awareness of what they secretly hunger for out of their spiritual anorexia? Does the Eucharist "draw them into their Friend's presence, looking long and lovingly into each other's faces and then parting silently, no words having been spoken or required but both touched to the depth by the other's presence?"[5]

These elements are the outward invitations to inward states of soul, to inward stages of experience, which, if they laid hold of the worshipers as they are intended to do, would bring these worshipers into the presence of the Listener and renew and refresh their lives.

How I value the way Douglas Steere tells the story of the Quaker tradition. "These first Friends who trembled with a consciousness of God's nearness to them . . . rightly got the name 'Quakers.' " There was One nearer to them than breathing who "spoke to their condition." They felt the healing of God drop upon their souls. The whole creation had a new smell. They were "moved" to their tasks.[6]

In *On Being Present Where You Are,* Douglas Steere speaks of presence as

> a readiness to respect and to stand in wonder and openness before the mysterious life and influence of the other. It means to be sure, a power to influence, to penetrate, to engage with the other; but it means equally, a willingness to be vulnerable enough to be influenced by, to be penetrated by, and even to be changed by the experience.[7]

Solitude

In all of Douglas Steere's writings he has some plain words for the universality of the contemplative and mystical dimension in the heart of every person. So characteristic of his modesty is his way of frequently quoting another to describe his own insight, intuition, and experience. As Evelyn Underhill has said, "Ordinary contemplation is possible to anyone; without it, they are not wholly conscious, nor wholly alive. . . . The spring of the amazing energy which enables the great mystic to rise to freedom and dominate his world, is hidden in all of us, an integral part of our humanity."[8] Douglas does not let you focus or linger upon himself too long; he is always introducing you to another friend, whom he feels will have more to say.

Listening

In our day of verbal and image saturation, I envy the Spirit of the Quaker tradition:

> There are times when they do not want words even though they may be good words. They want to feel the fresh, free currents of life without any sound or voice. They have a fear of stopping with the outward symbol and of not getting beyond it to that deeper reality for which it stands. The result is that throughout their history, they have preferred to seek for the baptism of the spirit without the use of water and to experience a communion of soul with the living Christ without the use of bread and wine.[9]

Douglas is graced with great teachers, great friends. He takes people deep into himself and treasures their stories and wisdom. He quotes T. S. Eliot pointing out how often we find our true contemporaries not in our own generation: "they walk out of other ages and lay hold of us, are acutely present to us and we know them for our own."[10]

Douglas Steere's writings are always illuminated with the wisdom of so many. Seventeenth-century Quaker Isaac Pennington speaks again through Douglas. "There is that near you which will guide you. O wait for it and be sure that you keep to it." He was ready to recognize an echo in Thomas Merton: "You don't have to rush after it.

It is there all the time. If you give it a chance, it will make itself known to you."

When I first read "On Listening to Another," I was drawn deep into what I call the immense silence created by the Eternal Listener. "If we but knew the gift of God" and who it is who speaks to us, who gives himself to us, who dwells in us!

Our words are often halting and many times plainly not what we mean. Back of what we mean on the conscious level, there is almost always a deeper unconscious meaning that is at work. What a gift Douglas Steere has for describing "holy listening."

> To 'listen' another's soul into life, into a condition of disclosure and discovery may be almost the greatest service that any human being ever performs for another. . . . Is it blasphemous to suggest that over the shoulder of the human listener, there is never absent the silent presence of the Eternal Listener, the living God? For in penetrating to what is involved in listening, do we not disclose the thinness of filament that separates men listening openly to one another, and that of God intently listening to each soul? . . .
>
> Then suddenly the message-bearer drops out of sight and the man who a moment ago thought he was the listener is now face to face with the compassionate presence of the Listener from whom nothing is hid but who, in spite of all, loves and accepts him.[11]

And the transforming moment of Emmaus is awakened again and our hearts are burning within.

Attention

"At an early age," Douglas Steere wrote, "we have become afflicted with what could be called 'hardening of the categories,' a disease that has constricted the whole world's vision today so that we can no longer attend to persons and situations or see them as they really are. As Leon Bloy's *Woman Who Was Poor* says, 'There is only one unhappiness and that is not to be one of the saints.' Saints for him are ordinary people who are inwardly attending to the highest truth they know and who are prepared to let His truth have more and more undivided sway in their lives."[12]

Silence

A Swiss writer, Max Picard, suggests that "the perfect silence is heard to echo in the perfect word." Douglas adds,

> Back of language and clinging to it, when it is real, is the receptive sea of silence. Language is always tempted to make reality more articulate than it is. And the words of language are always being rebuked and overrun and swallowed up again by the silent ocean of existence from which they once emerged.[13]

"The mysterious thing of it all is that in God's eyes there are no 'little' things. Everything matters and everything leads to something further."[14]

So many people live at the spiritual poverty level—unaware and inattentive to the moment. Yet everyone is called to be an outlet of eucharistic life . . . to bask in the grace and joy of one another . . . to experience the outbursts of joy that well up, absorbing the radiance of the inner being and colliding with the inner beings of others, releasing new joy, new life, new faith, new love.

We are to be contemplatives, to look upon others with love and to experience Christ looking at us with love. In being attentive to the inner silence, we intensify in this world that communal world of love which is divine—the ultimate purpose of Eucharist. The cumulative indwelling of Eucharist is to be drawn into Christ's presence, love, tenderness, gentleness like rain into the ocean or our breath into the air . . . of being immersed and enveloped in the air around us, of being breathed by Another. Through Christ's cumulative presence, we are visited, called, connected, and related everyday to each person along the way. Each road becomes the Emmaus road, allowing us to experience something of Christ's hidden light and joy in every individual, in every particle of creation. We feel pierced by darts, beams of beauty, peace, joy, and love. We are always being drawn deeper and higher, increasing our love and joy capacity, and being led to new potential, new life.

One does not have to have been with Douglas Steere very long to realize the harmony of his words and his life. With gratitude and profound respect, let me conclude by echoing his own words, which resonate within my own heart:

Until I have been lured into the desert, until I have been brought in solitude to the very ground of my being, where I am beyond the grip of my surface self with all of its plans and distractions, I am not able to hear the divine whisper. . . . It is then I discover at the heart of things that my solitariness is transcended and that I am not alone.[15]

Notes

1. *Rites of the Catholic Church* (New York: Pueblo Publishing Co., 1990), vol. 1, no. 83.

2. Pope John Paul II, "The Holy Eucharist," Lenten Letter, Feb. 24, 1980, in *The Church Speaks* 25 (1980): 146.

3. Douglas V. Steere, ed., *Quaker Spirituality*, Classics of Western Spirituality (New York: Paulist Press, 1984), 25.

4. Ibid., 18.

5. Ibid.

6. Ibid., 276.

7. Douglas V. Steere, *On Being Present Where You Are*. Pendle Hill Pamphlet 151 (Wallingford, Pa.: Pendle Hill Publications, 1967), 9.

8. Douglas V. Steere, *Gleanings: A Random Harvest* (Nashville: Upper Room, 1986), 18.

9. Steere, ed., *Quaker Spirituality*, 279.

10. Steere, *On Being Present Where You Are*, 7.

11. Douglas V. Steere, *On Listening to Another* (New York: Harper & Brothers, 1955), 14, 15.

12. Ibid., 51.

13. Ibid., 112.

14. Ibid., 128ff.

15. Douglas V. Steere, *Together in Solitude* (New York: Crossroad, 1982), back cover.

9

Centering Prayer and the Friends

BASIL PENNINGTON, O.C.S.O.

In 1971, when the leaders of the Order of Cistercians of the Stricter Observance (Trappists) were meeting at Rome in General Chapter, Pope Paul VI welcomed them to the Vatican. The pope, who was the architect, under the Holy Spirit, of the renewal that was taking place in the Roman Catholic Church, in speaking to the abbots and abbesses, asserted that there could never be a true renewal if there was not a renewal in depth of the members of the church themselves and in their prayer life, their union, and their communion with God. He went on to urge those assembled, with their communities, to do whatever they could to help their fellow Catholics in the West to recover the contemplative dimension of their Christian life.

Abbot Thomas Keating and the monks of Saint Joseph's Abbey, in Spencer, Massachusetts, took this exhortation of the Holy Father very seriously. Examining the situation, they realized that they offered their guests a share in their silence and solitude. Good food was provided for body and soul. The guests were welcomed into the community's liturgical prayer. But in fact, the monks were in no practical and effective way, apart from example and space, offering their guests the opportunity to enter into the contemplative prayer of the brethren. It was time for them to look into the tradition that was alive among them to see how they might begin effectively to do this.

The Cistercians of the Stricter Observance seek to live more strictly or, perhaps it would be better to say, more fully, Benedict of Nursia's Rule for monasteries.[1] In the last chapter of this Rule, written around 525, Benedict humbly declares that he has written but a rule for beginners.[2] For more profound guidance, the saint sends his disciples first of all to the sacred scriptures: "What page, what passage of the inspired books of the Old and New Testament is not the truest of guides for human life?"[3] And then to the "Fathers," citing especially the *Conferences* of St. John Cassian.[4]

John Cassian was a brilliant young Dalmatian who went to study at Rome at the end of the fourth century. He did not find in the lecture halls what he was looking for, and, in the style of that time (and many other times including our own), he left the heady knowledge of the schools behind and headed east. John's search was a long one. For a time he settled in a monastery in the Holy Land. But it was finally in the remote deserts of Egypt that he found the spiritual fathers who initiated him into the wisdom he sought. In particular it was Abba Isaac, who was reputed to be the holiest, oldest, and wisest father of the desert, who taught him a simple and practical way of entering into deeper prayer, a prayer of quiet union and communion. When he returned to the West, Cassian, himself now a spiritual father, founded a community for women and another for men in southern France. For these he wrote his *Conferences*, seeking to make available to his disciples the wisdom he had found in the deserts of Egypt, a living tradition that went back to the earliest days of Christianity.[5]

The simple way of prayer that Abba Isaac taught John Cassian was practiced through the centuries by the daughters and sons of Saint Benedict and passed on by them to others. We find constant reflections of it in the writings that come to us from this living tradition.[6] An early expression of this in the English language is the unusually popular fourteenth-century *Cloud of Unknowing*.[7] This text, written by an anonymous spiritual father for his spiritual son, a young advocate, is not easily read or understood by a twentieth-century person. It presupposes the father's oral teaching and it contains the cautions fashionable at that period.[8] It was meant to support the daily practice of one already knowledgeable in the prayer. The whole method is there, but it has to be coaxed out.[9]

Centering Prayer

As the monks of Saint Joseph's Abbey set about responding to the exhortation of Pope Paul VI, they sought to pass on the traditional teaching of Abba Isaac, John Cassian, and *The Cloud* in the simplest way possible so that Christians of all ages and backgrounds could easily grasp it and begin to practice it in their daily lives. The monks were deeply conscious of the clear teaching of Paul: "We do not know how to pray as we ought, but the Holy Spirit prays within us."[10] The method did not have to teach all—it couldn't. Rather, it opened the space for the Spirit to pray within us. After a good bit of trial and error, sharing the prayer with many thousands, the presentation was refined to these simple points:

Sit relaxed and quiet.

1. Be in faith and love to God who dwells in the center of your being.
2. Take up a love word and let it be gently present, supporting your being to God in faith-filled love.
3. Whenever you become *aware* of anything, simply, gently return to God with the use of your prayer word.

At the end of your prayer time let the Our Father (or some other prayer of your own choosing) pray itself quietly within.[11]

This way of prayer has traditionally been called the prayer of the heart. But this name has its difficulties. Some of the great teachers of prayer through the centuries have used the name and given it very specific meanings, so that its use can be somewhat ambiguous. Moreover, modern Americans did not readily understand "heart" in the biblical sense of that deepest place within us, the core and center of our being, where we are in touch with the source of our life and life responses. Rather, they think more immediately of the cardiac organ and are distracted by the image. Inspired by the very popular writings of a modern-day Cistercian, Thomas Merton, those who learned the prayer began to call it "Centering Prayer."

Merton in writing about prayer said things like:

> The fact is, however, that if you descend into the depths of your own
> spirit . . . and arrive somewhere near the center of what you are, you
> are confronted with the inescapable truth, at the very root of your
> existence you are in constant and immediate and inescapable
> contact with the infinite power of God.[12]

He wrote to a Sufi friend:

> Now you ask about my method of meditation. Strictly speaking I
> have a very simple way of prayer. It is centered entirely on attention
> to the presence of God and to His will and His love. That is to say
> that it is centered on *faith* by which alone we can know the presence
> of God.[13]

Toward the end of his life, Merton, speaking to God the Father,
summed up his aspirations:

> To be here with the silence of Sonship in my heart is to be a center
> in which all things converge upon you. That is surely enough for the
> time being.[14]

This name, "Centering Prayer," has become quite popular. Unfortunately it has been applied to some other approaches to prayer,
which has caused some confusion. But, by and large, the name
"Centering Prayer" is understood to refer to the method of prayer
taught by the monks of Saint Joseph's, drawing upon the living
tradition of Abba Isaac, John Cassian, twelfth-century Cistercian
fathers, and *The Cloud of Unknowing*.

Centering Prayer and the Friends

Many, when they first hear about Centering Prayer and even when
they come to experience it, think of it as being similar to the way of
prayer practiced through recent centuries by the Friends. This is what
I would like to explore a bit here.

Douglas Steere has pointed out that Quakers generally are not too comfortable with methods of prayer.[15] Nevertheless, they do have a method of prayer. Is it really the same as what we have come to call Centering Prayer? The answer is perhaps both yes and no.

An important part of the Quaker witness, as Steere sees it, "is that the living promise of transformation is still accessible, is still going on here and now."[16] He states:

> Although Quakerism has never explicitly formulated the matter in any major statement with which I am familiar, many Friends feel themselves a part of something that is unwalled, that is a third force, that is neither Roman Catholic nor Protestant but a part of a Christian mystical stream that has nurtured and over and over again has renewed them all.[17]

Douglas Steere's presence at the Second Vatican Council as the Quaker observer may well have inspired Pope Paul VI in his reaffirmation of the importance of the contemplative dimension for the wholeness of the renewal. Certainly the pope's own Roman Catholic tradition has much to say about it. Contemplative communities present throughout the Catholic world are supposed to be living it and giving witness to it. Yet I believe it is Quaker practice that impacts most on our consciousness. The Friends are seen as a contemplative people whose quiet, effective action for peace and human betterment flows out of their contemplative experience.

Nonetheless, it seems to me that the Quaker way of sitting in the silence and opening to transcendence would in general be uncomfortable with the formulation of Centering Prayer, especially with the third point. The Quaker way is generally more open and flexible. Again let us listen to Douglas Steere:

> The manner of entering the silence varies widely and each person must find his [or her] own way into it. . . . Some give themselves to a wave of gratitude and thankfulness that they are loved and cherished by God, knowing, as William Penn once said, that "we can fall no deeper than God's arms can reach, however deep we fall."
>
> Some pour out their gratitude in the mood of the French poet Paul Claudel, who said that prayer is simply "thankfulness that God

is." They may even spend a few moments thinking what their lives
and future would be like if God did not exist. Some lift up their
hearts in thankfulness for members of the gathered company whom
they know, and hold each of them up in the Presence as they may do
with absent members who are in need. Some simply let go in the
silence and abandon themselves and their needs in much the same
way that we might do if we were walking with a dear friend and
found it unnecessary to talk but simply sensed the joy of the other's
presence. Others are troubled by all kinds of distractions that
intrude into this silence. . . . Friends learn not to try to suppress
them but to acknowledge their presence and abandon themselves
to being open to the inward Christ, the Guide, the Renewer, even if
the distractions continue to be there throughout.[18]

Communal sitting is very important to Quakers, and for many the
primary and even the only way they sit, though more frequent sitting
at home is certainly encouraged by the tradition. While those
practicing Centering Prayer usually find it a great help to sit with
others—there are currents of supportive grace as well as faith-
strengthening witness—the emphasis is on daily personal practice.
Twice a day for twenty minutes is the usual formula for beginners.
After some experience the person praying may decide for longer or
shorter periods. In time, with faithful practice, one's whole life seems
to become centered. God is perceived as present in everyone and
everything. But even then we are still encouraged to continue with a
couple of periods each day of just sitting with the Lord in the silence.
If we are urged to find or create a group to sit with, at least at times,
such is urged mainly to support us as individuals and keep us faithful
in our own daily practice.

In Quaker sitting another element is emphasized as much as
waiting in the silence, and that is obedience. As Steere puts it, "Fox
[George Fox, the man usually referred to as the founder of the
Quakers] thought that the Spirit that moved so fiercely in his heart
did not stop at giving him a bracing feeling that he was not alone. It
went further and laid on him things that were to be done."[19] As Isaac
Pennington, one of the early Quaker writers, put it: "There is that
near you which will guide you; Oh, wait for it and be sure ye keep
to it."[20] Quakers in their sitting, in their waiting upon the Lord,

wait for a word of guidance, for themselves personally and for the community.

Though in Centering Prayer we do not seek guidance or a word from the Lord, either for ourselves or for the community, at the time of prayer, we certainly cannot be closed to such guidance. In fact, in opening to the Spirit, through prayer, we are seeking the growth of the constant activity of the Holy Spirit in the whole of our lives, guiding us in all that we do. Merton states the matter quite forcefully and succinctly:

> A man cannot enter into the deepest center of himself and pass
> through the center into God unless he is able to pass entirely out of
> himself and empty himself and give himself to other people in the
> purity of selfless love.[21]

But during the few minutes given to this particular form of prayer, instead of seeking any leading or any other word from God, those centering are seeking only God, to be with them in silence, in a complete communion of love. I might liken it to certain moments in the living out of the relationship between a married couple. In the Scriptures God has often enough used the image of lovers to depict the relationship God wants to have with us. Openness to sharing their thoughts and concerns is extremely important to a married couple. Nonetheless, there are those moments when they just want to be together in the embrace of love and leave everything else aside. These moments are supremely important in themselves. But also, who can say how profoundly they nurture the listening of other times? In Centering Prayer we are seeking these moments of quiet, all-absorbing embrace. Of course, if we are wholly attentive to God there is nothing to prevent God from infusing into us knowledge or guidance. We can remain wholly attentive to the Lord during this time of prayer. What God has given us will be there later when we need the guidance and need to put it into effect.

The third point or "rule," if you would, of the Centering Prayer method does not want to inhibit the free activity of the Spirit, or try to predetermine what the Spirit will do during our prayer. Rather, the third point acknowledges the proneness of rational discourse to take over in our lives. What begins as listening to the Spirit can quickly become listening to ourselves or a rich theological or practical development of what the Spirit has had to say to us. Our prayer time can quickly become a planning session instead of a quiet loving resting in God, letting God enjoy us and us enjoy God. Most of us tend to orient everything very quickly to human activity. The false self is made up of what we do, what we have, and what others think of us. This is the self that Jesus said must die. By insisting that at the time of prayer we deliberately lay aside all thoughts about our doings and havings, we engage in a process of dying to the false self so that the true self can emerge in God.

Quakers, supported not only by the clear teaching of their tradition but by the regular practice of the weekly meeting, may not be in as much danger of getting lost in self. Therefore, they do not need this sort of absolute insistence on a time of prayer when all thought is laid aside. Those coming from more actively oriented traditions may have less of a hold on the contemplative dimension. The need for insistence upon this third point becomes less important as our lives become more and more constantly centered and the Spirit is constantly at work within us. God is seen and heard in all at all times. Yet when we come to this centering, we more and more want and enjoy simply resting in God.

There is another somewhat more subtle end being aimed at in this third point. I like to try to bring it out in this way: What we are trying to do in Centering Prayer is obey the first commandment: to love our God with our whole mind, our whole soul, our whole heart, and all our strength. In other words, to be all there. Most of the time we are not all there. Most of the time we have one eye on God and the other on ourselves, watching what we are doing, what we are getting. In Centering Prayer we try for a bit to put both eyes on God. When we are looking for something for ourselves, even divine guidance, we are prone to turn back on ourselves. When we have both eyes, all our attention, on God, then we are not self-aware. God has our complete attention and can communicate to us at will. As soon as we become aware of anything else, God no longer has our complete attention. During the little time we set apart for this particular form of prayer, we want to give God our complete attention, be all there for God so we can receive God fully. To do this, to try to be completely there for God, during this prayer whenever we become aware of anything, we simply, gently turn back to God, with the use of our word of love.

This total attention in no way limits what God can do with us and in us during our prayer. To the contrary, it gives God total freedom to act in us, without in any way being limited by our self-reflection. God can give us guidance and we are all there to receive it. God can give us a word for the community and we unself-consciously give voice to it and pass it on to the community in its full clarity and purity.

When self-reflection is present, we begin to think how good the word we have received will sound and how well the community will think of us or how foolish the word might appear and what a fool we will seem to be. The word from God begins to be colored by our reflections. We need a very pure heart to let the divine light flow through undistorted. In Centering Prayer, by seeking to let go of all our thoughts and reflections and judgments, we are trying to move toward purity of heart, trying to become clear windows through which the divine light can shine undisturbed. In Centering Prayer we simply seek to be totally present to God in faith and love—and leave the rest to God.

Does the renewal of this particular little practice from our im-mensely diverse and rich Christian tradition have anything to offer our Friends? I think some Friends might find the Centering Prayer method of use at times.

Douglas Steere notes: "Some [Quakers] who have learned med-itation techniques for stilling the body and the mind make use of them to center themselves in readiness to sense the Presence."[22] Sometimes we come to prayer and our minds are racing. A million cares or worries are pressing on us. Or we are having very strong feelings, good or bad, about another or our life situation. And so on, and so on. A method that will help us to quiet down and let go of all this can be a real help at such times. And Friends might be more comfortable with a method that comes from our own ancient Christian tradition than one borrowed from a more foreign culture and religious outlook.

After entering into the Presence some might find using a love word supports their remaining quietly in that Presence, totally attentive so that the Divine can transmit to them and through them whatever guidance God wishes without any interference from the reflective self. But this seems a natural thing to do rather than a particular method. The Centering Prayer is so simple and so natural, it is almost not a method.

I realize that I write here about Quaker prayer and tradition without that personal experience that comes from sitting in meeting and imbibing the wisdom of the tradition that comes from the sharing of the elders. My many years of friendship with Douglas and Dorothy Steere have given me many insights into the Friends and have greatly enriched my life. Nonetheless, as one writing from outside, I wholly and happily submit my reflections to the judgment of my Friends. Because of my deep friendship with Douglas, I am happy in his honor to offer to our Friends this gift from our common ancient heritage which I have received and have been privileged to share with others. I am far more the debtor in all that I have received from the Friends through Douglas Steere.

Notes

1. Benedict of Nursia, *RB 1980: The Rule of Saint Benedict in Latin and English with Notes,* ed. Timothy Fry, O.S.B. (Collegeville, Minn.: Liturgical Press, 1981).

2. Ibid., ch. 72, 295.

3. Ibid., 295ff.

4. Ibid., 297.

5. For a good but incomplete translation of the *Conferences* see John Cassian, *Conferences,* trans. Colm Luibheid, The Classics of Western Spirituality (New York: Paulist Press, 1985). The collection does contain the pertinent second conference of Abba Isaac, 125ff.

6. See "Handing on the Gift," ch. 3 in M. Basil Pennington, *Centering Prayer* (Garden City, N.Y.: Doubleday & Co., 1980), 39ff.

7. *The Cloud of Unknowing and the Book of Privy Counsel,* ed. William Johnston (Garden City, N.Y.: Doubleday & Co., 1973).

8. Many moderns have been put off by the warnings given by the father in the foreword and in the last chapter, ch. 75 (ibid., 43–44, 144ff.). These have to be understood in the whole context of the volume as well as of the times. See M. Basil Pennington, *Centered Living: The Way of Centering Prayer* (Garden City, N.Y.: Doubleday & Co., 1986), 155f.

9. Using quotations from Johnston's edition of *The Cloud of Unknowing,* the whole of the method can be presented in summary fashion:

Simply sit relaxed and quiet. (ch. 44)

It is simply a spontaneous desire springing . . . toward God. (ch. 4)

Center all your attention and desire on him and let this be the sole concern of your mind and heart. (ch. 3)

The will needs only a brief fraction of a moment to move toward the object of its desire. (ch. 4)

If you want to gather all your desire into one simple word that the mind can easily retain, choose a short word rather than a long one. . . . But choose one that is meaningful to you. Then fix it in your mind so that it will remain there come what may. (ch. 7)

Be careful in this work and never strain your mind or imagination, for truly you will not succeed in this way. Leave these faculties at peace. (ch. 4)

It is best when this word is wholly interior without a definite thought or actual sound. (ch. 40)

Let this little word represent to you God in all his fullness and nothing less than the fullness of God. Let nothing except God hold sway in your mind and heart. (ch. 40)

No sooner has a person turned toward God in love than through human frailty he finds himself distracted by the remembrance of some created thing or some daily care. But no matter. No harm done; for such a person quickly returns to deep recollection. (ch. 4)

Should some thought go on annoying you, demanding to know what you are doing, answer with this one word alone. If your mind begins to intellectualize over the meaning and connotations of this little word, remind yourself that its value lies in its simplicity. Do this and I assure you these thoughts will vanish. (ch. 7)

You are to concern yourself with no creature whether material or spiritual nor in their situation or doings whether good or ill. To put it briefly, during this work you must abandon them all. (ch. 5)

(From *Centering Prayer*, 34f.)

10. Rom. 8:26.
11. Pennington, *Centered Living*, 199.
12. From *The Contemplative Life* as cited in ibid., 68.
13. Letter to Aiz. Ch. Abdul, quoted in ibid., 69.
14. From *Conjectures of a Guilty Bystander* as quoted in ibid., 81. We can see from these few quotations that Merton saw this method of prayer as

"centering" in a number of ways. The pray-er centered his or her attention on God alone—in faith. God was localized as being at the center of the pray-er. ("The Father and I will come and dwell within you." "The Kingdom of God is within.") United with God and the activity of God, the pray-er is with God at the center of all that is.

15. Douglas Steere, ed., *Quaker Spirituality: Selected Writings*, Classics of Western Spirituality (New York: Paulist Press, 1984), 5.

16. Ibid., 17.

17. Ibid.

18. Ibid., 27f.

19. Ibid., 29.

20. Isaac Pennington, *Works* (New York: Sherwoods, 1863), vol. 3, 520.

21. From Thomas Merton's *New Seeds of Contemplation* as quoted in Pennington, *Centered Living*, 68.

22. Steere, *Quaker Spirituality*, 27.

10
Spiritual Perspectives on Peacemaking

TILDEN EDWARDS

God's glory is humanity fully alive.
—*St. Irenaeus*

The Human and Spiritual Quest to Become Fully Alive

Built deep into our nature is the desire to be fully alive. If we are to understand what makes for war and peace, we first need to understand how this relentless desire shows itself in us and in our neighbor.

Much in our biological, psychological, and cultural conditioning leads us to look for aliveness in such things as the accumulation of knowledge, goods, sensually exciting events, ego-reinforcing relationships, influential roles, and self-securing definitions of good and bad, true and false, self and other. When these are denied us, our innate aggressive instincts easily turn to subtle or blatant violence against whoever or whatever is behind the denial, and toward a quest for greater power as a means of securing what we want. If we already have a lot of legitimated power (individually or as a group), then instead of direct violence we can turn to established authority when what we want is threatened (for example, to police or other governmental forces). This is the kind of hidden violence of power used for oppressive purposes that scripture repeatedly condemns.

141

Looking for aliveness in such conditioned forms is part of the human journey for all of us, whatever our social position. Somehow God can be at work in all of them, drawing us through their disappointments, anxiety, satiety, and restless drivenness toward the enduring ground of real aliveness in divine love. The deeper we go in our intimacy with God, the more our sense of deep aliveness shifts away from these conditioned quests based in a possessive ego-identity. Our aliveness, rather, comes from our orientation toward the overwhelming and ever-present divine love that we have come to experience, yearn for, and trust as the seedbed of our true identity.

As this process evolves, we no longer can rest satisfied with an identity exclusively defined by biology, personality, gender, family, culture, nation-state, or even institutional religion. All such dimensions of our identity become distinctive vessels of a larger identity with the great mysterious love that reveals itself in and beyond them. Our personal identity, as Paul might say, is more and more hidden with God in Christ, and we find ourselves desiring to see life through God's eyes rather than through any ultimately separate eyes of our own. We are willing to die only for what those eyes see as belonging to love's way.

Our transformation from the old insular self to a more expansive awareness of self-in-God never seems to be complete in this life, though. In our freedom and confusion, we continually find ourselves trying to carry a new sense of self in old wineskins. At times we still want to protect our old ego identity from perceived external threats, sometimes at all costs. We are tempted to turn the unfamiliar and challenging forces both inside and outside us into enemies to be destroyed. That feels much easier and safer than any trust-stretching, sustained attempt imaginatively to find deeper common ground together. Something in us wants to hold onto that which is exclusive and understood in a certain narrow way. We are threatened when anyone tries to relativize these constants to a larger, less definable, and less ego-securing reality. Somewhere inside we know better, but there is a stubborn hold-out by the old "Adam" in us.

This internal split is the creator of spiritual combat, which many spiritual giants of the church since Origen have proclaimed as the realm where other humans are made into enemies. It is the arena where peacemaking begins. On one side of this inner struggle is the desire to cling to the familiar and definable little loves, treating any threat to them as an enemy. On the other side is the desire to open these loves in trust to the larger, less-known land of uncontrollable great love. Drawn into awareness of that land kicking and screaming, we slowly come to realize that there is no real freedom, joy, liveliness, and reliable belonging anywhere else. As we are empowered and ready, we gradually loosen our grip on narrowing identities held apart from that great love. As we do so we find that we are also able to loosen our sense of "enemies," freeing our hearts for reconciliation.

The Thrust of Scripture Toward a Lively Shalom

Such interior conversion turns us into subversives of any finite order that would demand our allegiance untested by that larger love. We see this subversive quality in the Hebrew prophets and in Jesus, as we see it in many great spiritual leaders throughout history. *Shalom* is the biblical sacred word that described the quality of life present when this larger love is full, when God truly reigns. It is an unpossessive, agapic, lively, just peace reflected in the fruits of the Spirit (Gal. 5:22; 1 Cor. 13) and the Beatitudes (Matt. 5:1–12). Biblical writers in their experience of God sensed its presence in our original Edenic relation to God. They felt its loss in our embraced freedom to choose a narrower ego love fallen away from the larger love. Biblical writers also again and again revealed the divine call for us to choose that larger liberating love that would put us on the path of shalom. Finally, they gave us hope for the fullness of that shalom when God is all in all.

As scripture progresses, we find less and less room for violence as an instrument of shalom. Retaliation and the use of violence are seen as leading people away from God.[1] Trust in God and embracing virtue and justice, rather than trusting in our instruments of war, is the way to shalom (Psalm 33 well summarizes this view). Eventually in second Isaiah we find the new figure of the suffering servant who absorbs violence in a redemptive way instead of striking back. This is offered in the context of Israel's call to be a community marked by sharing, justice, compassion, and acceptance of the stranger.

This thrust toward peace as the way to peace is brought to greater intensity in the New Testament. Jesus extends the sense of covenant to include even our seeming enemies. He refuses ego-enhancing power as a way to life and guides us instead to the liberating fruits of radical trust in God. This trust involves something very important to the way of peace: repentance. There can be no real communal peace unless we are willing to let God empower our capacity for forgiveness and stop the vicious cycles of revenge and the dominating acts of exploitation that help to perpetuate conflict. We are called to embrace God's proffered compassion and let it flow through us for others. As this happens, what we have destructively held onto from the past can be released. A new life and community grounded in God's gracious guidance is possible.

This new way is not marked by passivity or harmony at all costs. It is marked by a symbolic sword of righteousness that cuts to God's truth. It involves compassionate peacemaking and justice-seeking actions that grow out of our turning to God rather than out of autonomous, willful attempts to make things happen. Jesus' act of upsetting the money changers' tables in the Temple, so often used to support violence as a way to peace, can be seen in this light. That event happened in the context of a ministry grounded in Jesus' identity with the eternal liberating divine Lover of humankind, a ministry of proclamation and healing in relation to that Lover. He refused to let himself be violently defended by his disciples when he was arrested. In the Temple event, we see his felt sense of contradiction of the divine and just Lover he knew as he saw the money changers' presence and behavior, there in the very place that proclaimed that Lover. His shock treatment does not speak of physically maiming, killing, or even touching anyone; indeed, it speaks of Jesus immediately curing blind and lame people, a more fitting way than the money changers' of showing forth the merciful God worshiped in the Temple (Matt. 21:12–17).

The culmination of Jesus' way is found on the cross. For spiritual seekers of all times the cross has shown us a way of self-emptying as the way to life and peace, a way that contradicts the world's way of striving to find life by self-seeking, self-filling, self-expansion, self-preservation. The cross helps to free us even from clinging to physical life as necessary to "life." Divine love alone is necessary to life, alone is truly life-giving, and that love includes our death and whatever lies beyond. When we are graced to accept this radical reality of faith, we are free of one of the major barriers to communal shalom: the sense that physical life and its enhancement must be clung to and killed for at all costs. At the same time we are free to more fearlessly foster the world's true life in the great love the cross reveals.

The Divided Response of the Church in History

Jesus' sacrifice on the cross released enormous divine energy into the world. "Through his wounds we are healed"—given peace (Isa. 53:5, JB). It underscored the great, mysterious "peace that passes understanding" that Jesus brought, a peace that comes from our empowered surrender to the divine love. Christian martyrdom in witness to that truth in the centuries that have followed has always been held in great honor. To die for the faith has never been of questionable merit in Christian tradition, but the merit of killing for the faith has always been controversial: it was not the way of Christ. In the first few centuries of the church, until after Constantine began its imperial establishment in the Roman Empire, the church was essentially a pacifist community that normally forbade the profession of combatant soldier to its members. Christians were to be the new community of God's shalom, and no secular power was given the right to compromise what it had been given as the way to true life.

After Constantine and up to this day the church has divided into three positions, each of them seeking some kind of scriptural warrant.[2] The church's intensive spiritual life in religious communities followed the way of self-relinquishment; there was no place or need for violence when these communities were true to their calling. Their members, along with the professional leadership of the whole church, normally were forbidden to bear arms. Churches growing out of the Radical Reformation, such as Mennonites, Brethren, and Quakers, joined these older religious communities in renouncing violence as a means to peace. Disputes were to be settled in an atmosphere of mutual respect, humility, and love.

The second position, defense of the "just war," was first elaborated by Augustine. If love is the motive, and justice is only on one side, then, with certain testing guidelines, a war by the state can be justified. Major problems with this theory historically have included the reality that justice has almost always been on both sides to one degree or another, and the meeting of the many vague guidelines for a just war is in effect arbitrarily determined by the states involved. The guideline that the perceived good of a war would outweigh the likely evil is particularly problematic today, where our technological capacity to kill and destroy on an indiscriminate mass scale makes it virtually impossible to foresee the many possible devastating turns and consequences of a war, especially if the arsenals of both sides are massive.

The third position was the crusade, where a righteous war against any group that did not properly honor the Christian God as determined by the church's leaders could be fought, with great spiritual merit for the Christian participants. These wars have proven to be more brutal and savage than any of the merely political wars in Western history. Nothing unleashes human capacity for uncontrolled violence as much as an enemy operating with divine sanction.

The Spiritual Attraction of War

The ambivalence about war in Christian history and experience can be explained a bit by looking at the potential spiritual attractiveness of war. War can be seen to offer a distorted mirror image of what everyone wants deep down in peace: a chance to be fully alive and in intimate community, the foundational goal alluded to at the beginning of this chapter. Let me give an example of this war-induced aliveness from my own experience.

The news of the Persian Gulf war came to me in a semi-darkened chapel in the middle of evening prayer with about thirty people who had gathered from around the country for a Shalem Institute spiritual guidance program. Tears began to flow, people embraced one another, and spontaneous prayers for mercy were offered. We collectively bore our pain and hope to God. Our personal concerns that had seemed so important a moment before suddenly felt petty before the enormity of what was happening. We were galvanized into an intimate community that transcended our differences.

We were somehow more "alive" than before the announcement as we faced the unpredictable life-and-death realities of a major war, just as we become more alive when we confront individual life-and-death issues. But this was a *shared* aliveness—a whole *nation's*, a *world's* aliveness . . . something big was happening. Whether or not we agreed with it, we could not ignore its impact. People at this moment were being asked to sacrifice their well-being and lives for something beyond themselves. Our own often over-securing concerns and unadventurous lives were exposed. Here was a chance, for all its horror, really to live into something vibrant together that transcended our self-centeredness.

In such a time many people can sense the excitement of something new, the vaguely conscious possibility of some breakthrough perhaps in stuck places of individual and public life. Somewhere inside us we all know we need something new: new justice, new aliveness, new community, and who knows what else that causes our inner restlessness. We can forget all the patient diplomacy, compromises, interior spiritual struggle, and slow movement of things in "normal" times. War feels like an opportunity to break through barriers, to explode our way into some new possibilities that we hope will bring greater freedom and happiness to us and others.

For those on the front lines of battle, notwithstanding all the terror and disgust, there can be an even more intensive sense of aliveness than for those behind the lines. Tim O'Brien, a Vietnam veteran, speaks to this:

> At its core, perhaps, war is just another name for death, and yet any soldier will tell you, if he tells the truth, that proximity to death brings with it a corresponding proximity to life. After a firefight, there is always the immense pleasure of aliveness. The trees are alive. The grass, the soil—everything. All around you things are purely living, and you among them, and the aliveness makes you tremble.[3]

Each of us could bring our own different description of the strange attraction of war as a way to spiritual fulfillment, even as we would recoil from its horror and deny its efficacy. There are indeed ways in which the stretching experiences of war can deepen some people's relation to God, life, and one another, but, being war, it is finally at the expense of someone else. War, I think, more likely will lead to the destruction or warping of our relation to God and one another amid war's disruptions, deceptions, and brutalities. God's redemptive hand can open the way for us again in time, but a terrible price will have been paid already.

The long history of war, in one sense, is the history of a mass, delusory, reflex response to organized homicide as a way to fuller life. War continues to promise far more than it can deliver, but it is pursued until people become so disillusioned with its consequences that they finally vow to give it up. Then after a few years' rest, we forget the consequences and begin to trust the magical promises of another explosive fix. Seventy percent of U.S. research and development resources pour into preparation for war while almost none is allotted to imaginative and just peacemaking. When rationalization for the act of war comes, we secretly hope that this new high will bring us a great shalom, the "new world order" that our restless hearts crave. Just as with addictive behavior, we discover in time that it is one more substitute for the real way to transformed life. It cannot deliver what we seek. It cannot bring real shalom. We need to exorcise our fascination with war as a valid way to fuller life and shift our energy to the inclusive, collaborative way our experience with God reveals, a way that exposes all war as civil war.

The Interior Orientation of the Peacemaker

The deep spiritual life brings some special gifts to peacemaking that are implicit in what has been said thus far. First, it often brings an experience of God as an inclusive lover, yearning for all that is real to be brought to its intended full liveliness and compassionate interdependence with the rest of creation and the Creator, yearning thus for an inclusive shalom. Second, deep spiritual life brings a personal identity so grounded in God, so yearning for God's fullness, that it does not depend on the enhancement and preservation of the ego-self for a sense of aliveness. Such a person is free to die as well as to live for God's shalom. That person also is free to embrace poverty and service as these may be called for in the way of shalom, and to use power and riches expediently to serve that shalom.

The long interior struggles of the spiritual life eventually reveal more of the peaceful, God-connected side of the psychic forces that we may have treated as enemies to vanquish or evade within. Then there is less temptation to blindly project our inner war outward and treat the world likewise, to yield to the desire to wipe out what we don't understand and don't like. Such experience counsels that peacemaking begins by asking God to help us tame our killer instinct within. Taming that instinct means directly opening it to the great love whenever it appears. With grace and courage, the violent and truth-denying forces within us can be slowly transformed into a lively interior shalom.

Instead of looking for enemies without, the experience of graced interior trust and reconciliation is projected into the world. We more and more desire to see the beauty and preciousness of life through God's compassionate eyes, and to be energetic and willing vehicles of God's shalom as we are called and empowered. The need for empowerment and God's timing are seen as essential. We do not create shalom separately from God. We want to live out an intimate cocreativity, a moment-by-moment dance led by God's embracing Spirit.

The Practice of Peacemaking

Our best guide as to what we are to do will be our own constant prayerful turning to God, expressing our desire to live and foster shalom and asking to be shown the way day by day. Beyond this essential ongoing practice, there are many practical dimensions to ponder, some of which I will offer here for our consideration.

First, there is our own need and others' need for *support* in caring about peace as the way to peace. On one level this might involve a regular relationship with a spiritual friend and/or small group where everyone's primary concern is a deepening relationship with God and the truth of our own souls. We may never discuss strategies of peacemaking with such people, but we would find support and prayer for the ground of all peacemaking: our yearning for God. In letting our deepest identity be *in* God together, we can come to share God's pain in the suffering and violence we see in the world rather than shying away from its horror. That is an important step toward our freedom for peacemaking: we must first be free to touch and not run from the pain, and sense that it is God's pain in us.

With such people we also could test out some sense of our particular *callings* to peacemaking. We need a listening and encouraging ear to help us sift through our feelings, doubts, hunches, fears, and "drawnness," and discern what our particular calling may be at a given time.

On another level we need the stimulus and practical support of people, knowledge, and ideas concerning the specific *tasks* of peacemaking. We need mutual reinforcement as we seek to perceive and embrace God's shalom interiorly, among family and friends, in work, community, and church settings, as well as in national and international social and political arenas. Attention to peace as the way to peace in each one of these dimensions of our lives has a way of reinforcing peace as the way in all other dimensions.

One source for such ongoing support can be found in such periodicals as *Sojourners, The Other Side,* and the Fellowship of Reconciliation's magazine *Fellowship.* Not only do these provide often spiritually grounded and informative articles, but among them they review many of the books and other media available about peacemaking. They also carry notices of relevant national meetings, organizations, and peace activities.

It is no accident that serious reading in this area again and again encounters claims for the necessity of *justice* for an enduring peace. Anyone called to work for real social and political justice also is working for peace, so long as the way to justice does not depend on ultimately demonizing and destroying any group and looks toward an inclusive and mutually respectful society.

Historically a distinction has often been made between the peace and justice possible and called for within the committed church and what is possible in the larger society. This is especially strong among the historic "peace" churches. Perhaps the greatest distinction comes in the church's seeing our ego-identity with all its grasping for security relativized to our larger, freer identity in God. Realistically, an experiential understanding of that difference may belong to only a small minority of people in any church, but at least there is a theology and history to call upon, including a shared concern for all God's people.

Such themes of peace, justice, spiritual identity, and inclusive love can be given weight in the church's life, liturgy, preaching, religious education, and social action. Special help can be given in the practice of nonviolence. Given the strong cultural conditioning of most church people that often challenges these themes, the themes need to be introduced in challenging and prayerful dialogue with dominant cultural views, a process that in time might help more people to feel free to affirm the church as a truly alternative community of faith with its own liberating integrity and vision of true life.

Even though the church's struggle to be faithful to these concerns cannot be depended upon in the larger society, we nonetheless are dealing with the same God-impregnated human beings whose yearnings for a lively and just peace beneath all their ego-vested interests can be tapped as willingness and grace coincide. In both church and larger society there is the same need to foster whatever is truly life giving for people that does not come at the unnecessary expense of others. There is the need to foster whatever helps people to appreciate the giftedness and preciousness of the life before them day by day, and whatever helps them move toward mutually respectful and just relationships and social structures. This means a discouragement for whatever is death dealing, over securing, suppressive of our gifts, denying of our God-given rights, and involves aggressively lording it over others.

It is important to be realistic about the strong societal values that counter this way of and to peace. Our national valuing of at least a secular view of peace, justice, and mutual respect is more than countered by long-enduring national political policies based on our own military force, on military support for pliant client states regardless of their support of justice, and on disregard of the kind of interdependent world we have become. It is a world in desperate need of visionary leadership that can humbly listen to the Holy Spirit nudging us toward some fundamentally different ways of relating and approaching problems of conflict and injustice.

Instead, our dominant political forces demonstrate that their overarching values involve a sense of American right to maintain massive waste of the earth's resources and massive world-encompassing military power far beyond our economic means or reasonable need to sustain (with the consequent serious impoverishment of human and infrastructural resources and a huge national debt). Given the fairly wide public support of or indifference about these values (though with slowly growing countertrends), we need to realize their deep cultural reinforcement in our materially oriented societal values and in our conditioning to try to force what we want intrapsychically, interpersonally, and politically. Such an orientation has led us to be one of the most violence-prone societies in the world, in every area of life. We are not conditioned to accept limits easily, and perhaps we would rather keep the illusion of omnipotence and a desire to dominate the world, and be willing to kill for that vision, than face the call to find our responsible place and limits in an interdependent world and society.

We see these dominant values clearly shining through the surface rhetoric of peace and justice in the Persian Gulf War, a war rightly resisted on theological grounds by the national leaders of most mainstream American denominations. We desperately need corporate prayer for the courage and imagination to let go of this reliance on great explosive power and material ambition at the expense of our own and the world's true justice and peace, and move toward reliance on God's different way to real life shown us in Christ and the great saints of all deep religious traditions.

We already are moving well beyond the nation-state as the only significant actor on the international stage, with international corporations, with religious, cultural, and ethnic bodies, and with growing regional networks of all kinds. Just as religious denominations are hearing and learning from other religious bodies around the world, so is this happening in other social realms. Despite the frequent drag of national regimes, we are all slowly becoming internationalized, finding ourselves mixed up with the rest of the world's richness and sorrows. I sense God's Spirit is slowly drawing us together, despite our fears, resistance, and many differences.

This is happening, though, with the nation-state still reliant on massive military and secret agent and police powers, and an outmoded view of a balance of terror between nation-states that can seriously retard so many of our needed moves toward a humane planet of shared resources, personal freedom, and mutual honor. Think how much more motivation there would be for such constructive moves internally and internationally if we and other states did not have such massive and lethal military and police forces quickly to turn to when negotiations threatened illegitimate political dominance; then we might take more seriously the legitimate political, social, economic, and ecological concerns of one another.

I say this with an awareness that military and police structures in themselves are no worse, and in some ways are better, than many other social structures, apart from the dangers inherent in their cultivation of blind obedience to authority. All societies in the light of human conflicts need a certain capacity to maintain a minimum (though it often becomes an oppressive maximum) order that prevents the kind of helpless chaos in the face of various natural and internal and international social crises that can paralyze or destroy a society. These ordering structures particularly hold up a discipline and commitment that implies that there is something larger than one's ego-self to live and die for. In the American military, there is also the admirable quality of bringing people together from a wider range of ethnic, class, religious, and racial backgrounds into a close collaborative relationship with more equal opportunities for advancement than is available in most other institutions.

The question for us is how we can encourage such positive things in our social institutions without the necessity of envisioning an enemy as the cohesive factor. Military forces, with courageous international political sanction, can begin making the effort to move toward a common commitment to the well-being of the human family as their primary loyalty and to the nation-state secondarily, seeing themselves as part of a world peacekeeping force. Some visionary military officers and political leaders I believe do realize the need for this shift of primary loyalty. Such a courageous and sane step could make easier the task of reducing massive, resource-sapping national forces (which currently number 26 million worldwide in the regular armed forces, with sixty-six countries in the lucrative business of peddling arms to them). Spiritual leaders can help lead the way in bringing such proposals crucial to world peace from cautious whispers to real public dialogue and evolution.

The Mennonite theologian Duane Friesen has listed some specific dimensions of international peacemaking that we would do well to support.[4] These include the recognition that war is made possible by:

1. unresolved deep conflict
2. religious/ethical legitimizing of preparation for war that breaks down taboos against organized violence
3. institutional structures that can implement these preparations

4. the absence or failure of institutions to resolve conflict peace-
   fully

The temptation of war can be reduced by modifying any of these
factors. We badly need new and strengthened institutional structures
for dispute settlement and for the policing, monitoring, and minimali-
zation of war industries around the globe. The so-called realism of
current balance-of-power policies has brought us increasing terror
and impoverishment as massive resources continue to flow into the
military and espionage establishments, even after the collapse of the
Cold War. "Realism" today requires imagination and courage to
follow the Spirit's lead toward political values and structures that
serve rather than inhibit a just and livable planet, and toward the
elimination of war, that is, coordinated, impersonal human slaughter,
as a legitimate social institution.

Suggestions for Peacemaking

As spiritually motivated people it is important for us to witness to
alternative ways of living and structuring human life. We need to
uphold an "aliveness" that does not depend on dominance, destruction, and maiming of others. Among the things we can do that may
show themselves in our prayer as particular callings are the following:
   *We can recognize, embrace, and advocate the power of the church's
re-presentation of Jesus' sacrifice on the cross in the eucharistic
liturgy.* Among the endless depths of benefits flowing from this act is
the way it can expose the demons within and around us, calm their
violence, strengthen our resolve for a just peace, and show us Christ's
ego-emptying way to true and enduring aliveness.[5]
   *We can educationally foster nonviolent and just conflict tolerance
and resolution in the family, church, and schools.* Conflict is inherent
in human life. The question is how we are helped and encouraged to
bear and resolve it, within the limits of our capacities in this volatile
and ego-prone, yet God-ward world. This educational process needs
to include attention to the ways we are conditioned to violence in our
culture, particularly men. The new "men's movement," which has
risen partly in relation to the revolutionary women's movement of
recent decades, is helping to unmask this dimension as it seeks to help

us redefine and foster an authentic manhood that is not based on control and domination, but rather on a new combination of compassion, vulnerability, and responsible toughness.[6]

We can take up a martial art like aikido, which came into existence as a means of self-defense that cultivates compassion and non-destruction of the attacker. It can help to condition us to move *with* what comes to us rather than pitting ourselves *against* it, cultivating qualities of sharp awareness, courage, and gentleness, which could be called authentic "peace warrior" virtues.

We can be involved in organizations that support fundamental human rights and needs, which in the long run will aid in reducing the grounds for conflict. We can encourage an international policy of recognizing the legitimacy only of nations that guarantee human rights to their citizens.

We can support a just legal system, the law being one of the fundamental means historically of defending the weak in a nonviolent process. As Roland Bainton has said, war primarily is self-vindication without due process of law, and especially in modern warfare, without discrimination of the specific offenders.[7] We especially can foster strengthened international agencies that will support a modicum of justice and conflict mediation between nations, ethnic groups, and other bodies, encourage and monitor arms reduction, and be given policing power to reinforce their decisions.

We can seek to influence public policy at every level with our support of candidates, organizations, and proposals that contribute to justice and the way of peace. Certainly this would include fostering the transfer of monies from still highly inflated military and espionage budgets toward desperately needed social services, ecological cleanup and support, the expansion of an ecologically sound mass transportation system, and international economic stabilization. It also could include monies for research into nonviolent means of national defense, as some Scandinavian countries have included in their military budgets for some years now.

All of this involves a sense of call toward a planetary reconstellation of political structures that will recognize and foster what will allow us to approximate a just and peace-seeking human family. It is in God's hands to bring about the fullness of shalom. We cannot expect more than a fragile approximation of a viable world social order short of that full empowerment, but we certainly can pray, hope, and work with God's Spirit for more than the dangerously inadequate structures we have now. The new window of opportunity given us by the end of the Cold War, and by our awareness of the impersonal and indiscriminate power of modern weaponry, can be seen as providentially given.

We can support mass media productions that provide an alternative to the dominant ones in our culture that glorify violence against other people and nature as legitimate, strategic, easily chosen, even recreational ways of attaining human ends, especially ones that glorify the quest for idolatrous personal power at the expense of others, which I believe is the greatest breeder of long-term violence.

We can support games, festivals, and art forms that sublimate our deadly serious instinct for violence into playful, creative aggression and bodily expression.

We can foster mutual respect, learning, and peace among the world's religions; that is a special responsibility of religious people. A new world interfaith body is needed that is dedicated to evolving a shared vision of reconciled human life grounded in the historical inspirations of deep spiritual awareness.[8] This is happening on an informal and spasmodic level now, inspired by such people as the Dalai Lama, by recent papal pronouncements and meetings, and particularly by leading monastic figures in Christian and other traditions.[9] A more visible and enduring forum is needed now. Perhaps the psalmist's rejoicing in "How good, how delightful it is for all to live together like brothers [and sisters]" (Ps. 133:1, JB) can take on planetary-wide meaning through such a body.

We can foster a sense of God's covenant with the whole of humanity in the creation and flood stories, letting these take precedence over later more exclusive covenants, in whose light they are to be interpreted.

We can support and selectively visit those retreat centers, monastic-inspired communities, base communities, and other spiritual sub-cultures around the world where we find deep, shalom-invoking, prophetic spiritual awareness and inspiration, assisting their influence in our churches and broader society.

We can support a rhythm of ministry and Sabbath time: learning in receptive Sabbath time the value of relaxing our violence-prone drivenness, letting life be for a while in a particularly appreciative, nonmanipulated, restful state. We can let our ministry time stay close to our desire for God's cocreativity with us.[10]

We can practice observation of our emotions and behavior related to violence, looking at what in our attitudes and life-style cultivates polarization and the desire to wipe out any kind of opposition. As such realities show themselves, we can open them to God and ask that we be empowered to see our interdependence even with so-called enemies (within and without), and to empty them of their power to divide us from compassion, even when they need to be resisted and transformed.

Where we must accept killing as part of God's way for sustenance of life, as with our food (whether animal or vegetable), we can accept it with gratitude for what has died for us, and commit ourselves to no unnecessary killing of any living creature of God (that is a realistic way of reading the Sixth Commandment).

Where we or others fail in compassion (as will often happen), we can recognize that fact with simplicity and ask for and offer forgiveness as we are authentically enabled, rather than focusing on justification of what we have felt or done, which can simply increase the polarization. If we are dealing with systemic issues of oppression, we can resist oppression firmly and work energetically toward a new social order, but still from an ultimate motivation of compassion for everyone involved, looking for final reconciliation with oppressive forces wherever possible.

We can nourish an interdependent appreciation and respect for our earth's living ecosystem, including it in our understanding of shalom (see Hos. 2:18–19).

Through all of the above, we can maintain a sense of humor and irony rather than a heavy self-righteousness that can unnecessarily polarize our dialogue with those who disagree. Humor and irony also help to preserve our humility, reminding us that the fullness of the truth, including the truth about the ancient, complex, multidimensional realm of violence and peace, is always beyond our full conceptual grasp, and that God needs to be trusted as the one who will finally free the fullness of peace in God's own mysterious way. We each have our place in that process, but it may prove to be very different from what we had planned at a given time.

We can't do everything, but we can do something. That's why it is important to start with a few people who can support us in discerning what that "something" is meant to be for us at this point. Whatever it is, we need to pray for our actions to be empowered from a God-centered, God-desiring, God-inspired, pain-bearing, loving, forgiving, life-appreciating heart, rather than out of hate, fear, and desire for personal or institutional power. We also need to be willing to suffer with Christ, if necessary—materially, physically, and/or emotionally—for a God-called witness to the way of shalom. This willingness to have a casual attitude toward our own well-being and bear hard things will be easier and lighter if we can trust that creation, for all its ambiguity, stems from a divine loving source that truly wills shalom.

Finally, we need to act without attachment to the results, but from the simple willingness to act as we have been led to act, leaving the fruits in God's hands. God is the peacemaker, living through us in mysterious ways, drawing creation toward its full and true aliveness. In that fullness of time we are promised that God will live in every heart, and there will be no more training for war (Micah 4:3).

Notes

1. Biblical scholar Donald Senior supports this thrust of scripture toward nonviolence in "What the Bible Says on War and Peace," *Praying*, May-June 1991.

2. See Roland Bainton's classic *Christian Attitudes Toward War and Peace* (Nashville: Abingdon Press, 1960) for an enlightening history of this theme.

3. Tim O'Brien, *The Things They Carried* (New York: Penguin Books, 1990), 87.

4. Duane Friesen, *Christian Peacemaking and International Conflict* (Scottdale, Pa.: Herald Press, 1986); see esp. pp. 176–241.

5. Paul Tournier, *The Violence Within* (San Francisco: Harper & Row, 1978). Tournier gives an excellent analysis of the psychological and spiritual relationships of sacrifice, violence, and power. See esp. pp. 73–118.

6. For a list of reading and other resources on the men's movement, refer to the July-August 1991 issue of *Creation Spirituality*; also the May 29–June 5 issue of *The Christian Century*.

7. Bainton, *Christian Attitudes*, 240.

8. See Wayne Teasdale's brief suggestion in "Contemplation as a Way to Peace," *The American Benedictine Review*, 42, no. 1 (March 1991).

9. One such group, the North American Board for East-West Dialogue (composed of Christian monastics), along with the Dalai Lama, signed in October 1990 a "Universal Declaration on Non-Violence," which declares that religion can no longer be an accomplice to war, terrorism, or any other form of violence against any member of the human family. The full text was published in the April 12, 1991, issue of the *National Catholic Reporter*.

10. See my *Sabbath Time* (revised edition; Nashville: Upper Room, 1992) for ways of living out a rhythm of Sabbath and ministry time.

11
Letters for
Spiritual Guidance

E. GLENN HINSON

Next to personal, face-to-face encounter, letters have served as the main medium of spiritual guidance throughout the centuries. Only time will tell what further benefits may come from the ongoing revolution in communications technology, which puts people face-to-face over long distances, but letters may still make special contributions even in a world quick to experience "the personal touch" of the telephone or other audiovisual devices.

For one thing, letters leave a more permanent record. Those who receive them can turn to them again and again and share them with others. What a great loss to later generations if superlative spiritual guides of the past such as Augustine or Bernard of Clairvaux or Francis Fénelon, to name but a few, had left no letters because they transacted everything by phone!

From the point of view of the spiritual director or directee, moreover, letters encourage greater care and conciseness, a certain economy of words and preciseness of thoughts. Conversation can and often does ramble. Counsel may have to come too quickly to permit the wisest response to queries and needs. Exchange of letters allows for, indeed almost forces, extended reflection. By its very nature spiritual guidance needs fallowing time, as the great spiritual masters repeatedly underline. Hiatuses between letters may tone down a notch or two the universal tendency to expect immediate spiritual maturity, as if guidance were a kind of spiritual steroid. All have to recognize, as Baron Friedrich von Hügel reminded his niece Gwendolen Greene, that human beings have to plod along if they expect to make any progress.[1] Like physical growth, spiritual growth takes time and requires patience, and few things impede progress more than prideful impatience.

Letters also permit some of the masters to expand the range of grace operative through them. Thomas Merton, for instance, although he was a Trappist monk and, for three or four years prior to his premature death, a hermit, engaged hundreds of persons in many walks of life around the world who could never have met him personally at the Abbey of Gethsemani. Other types of writing do not do what personal letters do, even in the case of a gifted communicator like Merton. At one time, on advice of a friend, Merton seriously considered letter writing as his vocation.

Two Masters

I will focus on two extraordinary spiritual guides through letters whose stories have intersected, Baron Friedrich von Hügel and Douglas V. Steere. Steere never met von Hügel, who died in 1925, but he wrote a Ph.D. dissertation on *Critical Realism in the Religious Philosophy of Baron Friedrich von Hügel* (Harvard University, 1931) and published a volume of selected letters and spiritual counsels prefaced by a brilliant essay, "Baron von Hügel as a Spiritual Director."[2] Those who know Douglas Steere and have benefited from his counsel will readily recognize a preeminent source of Steere's philosophy and style of spiritual guidance, whether of an extended or more casual sort. In his essay on the Baron, give or take a few strokes here or there, Steere painted his own portrait.

Friedrich von Hügel was born May 5, 1852, in Florence, where his father, Carl, served as Austrian ambassador to the court of Tuscany. His father was Roman Catholic, but his mother, Elizabeth Farquharson, was a convert from the Scottish Presbyterian Church. The family later moved to Belgium and then to Torquay in England. As a consequence of his cosmopolitan education, Friedrich gained proficiency in German, French, Italian, and English as well as Greek, Latin, and Hebrew. An attack of typhus at age eighteen caused severe hearing impairment and weakened his health permanently. A Dutch Dominican, Raymond Hocking, helped to rescue him from the religious crisis brought on by this. In 1884 he met Abbé Huvelin, whose spiritual guidance also deeply impressed him.

Von Hügel combined spirituality with a keen interest in science, philosophy, biblical criticism, and history. Early on convinced of the validity of historical criticism, he was pulled into the Modernist Movement in the Roman Catholic Church and became a spiritual mentor to leading modernists, notably George Tyrrell and Alfred Loisy. In 1905 he founded the London Society for the Study of Religion, which he credited for shaping much of his own thought. With the appearance in 1908 of *The Mystical Element of Religion,* a study of Catherine of Genoa, he gained a reputation as a premier theologian and religious writer. He enhanced his reputation further with essays on the Gospel of John published in the *Encyclopaedia Britannica* in 1911, an article intended for the Hastings *Encyclopedia of Religion and Ethics* that grew into the book *Eternal Life* in 1912, and *Essays and Addresses on the Philosophy of Religion.* Failing health prevented his giving the Gifford Lectures at Edinburgh, 1924–1926. He died on January 27, 1925.

From the beginning of Douglas Steere's story one would hardly have expected his path to cross von Hügel's. Born in Harbor Beach, Michigan, August 31, 1901, he could not claim impressive family credentials such as von Hügel had. His father, Edward Morris Steere, worked thirty-seven years as a night clerk for the Michigan Central Railway. Offended by deprivations suffered as a "preacher's kid" in the Free Methodist Church, Douglas's father distanced himself from religion throughout most of his life. From his mother's side of the family, however, Douglas tasted a bit of the ecumenism that has characterized his own outlook.

Graduating from high school at age sixteen, after skipping one year, Douglas Steere compiled an outstanding record at Michigan Agricultural College in Lansing (now Michigan State University), working each summer as a potato inspector and interrupting his degree program to teach high school one year. Encouraged by one of his professors, he began the study of philosophy at Harvard under William Ernest Hocking, Clarence I. Lewis, and, later, Alfred North Whitehead. In 1925 he won a Rhodes Scholarship to study at Oxford University, where he earned a B.A. and established his first contacts with Quakers. The latter opened the way for an invitation to join Rufus Jones at Haverford College when he completed his stay in Oxford in 1928. Having already passed qualifying exams for the Ph.D. at Harvard, he elected to write his dissertation on the religious philosophy of Baron Friedrich von Hügel. He received his degree in 1931.

Douglas Steere taught at Haverford from 1928 until he took early retirement in 1964 so as to attend the Second Vatican Council as an official observer on behalf of the Friends World Committee for Consultation. From the very first he and his wife Dorothy had taken an active part in the founding of Pendle Hill, the Quaker Center that has done so much to foster the contemplative life not only among Quakers but among other believers as well. In 1937 he felt a strong leading to visit Quakers in Nazi Germany and the Scandinavian countries, a trip that opened the way to one of his most notable achievements. During and after World War II he became keenly sensitive to the plight of Finnish peoples and organized a massive relief effort, which the Finnish government belatedly recognized with a medal in 1990. He and Dorothy became ambassadors at large for the Friends World Committee in South Africa during the fifties. Douglas served as president of that committee from 1964 until 1972.

Qualities of Literary Master Guides

In his essay "Baron von Hügel as a Spiritual Director," Douglas Steere has ascribed to him four gifts that set the Baron apart as a master of spiritual direction. All four would apply to Douglas Steere as well.

First, "he was saturated with an awareness that God was at work, that he is present and operative and laying siege to every soul before, during, and after any spiritual director might come upon the scene."[3] Like Bernard of Clairvaux, both von Hügel and Steere would place their confidence in God as the initiator, the Hound of Heaven. Von Hügel needed two "lifts," he explained to one correspondent, "a lift which is always going up from below, and a lift which is always going down from above."[4] In his classic *On Listening to Another,* Douglas Steere reminds us that the task of the listener is always to bring the other person to an encounter with the Eternal Listener. Realizing our limitations, we recognize with seasoned spiritual guides that our task is "to take men [and women] to Christ, to bring them to the living Listener, and to leave them there."[5]

Second, "he knew himself what it was to be a needy one." Repeatedly in his letters von Hügel underscored the importance of religion. To those who wanted to know what value there was in religion, he replied, "I simply cannot say more than this—that I simply cannot get on without it. I must have it to moderate me, to water me down, to make me possible."[6] Although Douglas Steere seldom speaks long about his own experience, even when prompted to do so, those who know him know that his unending quest has been "the love which is at the heart of things," an oft-sounded phrase on his lips. In an autobiographical address at Wake Forest University in 1983 that he later titled "Mind Your Call That Is All," he quoted a brief statement he had once made about what the Quaker meeting meant to him.

> The meeting for worship has sent tears down my cheeks. It has given me specific things to be done and the strength to undertake them. . . . It has rested me. It has upset my sluggish rest. It has helped prepare me to live.
>
> It has sacrificed me and broken down the hull of my life and shown me how I might live. It has warned me that I am too cowardly to live that way, but reminded me for good measure that it is not what I give that makes me suffer but what I hold back! It has comforted and quieted me when I was torn and hurt, and it has dug up the garden of my soul when I thought the present produce was all I could manage.[7]

Third, "he also had a profound reverence for the differences in souls." Von Hügel felt keenly his failure in attempting to impose his own pattern upon his oldest daughter, Gertrud. Early in their development of friendship, George Tyrrell rebuked the Baron gently for expecting too much of himself out of his equally brilliant daughter. He warned that,

> in your enthusiasm and intensity with regard to all that concerns the Catholic faith and the cause of truth, and in the natural desire you have to make your daughter a sharer of all your views and hopes, your very affection seems to blind you to the fact that, after all, your Gertrud is years and years younger than you are, and that the fibre of even the best mind at 20 is feeble compared with that of an equally good mind at 45.[8]

He went on to suggest that her physical illness came from her spiritual condition. The Baron responded with an admission of the "undermining character of my influence" and hoped Gertrud would come through despite him.[9] "Souls are never dittos," he reminded his niece in his last days. "There are such differences of soul."

Douglas Steere likes to quote Martin Buber's word in a Quaker meeting that "the greatest thing a man can do for another is to confirm the deepest thing in him."[10] Both Douglas and Dorothy Steere have a gift for uplifting other persons through affirming "that of God" in them. One never goes away from a meeting with them or from reading a letter, even a small note, without taking on more fuel for one's journey. They, too, prize the variety of souls.

Fourth, "von Hügel was himself expendable in the business of guiding souls." They could get along without him. Yet he seemed to sense the need of others even at a distance and made himself entirely accessible to those who sought his counsel. He opened a letter to George Tyrrell,

> My very dear Friend,
> —I hardly know exactly *how* or *why*, —unless it be in part your, after not long, silence, —I come to have a strong and abiding, unreasoned and, so far, irrepressible impression that you are in interior trouble and trial, —of a specially strong kind or degree; but I know that I *have* this impression.[11]

At any rate he decided to lay aside his own work and write, adding,

I need not say, I hope, that, if and when you like, I would listen, so affectionately and respectfully, to anything you might have to say, and I could promise, I think, ever to learn before answering, and not necessarily to say anything at all.[12]

Though in his late years burdened with failing health, a heavy workload, and difficulty in hearing, he insisted that friends call on him. To Evelyn Underhill, he wrote,

Do not, I pray you, if ever you feel at all clearly that I could help you in any way—even if by only silently listening to such trouble and complications as God may send you—do not because I am busy, shrink from coming to me, or letting me come to you. We are *both* busy, so we have each the guarantee that we will not take up each other's time without good cause.[13]

He chided his niece, Gwendolen Greene, for having written "pathetic little lines" because she claimed to be overwhelmed with work. "I too am overwhelmed with work," he replied. "And your and my work is *just the same,* if we learn to do it simply for God, simply as, here and now, the *one* means of growing in love for Him."[14]

Those who know Douglas and Dorothy Steere sense an intuitive timing about letters and notes they receive. When I was trying to decide whether to accept an offer of a professorship at Wake Forest University in the fall of 1982, I received a letter from Douglas penned at the Abbey of Gethsemani. "I have wondered how your inner leadings were guiding you," he wrote without weighting his inquiry either way.[15] A month or so later, he wrote again, this time with a telling word.

I have thought often of your difficult decision in this matter of your future teaching post. You recall old Berulle's word in late 17th century France to a group of "religious" who were going off to the Far East and were sitting in the final service with a group of their brothers who had not been chosen to go, and who looked on the travellers with much envy. Berulle said, "To go or to stay is the same." The real issue is the *willingness,* the *abandonment* to go where they were led.[16]

When Henri Nouwen invited Douglas Steere to speak to a class on spirituality he was conducting at Yale, Nouwen went to meet Steere's train to New Haven. Looking down the platform as the passengers disembarked, he spotted him carrying two heavy suitcases for someone else! That is the kind of humble accessibility he has brought in spiritual guidance.

Principles of Spiritual Guidance Through Letters

Spiritual guidance through correspondence requires special gifts and skills and insight. Douglas Steere has spelled out the major ones in his classic *On Listening to Another:* (1) vulnerability, (2) acceptance, (3) expectancy, and (4) constancy. Both he and von Hügel give evidence of these qualities throughout their letters of spiritual counsel.

Vulnerability

Great spiritual guides like von Hügel and Steere have a way of exposing their humanity, letting others see that they have walked the same way, known the same joys and sorrows, and experienced the same struggle. Von Hügel's early hearing loss and ever frail health, once accepted, tore down some of the defenses other people erect. He learned through what he suffered not to cover up, and his letters are rich in confession of his own struggle. Responding to queries of his niece, Gwendolen Greene, about how to respond to "the stress of darkness and dryness," he cited personal images that had helped him at three different stages of his life. At eighteen he learned from mountain climbers to wait until the fog lifted before he tried to climb higher. In his thirties he imitated sea travelers who selected a few things and secured them to their cabins to weather storms. In his forties he took his cue from bedouins who, during sandstorms, dismounted from their camels, fell prostrate face down on the sand, and covered their heads with their cloaks until the storm passed. What he had learned, he went on to say, was "to form no conclusions, to take no decisions, to change nothing during such crises, and, especially at such times, not to force any particularly religious mood or idea in oneself. . . . It is far, far more God Who must hold us, than we who must hold Him."[17]

Sometimes von Hügel was even more confessional, as here to his niece:

> My doings have cost me a good deal. I know why. The fact is that, like all three of my daughters but quite unlike their mother, I have a very vehement, violent, over-impressionable nature, which, on such occasions, gets ridiculously over-roused, jarred, confused. Hence I have then a big job (quite apart from all visible doings) to drop, drop, drop all this feverishness, and to listen, as docilely as I can, to think, will and pray, with only *"la fine pointe de l'esprit"* as St. François de Sales and Fénelon never weary in recommending.[18]

As this quotation shows, von Hügel had such a rich lode of personal experience he naturally brought those he guided into a much larger company of saints.

The same characteristic is visible in the letters of Douglas Steere. A lover of "wisdom in human hide," Steere sprinkles his conversation and letters with personalia, but, like von Hügel, he always lets his personal story glide into a larger story, insights he has gained from others reinforcing those which have forced themselves into his own experience. Scrupulous journal keeping has enabled him to keep a remarkably full account of conversations with others whose perspectives enlarge his own—Albert Schweitzer, Paul Tillich, Martin Buber, Pope John XXIII—in a natural, unaffected way. Many are those who have received letters enriched by Schweitzerisms, for example, drawn from visits to Lambarene in May of 1953 and 1954. Douglas Steere embodies in his own life Schweitzer's characteristic sense of presence to other persons, but he modestly prefers to let a story make the point for him.

Acceptance

Saints who want to serve as companions on the way have to have sufficient love for others that they will not try to reshape them in some other mold but rather to affirm what is deepest in them. This will not mean "toleration born of indifference," as Douglas Steere points out,[19] but appreciation for the gift of God in the other person.

Von Hügel operated on two basic principles in guiding others, he explained in a letter to Maude Petre, who later wrote his biography: that religion is the starting point of everything and that one should never begin with negatives. His objective was to begin where people were and take them to a deeper level.[20] He scrupulously avoided trying to convert people to Roman Catholicism even though he had a deep love for the church. He would do what he could "to feed in such souls the true and deep, in their degree, Catholic instincts and practices that I find in them" but he would not go beyond that.[21]

Von Hügel reveals best his capacity for acceptance in his sensitivity to numerous youth who sought his guidance. Speaking of efforts to direct a twelve year old, he confided to Professor Clement Webb that he had failed miserably in communicating "adult apprehensions" and thus had learned "to clothe the selection in childish imagery, illustration, limits and deflections of various kinds," even though he knew that what he said was "only roughly connected with what I know to be the more accurate conception."[22] He spoke ever so lovingly to a young woman who felt unworthy to take communion after a four-year hiatus while her life drifted religiously. "Oh! I just loved *that:*" he replied, "not, of course, the past drifting in itself, but the humility and frankness and, above all, the sense of need of that dear strength not your own." Nothing would please him more, he added, than to see her put the past behind and go forward.[23]

Douglas Steere may defy expectations some will have for contemplative types in the way he not only accepts those who seek him out but also in the way he reaches out to others, especially by letter. As a Professor of Philosophy at Haverford College, he established personal contact with many of the leading thinkers of the twentieth century who could enrich the lives of his students—Martin Buber, Paul Tillich, Gerald Heard, Howard Thurman, Emilia Fogelklou, Albert Schweitzer, Thomas Merton—as well as persons who could assist in carrying out projects he initiated, such as relief for war-torn Finland after World War II. Like Baron von Hügel, he also possessed a gift for participating in and generating groups of horizonal contributors to spirituality, such as the Ecumenical Institute of Spirituality. Beyond these things, Douglas Steere constantly has been a spiritual radar beaming out toward needy persons who had yet to discover some of the depths in themselves, maybe, as in my case, because they were shy or introverted.

The Steere files overflow with correspondence from and to "ordinary saints" who have come to a Steere lecture or read one of his writings or been touched by him through someone he has influenced. Although his correspondence has not yet become public, I think I can say from extensive reading in it that Douglas and Dorothy Steere take the same care with the ordinary that they do with the extraordinary. No serious question is shrugged off, no concern ignored. In numerous cases they have taken initiative to write when they became aware of a concern.

In a lecture on ecumenism Douglas Steere may give a clue to what lies behind this principle of acceptance. In dialogue between Christians and non-Christians, or simply among Christians, he suggests "mutual irradiation." According to this concept, those involved in dialogue "would try to provide the most congenial setting possible for releasing the deepest witness" others had within them.[24] Within every person shines the love of God that is at the heart of things; consequently, our task is to affirm and evoke that of God in the other.

Expectancy

Spiritual guides who have really helped others have had a way of generating hopefulness or, perhaps better stated, bringing others to the Source of hope. In both Friedrich von Hügel's and Douglas Steere's letters expectancy comes through in a powerful accentuation of grace, God's presence. Even in his last years when he battled a succession of illnesses, von Hügel sounded upbeat in his letters. Steere is blessed with a gift for uplifting others.

The note of uplift sounds in von Hügel's adherence to the principle that he would always begin with something positive, even when he meant to confront the other person in a serious way, as he often did. The negative took the form of expectation. In a quite serious engagement with the brilliant New Testament scholar Claude Montefiore, for instance, on the place of Judaism, von Hügel took care to lay the ground for possible improvement. "Let me first underline what I specially admire here—much the most of the whole," he wrote. "And let me then indicate the three or four places where I hope you may eventually put things somewhat differently: in each of these places the modification I wish for, is evidently well within the Jewish conviction and *Welt-bild*."[25]

In more personal and less academic letters von Hügel sought to recall the reader to sources he had found helpful. Shortly after the death of his eldest daughter, Gertrud, he described to Maude Petre her last hours of life and the childlike faith she had exhibited, then added, "And thus, in the midst of one's literally irreplaceable loss, there well up springs of water of eternal life; and we can stand most bracingly abashed before God's goodness working in and through her."[26] Von Hügel made much of the value of suffering, particularly as he sought to encourage the suffering. All souls are interconnected and can share suffering; that is what the church is.[27] To a friend suffering a terminal illness he recalled how he had held out hopes for Gertrud. In retrospect he was thanking God

> that, given the suffering and trials which God then sent or permitted, He also soon gave her a light, far more vivid and continuous than it used to be, and an evergrowing acceptance and active utilization of it, as to the place, meaning and unique fruitfulness of such suffering, thus met (as it were) half-way, in the mysterious, but most certain, most real scheme of the deepest life and of God.[28]

"Holy suffering is the very crown of holy action," he told his niece.[29]

The accent on suffering is more subdued in Douglas Steere's letters, but one will find in them otherwise a remarkable congruence with von Hügel's approach: the positive first and a search for the hopefulness in even the bleakest situation. In the Douglas Steere Lectures at Bay View, Michigan, in the summer of 1984 I gave one of my five lectures on Douglas Steere himself. In preparation for that lecture, unfortunately, I did not have access to extensive biographical information and made several slips on details. When Douglas wrote later to express appreciation, he made some warm comments and asked if he could photocopy it for a doctoral candidate who wanted to do his dissertation on some aspect of Douglas's thought. Then, in his gentle way, he asked, "Would you mind if I corrected two or three very small things in your most thorough presentation?" The corrections took almost a full page! But with such gentle handling I felt uplifted and determined to do better.

Douglas Steere's personal notes and letters, like von Hügel's, are replete with uplifting words, not glossing over reality but calling attention to experiences in which one could rejoice. In January 1986 at a meeting of the Ecumenical Institute of Spirituality, Tom Kilduff, a cherished long-time and faithful member, announced that he had inoperable cancer. Since my teaching schedule prevented my attendance, Douglas took time to share with me what had transpired and in a postscript pointed to a ray of light peeking through dark clouds.

> Dear Tom Kilduff has cancer of the liver which is inoperable. He shared what it is like to face certain death. He ministered in the mass that closed the meetings and it was an experience that was indescribably wonderful. He is not in pain now but to have him there with us for probably the last time was itself a gift beyond measure.[30]

Douglas Steere never stops on the gloomy note; a profound confidence in God's inescapable nearness evokes something hopeful.

Constancy

In the long run spiritual guidance depends on patience, standing *with* another, stick-to-it-iveness. The slow pace of spiritual growth will discourage many whose faith has not yet matured enough to wait for God to work in their lives, so spiritual guides have to model constancy. Even the best guides will experience failure in this.

Baron von Hügel confessed to his niece that "a couple of attempts to help souls seem to have gone awry with me just now." He held out a bit of hope for the first case, in which he tried to dampen a speculative and enhance a devotional bent. "He is a well-intentioned man," von Hügel proceeded to reassure himself, "and God will bless even unlikely-looking happenings."[31] The other one, in which he had commended the poetry of Robert Browning to a young woman who had given up on religion, did not prove so hopeful, and he had to be content with the judgment that he had done his "little best."

Neither von Hügel nor Steere let the whole weight, or even most of it, rest on their personal counsel by letter or face-to-face contact. Von Hügel repeatedly emphasized balance between the rational, the mystical, the institutional, and the social elements of religion.[32] Where he detected an imbalance, he tilted those he counseled toward other elements. He relied heavily on well-selected reading not merely in devotional literature but in the whole broad spectrum, sending personal copies when directees might have trouble finding them. Devotional reading, he advised his niece, "should always be select, slow, ruminating, and given to comparatively few books or papers."[33] He also strongly encouraged attendance at church, not meaning Roman Catholic Church but whatever communion the person felt at home in.

> As for myself, I find myself inclined to be very zealous to help souls to make the most of what they already have; and, if they come to think of moving, to test them to the uttermost. And again, to do all I can to make the old Church as inhabitable *intellectually* as ever I can—[34]

Although von Hügel and Douglas Steere belong to quite different religious bodies, both appreciate the continuity of Christian tradition. Steere has rendered a service to thousands by introducing them to the classics of Christian devotion through the classroom, translations, introductions, and sharing of insights drawn from them. His letters, like von Hügel's, are rich in the treasures of the church universal.

Minding a Serious Calling

Friedrich von Hügel and Douglas Steere have brought to spiritual guidance the rare combination of qualities that von Hügel discerned in Francis Fénelon, who was to him the guide par excellence: "a light and elastic open temperament with an earnest will and gently concentrated determination."[35] Both know from experience that growth is of God and the key to growth is to get people in touch with the working of grace in their lives. Their letters have few "musts" and "have to's" and even "oughts." They share themselves and their experience. They affirm and encourage. They point up signs of hope. They stand with those who seek their counsel.

What has equipped them as superlative guides? Reading programs such as those outlined for others by von Hügel? Faithful participation in the body of Christ in its many expressions—from the Catholic mass to the Quaker silent meeting? Inward exercises and habits of mind in attentiveness to God personally present? Active involvement in the press and struggle of human beings in urban ghettos and slums, as von Hügel advised Evelyn Underhill? Natural gifts of mind and spirit? All of these surely had something to do with Friedrich von Hügel and Douglas Steere as spiritual guides. In the long run, however, I suspect we can never answer the question except to say that the Master of souls has called them to this task and they have minded the call. We are fortunate to see how the call comes through in their letters of spiritual counsel.

Notes

1. Letter to Gwendolen Greene, Jan. 26, 1919.

2. *Spiritual Counsel and Letters of Baron Friedrich von Hügel*, ed. Douglas V. Steere (New York: Harper & Row, 1964).

3. Ibid., 10.

4. Letter to Mrs. Lillie, April 20, 1922; in *Baron Friedrich von Hügel: Selected Letters, 1896–1924*, ed. Bernard Holland (London & Toronto: J. M. Dent & Sons, 1927), 354.

5. Douglas V. Steere, *On Listening to Another* (New York: Harper & Brothers, 1955), 27.

6. *Letters from Baron Friedrich von Hügel to a Niece*, ed. Gwendolen Greene (London: J. M. Dent & Sons, 1928), xxv.

7. Douglas V. Steere, "A Quaker's View of Transcendent Experience," in *Civil Religion and Transcendent Experience*, ed. Ralph C. Wood and John E. Collins (Macon, Ga.: Mercer University Press, 1988), 146.

8. Cited by Bernard Holland, ed., *Baron Friedrich von Hügel: Selected Letters, 1896–1924* (London & Toronto: J. M. Dent & Sons, 1927), 8.

9. Letter to George Tyrrell, Jan. 26, 1898; ibid., 9ff.

10. Douglas V. Steere, unpublished autobiography, p. 548.

11. Letter to Father Tyrrell, Dec. 4, 1902.

12. Ibid., 114.

13. Margaret Cropper, *Evelyn Underhill* (New York: Harper & Brothers, 1958), 70.

14. Letter to Gwendolen Greene, May 4, 1920, in *Selected Letters,* ed. Holland, 306.

15. Letter of Douglas Steere to E. Glenn Hinson, Nov. 3, 1982.

16. Letter of Douglas Steere to E. Glenn Hinson, Dec. 24, 1982.

17. Letter to Gwendolen Greene, April 21, 1920, in *Selected Letters,* ed. Holland, 305.

18. Letter to Gwendolen Greene, Oct. 4, 1920, ibid., 309.

19. Steere, *On Listening to Another,* 12.

20. Letter to Maude Petre, Nov. 17, 1910.

21. Letter to a lady, May 22, 1911, in *Selected Letters,* ed. Holland, 187.

22. Letter to Professor Clement Webb, Oct. 13, 1916, ibid., 236.

23. Letter to J.M., Epiphany, 1921, ibid., 322.

24. Douglas V. Steere, *Mutual Irradiation: A Quaker View of Ecumenism* (Wallingford, Pa.: Pendle Hill Publications, 1971), 8.

25. Letter to Claude Montefiore, Oct. 28, 1916, in *Selected Letters,* ed. Holland, 239.

26. Letter to Miss Maude Petre, Sept. 14, 1915, ibid., 223.

27. Letter to Gwendolen Greene, Apr. 7, 1919.

28. Letter to a friend in his last illness, 1916, in *Selected Letters,* ed. Holland, 226f.

29. Letter to Gwendolen Greene, Oct. 7, 1921, ibid., 340.

30. Letter of Douglas Steere to E. Glenn Hinson, Jan. 12, 1986.

31. Letter to Gwendolen Greene, Jan. 29 and Feb. 2, 1921, in *Selected Letters,* ed. Holland, 324.

32. Von Hügel did not include the fourth dimension in the list he frequently cited, for example, in a letter to the Rev. Canon Newson, July 7, 1911, but he directed Evelyn Underhill to spend two afternoons a week in the slums so as to "de-intellectualize" her. This procedure, he explained, "will, if properly entered into and persevered with, discipline, mortify, deepen and quiet you. It will, as it were, distribute your blood—some of your blood—away from your brain, where too much is lodged at present." Cropper, *Evelyn Underhill,* 75.

33. Letter to Gwendolen Greene, Jan. 2, 1920, in *Selected Letters,* ed. Holland, 299.

34. Letter to Gwendolen Greene, Dec. 9, 1921, ibid., 347.

35. Letter to Gwendolen Greene, Nov. 23, 1920, ibid., 315.

12
Along the Desert Road: Notes on Spiritual Reading

JOHN S. MOGABGAB

"Show me your ways, O Lord, and teach me your paths" (Ps. 25:3, JB). The ancient longing expressed in the psalmist's words is being felt with new intensity in our day. A more intimate acquaintance with God's ways in the world and a more informed knowledge of sources that help us walk those ways have become major concerns of clergy and laity across denominations. Indeed, a renewed flowering of ecumenical Christian encounter is occurring around a deep yearning for guidance in the spiritual life.

Seekers in every age of the Christian era have found such guidance in spiritual reading. Although the primary focus of this discipline has always been scripture, it can encompass a wide range of literature. Poetry, drama, biography, and prose fiction as well as explicitly religious or devotional texts all may find a place in the practice of spiritual reading. In spite of its long history, however, spiritual reading may yet remain an undiscovered source of growth for many people. Perhaps this is because the pace and complexity of life cause us to think that we have little time for reading. It may be, too, that in our culture reading tends to be either utilitarian or recreational; we read to acquire information or to be entertained. In view of these tendencies, how can we come to appreciate the place and importance of spiritual reading in the life of faith? As I was thinking about this question, I came across the story of Philip and the Ethiopian eunuch in the book of Acts.

Philip and the Eunuch

Perhaps this ancient story can offer us helpful images for envisioning the role of spiritual reading in the journey to fullness of life with God.

> The angel of the Lord spoke to Philip saying, "Be ready to set out at noon along the road that goes from Jerusalem down to Gaza, the desert road." So he set off on his journey. Now it happened that an Ethiopian had been on pilgrimage to Jerusalem; he was a eunuch and an officer at the court of the kandake, or queen, of Ethiopia and was in fact her chief treasurer. He was now on his way home; and as he sat in his chariot he was reading the prophet Isaiah. The Spirit said to Philip, "Go up and meet that chariot." When Philip ran up, he heard him reading Isaiah the prophet and asked, "Do you understand what you are reading?" "How can I," he replied, "unless I have someone to guide me?" So he invited Philip to get in and sit by his side. Now the passage of scripture he was reading was this:
>
>> Like a sheep that is led to the slaughterhouse,
>> like a lamb that is dumb in front its shearers,
>> like these he never opens his mouth.
>> He has been humiliated and has no one to defend him.
>> Who will ever talk about his descendants,
>> since his life on earth has been cut short!
>
> The eunuch turned to Philip and said, "Tell me, is the prophet referring to himself or someone else?" Starting, therefore, with this text of scripture Philip proceeded to explain the Good News of Jesus to him.
> Further along the road they came to some water, and the eunuch said, "Look, there is some water here; is there anything to stop me

being baptized?" He ordered the chariot to stop, then Philip and
the eunuch both went down into the water and Philip baptized him.
But after they had come up out of the water again Philip was taken
away by the Spirit of the Lord, and the eunuch never saw him again
but went on his way rejoicing. Philip found that he had reached
Azotus and continued his journey proclaiming the Good News in
every town as far as Caesarea (Acts 8:26–40, JB).

Recognizing a Hunger

We meet the Ethiopian eunuch in the midst of a pilgrimage, one of
the oldest and most universal forms of religious quest. He has been to
Jerusalem to worship and is now returning home along the desert
road that descends from Jerusalem to Gaza. As he travels along in his
chariot, the eunuch sifts through pages of the Hebrew scriptures. This
activity reflects the larger search that has brought him such a great
distance from the scented court of the Ethiopian queen.

Who is this person, and why has he undertaken this arduous
journey? The story offers few details. He is chief treasurer in the
government of Ethiopia, a capable man whose talent and discretion
make him worthy of the highest trust. In keeping with his high
position, this pilgrim seems to be someone of means, a person who
travels by chariot and somehow has acquired a precious scroll
containing the book of the prophet Isaiah. Quite possibly he is one of
the many "God-fearers" living in Ethiopia, Gentiles drawn to the
monotheistic faith of Judaism who keep the Sabbath and observe the
ritual laws of cleanliness. But soaring bannerlike above all these
sketchy details is the one central fact of this man's existence: he is a
eunuch. In the story he has no name. He is simply and definitively
"the eunuch."

What does this mean for the queen's treasurer? A eunuch is a
person quite literally cut off from himself. A part of him is missing,
lost. Moreover, because this Ethiopian is cut off from himself, he is
also separated from God and the people of God. Such was the ruling
of Israel's cultic law, expressed with finality in the book of Deuter-
onomy: a eunuch "is not to be admitted to the assembly of Yahweh"
(Deut. 23:1, JB). Moreover, this prohibition was only part of a vast

system of law that had segregated Jews from Gentiles for centuries, thereby protecting Israel against religious pollution. The words of *Aristeas* express clearly the Jewish viewpoint: "Our Lawgiver fenced us round with impregnable ramparts and walls of iron that we might not mingle at all with any of the nations, but remain pure in body and soul."[1] Perhaps the most concrete and potent symbol of this estrangement was the wall, some four feet in height, that restricted Gentiles to the outer court of the Temple in Jerusalem. Upon that wall were signs promising death to any non-Jew who violated the sanctity of the inner court (cf. Acts 21:28–29). Where our story itself remains silent, intuition suggests a possible motive for the eunuch's pilgrimage. If he was indeed associated with the Jewish community in Ethiopia, he would no doubt have been familiar with the cultic law concerning eunuchs. Experiencing his life as one cut off from himself, from others, and from God, the eunuch may well have known a hunger for something more than the status he enjoyed in the court of Ethiopia's queen.

In various ways, are we not all cut off from others, from God, and from ourselves? Like the eunuch's world, ours too is convulsed by estrangement and hostility. How many contemporary barriers perpetuate discord and isolate us from one another: ideological commitments as unyielding as the tanks in Tiananmen Square; nuclear weapons, those "impregnable ramparts and walls of iron" by which the nations hope to protect themselves from the evil of others; fear, ignorance, or religious zeal that cause people to shrink from contact with those whose ways offend them. Like the eunuch's religious life, ours too may be hemmed in by pain or misunderstanding. Perhaps suffering, tragedy, failure, or rejection has nourished deep feelings of anger or distrust toward God, feelings that have separated us from the Lord as effectively as the law barring eunuchs from Temple worship. Finally, we may resemble the eunuch in another way as well. Figuratively, a eunuch would be any person who is cut off from his or her own inner sources of creative, generative power. A eunuch is one whose life has been severed from those deep roots that bring spiritual vitality, color, and meaning to human existence. How many of us suffer from feelings or experiences of impotence in one or another dimension of our life? In sum, we may be as successful in our work as the highly placed eunuch and still remain inward wanderers searching for larger patterns of meaning, more empowering renditions of truth. It is the eunuch in each of us that hungers for wholeness, for fullness of life with God and with our neighbors. It is this hunger, recognized perhaps only as an inchoate yearning for "something more," that sets us on the pilgrim's quest.

The circumstances under which we meet the eunuch suggest an additional observation. The spiritual journey draws us away from the comfortable and familiar places, perspectives, and people that have shaped our lives. Whether we leave behind the beauty, power, and privilege of a regal court, the security and collegial support of a particular career track, or the hearthlike assurance of long-held beliefs, the path of pilgrimage is marked by increasing vulnerability. The protective layers of habit that have insulated us from our yearning slowly fall away. Ironically, however, sometimes the most obvious places to go for the wholeness we seek turn out to be wrong destinations. The eunuch may have discovered this at the Temple in Jerusalem, with its limited access to Gentiles. We may meet the same irony in churches suspicious of spiritual questions, clergy untutored in spiritual guidance, friends or family fearful of the challenges our growth places before them. And so, at some point along the desert road, we may find ourselves trying to decipher a mystifying text—the text of our own life story that we hold in our hands but do not understand. Here is one of the compelling motivations for the practice of spiritual reading. In this discipline, we take up a text to clarify the contours of meaning and milestones of truth in the narrative of our own existence. "As [the eunuch] sat in his chariot he was reading . . ." (Acts 8:28, JB).

Finding a Community

A yearning at the root of our being woos us away from the familiar and onto our own desert road. But if it is to be fruitful, our spiritual seeking must at some point cease to be merely individual and become instead a journey shared. As Philip approached the eunuch's chariot, "he heard him reading Isaiah the prophet and asked, 'Do you understand what you are reading?' 'How can I,' [the eunuch] replied, 'unless I have someone to guide me?' So he invited Philip to get in and sit by his side" (Acts 8:30–31, JB).

This is a critical moment. The eunuch is reading a text in which his own story and the larger story of God's ways in the world converge. Here God's history with Israel intersects (and will transfigure) the eunuch's history with the Ethiopian court. This history may have included parents who dedicated their boy-child to the court, the agonizing experience of castration, the impossibility of normal adult sexual intimacy, the snuffing of any hope for offspring. Imagine, then, the powerful attraction the queen's treasurer must have felt to the passage from Isaiah he was reading:

> Like a sheep that is led to the slaughterhouse, like a lamb that is dumb in front of its shearers, like these he never opens his mouth. He has been humiliated and has no one to defend him. Who will ever talk about his descendants, since his life on earth has been cut short!

The eunuch may well recognize a connection between his own story and the story he is reading, yet not understand what this bond means. He may sense the power of this text and yet not know why it stirs him. Again, the eunuch may be gripped by the account of someone whose experience so nearly conforms to his own. In any case, he turns to Philip and says, "Tell me, is the prophet referring to himself or someone else?" (v. 34).

Thomas Merton describes scripture as "the strange and paradoxical world of meanings and experience that are beyond us and yet often extremely and mysteriously relevant to us."[2] In response to the eunuch's question, Philip helps him recognize the reason for his attraction to this particular text. Philip shows the eunuch that what seems beyond his comprehension is, in truth, extremely and mysteriously relevant to him. "Starting therefore with [Isaiah], Philip proceeded to explain the Good News of Jesus to him."

Here Philip is an image of the author who joins us for a stretch of the way when we take up the practice of spiritual reading.

Spiritual reading introduces us to a community of pilgrims large enough and varied enough for all to find companionship and guidance. The marvelously diverse community we discover through spiritual reading will, in one way or another, always help us recognize the places where the great biblical drama of God's love for us is recapitulating itself in the pages of our own story. How, then, do we find our way into this community of saints? Among the most traveled paths are historical and systematic studies, meditations on scripture, reflections on the spiritual life, and explorations of prayer.

Historical and Systematic Studies

The eunuch from Ethiopia was seeking something. Moreover, his search was informed: He was on a road and he knew approximately where he was on that road. Historical and systematic studies of spiritual traditions and practices, of great spiritual literature and leaders, can aid us in locating ourselves amid what may sometimes seem like a vast expanse of beliefs, experiences, and questions. Especially now, when many new perspectives on the spiritual journey are challenging the reliability of familiar landmarks, some pilgrims may find just the orientation they need in such studies.

Where might we begin? One point of embarkation could be the recent volume *Christian Spirituality*.[3] In it, twenty-four scholars introduce the reader to one hundred and twenty-five of the most influential writings in Christian tradition. Starting with Clement of Alexandria's *The Instructor* and *Miscellanies* (190–200 C.E.), and concluding with Gustavo Gutiérrez's *We Drink from Our Own Wells* (1983), the volume encompasses a wide range of spiritual traditions. Each entry includes a short biography of the author, a classification of the writing under review, the date of its publication, its main themes, and a substantial synopsis of its content. The entry concludes with a short list of recommended readings.

This format is useful in several respects. It provides the reader with sufficient information about a spiritual classic to make an informed decision about whether and why to take up the original. Moreover, these reviews help the reader bridge the often considerable gulf between contemporary assumptions and values and those that inform a particular spiritual classic. Without such help, writings from earlier periods of Christian history may be misunderstood and dismissed as either irrelevant or unintelligible to contemporary concerns.

Christian Spirituality is an admirable companion to Thomas S. Kepler's *An Anthology of Devotional Literature*, originally published in 1947.[4] The theme unifying the one hundred and sixty-two excerpts from original sources is the fellowship of the saints. Kepler wants to guide us into this expansive community so that we too might become saints. Other works that can help us find our bearings within the community of saints are two rich introductions to selected spiritual classics: Douglas Steere's *Doorways Into Life* and E. Glenn Hinson's *Seekers After Mature Faith*.[5] Louis Bouyer's three-volume *A History of Christian Spirituality* remains indispensable for those who wish a detailed tour through the development of spiritual theology from its New Testament foundations to the nineteenth century.[6] Also noteworthy is the more recent three-volume *Christian Spirituality*, a collection of essays covering significant eras, themes, or figures in the history of Orthodox, Roman Catholic, and Protestant spirituality.[7] Finally, two informative studies of Orthodox spirituality deserve mention: Kallistos Ware's *The Orthodox Way*, and *Orthodox Spirituality* by a monk of the Eastern Church.[8]

Meditations on Scripture

John the Solitary, a Syriac spiritual writer active during the first half of the fifth century, commended careful attention to the words of scripture so that they might teach us "how to be with God."[9] Jesus offers an image of meditating on scripture that suggests how it accomplishes the work of forming us into companions of God: "If you make my word your home you will indeed be my disciples, you will learn the truth and the truth shall make you free" (John 8:31–32, JB). The prayerful reading of scripture involves entering what Karl Barth called the "strange new world of the Bible" with a regularity that allows us to feel increasingly at home in it. In this form of spiritual reading we step into the words of the text and allow them, chariotlike, to bear our attention toward God. Over time these encounters foster in us a vision of God and God's kingdom that will orient and energize our journey. And as this vision sharpens, we find that our journey is one of ongoing conversion—that transformation of mind and heart that enables us to discern God's will for us (cf. Rom. 12:2). In all these ways Jesus' promise is fulfilled: "You will learn the truth." But there is more. Such reading also readies us to accept the work the Lord has prepared for us to do: "The truth will set you free." A growing habit of receptivity to the liberating power of God's truth, which is nothing other than God's love, is learning "how to be with God."

Dietrich Bonhoeffer, the young German theologian who died resisting the Nazi perversion of church and state, understood this. He once described meditation on scripture as similar to reading a letter from a dear loved one. In such reading we savor the words, linger over the fragrance of their meaning, attune our senses to a truth larger than sentences can serve up. Bonhoeffer's classic work, *The Cost of Discipleship,* exemplifies this approach to scripture.[10] Written in the mid-1930s, when the National Socialists were busy twisting Christian theology into Nazi ideology, *The Cost of Discipleship* seeks to clarify the distinctive marks of Christian life.

Bonhoeffer pursues his aim by dividing the book into two parts, the first an extended meditation on the Sermon on the Mount, the second an exploration of Pauline theology. At the center of both Jesus' preaching and Paul's proclamation of the gospel, Bonhoeffer discerns the summons to break with one's previous existence and enter into full fellowship with Jesus. "When Christ calls [us], he bids [us] come and die." Bonhoeffer's rigorous contemplation, bracing as an Arctic cold front, awakens us to the radical depths of scripture. With Bonhoeffer by our side for a part of the journey, we may find ourselves being guided into such questions as, "What contemporary ideologies, subtle and alluring, am I confusing with the way of God's Spirit?" or "What parts of my life am I clutching so tenaciously that I cannot open my hands to receive the new life God desires for me?"

Meditations on scripture like Bonhoeffer's *The Cost of Discipleship* show us how God's word can lay bare the hidden wounds of personal or corporate life that daze our spirit and disorient our search for God. At the same time, such meditations reveal how the urgent questions of an era, echoing in the voice of an author, can breach the cool crust of conventional piety and release the molten flow of spiritual renewal. Thus Gregory of Nyssa's *The Life of Moses,* with its emphasis on asceticism and the cultivation of virtue, may cause us to consider what it means to follow God in the laissez-faire atmosphere of a consumer culture. Bernard of Clairvaux's *On the Song of Songs* evokes the full-bodied passion of intimacy with the living God. Meister Eckhart's *Sermons* proffers the arresting thought that, following the pattern of Mary, we are called to birth God in the world. In *Strength to Love,* Martin Luther King, Jr. reminds us that both strength and love are called for when we live with the God whose arms are justice and compassion. Contemporary works such as Renita J. Weems's *Just a Sister Away* open the door to the hitherto largely hidden but stunningly rich community of women in the Bible.

Reflections on the Spiritual Life

A Hasidic tale asserts that human beings were created because God loves stories. Fashioned in the image of this story-loving Creator, we too are drawn to the colors and cadences of human lives rendered in words. As the Ethiopian eunuch was discovering when Philip met him along the desert road, the chronicle of someone's experiences with God exercises a unique pull on our interest and attention. "Is the prophet referring to himself or someone else?"

Even as Philip's own witness to the good news of Jesus led the eunuch to a watershed in his pilgrimage, so the lives of those who have walked with God, depicted in biographies and autobiographies, journals and letters, can guide us further along our own desert road. There are seasons of life when discovering aspects of our own story in the experience of another seeker is just what we need to gain fresh insights into God and our life with God. Spiritual reading of this kind can result in a new birth of sorts; through our immersion in the life of another pilgrim we receive our own life back, newborn and ruddy, from the deep waters of our shared humanity. Here again, spiritual reading enlarges the circle of our community.

It might be stretching the limits of community for some contemporary readers to find a friend in Antony, the third-century founder of Christian monasticism, whose life was recounted by Athanasius.[11] Yet even such an apparently distant figure as Antony can help us articulate questions worth living into. For instance, Antony's experiment in monastic life began shortly after the death of his parents, when he was in his late teens or early twenties. Entering a church, he heard Matthew 19:21 being read, and perceived that these words of Jesus were meant for him: "If you wish to be perfect, go and sell what you own and give the money to the poor, and you will have treasure in heaven; then come, follow me" (JB). Antony heeded this message and soon began to live a life of great simplicity and self-denial in his village. Antony's experience prompts several questions: How have I experienced God's guidance? How have I responded to that guidance? Has God's word made a difference in how I live my life? Antony soon left his village in order to dwell among the tombs on the outskirts of town. There he was repeatedly and fiercely attacked by demons, although to no avail. The account of these travails offers us an opportunity to review the nature of our own spiritual struggles. What internal impulses or external circumstances inflame our anger, envy, lust, despair? What forces seem to separate us from a fuller life with God? How do we respond to these disruptive impulses, circumstances, or forces? A final example. Antony spent nearly twenty years alone in a deserted fort deep in the desert. When he emerged from his solitude, those who saw him were amazed at his healthy appearance. His experience may cause us to ask what conditions most foster our physical, mental, and spiritual health. Moreover, what steps might we take to ensure that these conditions have an appropriate place in our way of life?

Other sources for such questions would be Augustine's *Confessions*, Teresa of Avila's autobiography (*The Life of Teresa of Jesus*), Martin Luther's *Letters of Spiritual Counsel*, the journals of John Woolman and George Fox, the anonymous classic *The Way of a Pilgrim*, and Henri Nouwen's *The Genesee Diary*.

Reflections on the spiritual life may also take the form of commentaries and collections. These too may be quite personal, but their effect is to instruct us in particular patterns, schools, or disciplines. A list of influential books in this rather broad category would include *The Sayings of the Desert Fathers*; *The Philokalia*; *The Dialogues*, by Catherine of Siena; *Showings*, by Julian of Norwich; *The Cloud of Unknowing* (anonymous); *The Imitation of Christ*, by Thomas à Kempis; *Ascent of Mount Carmel*, by John of the Cross; *Introduction to the Devout Life*, by Francis de Sales; *Hymns of Divine Love*, by Symeon the New Theologian; and *Deep Is the Hunger*, by Howard Thurman. Lest such catalogues of spiritual classics smother our energy for spiritual reading, let us recall the wisdom of W. H. Auden: "The distresses of choice are our chance to be blessed."[12]

Explorations of Prayer

In one of his many pastoral letters, Martin Luther confided that "I have often learned more in one prayer than I have been able to get out of much reading and reflection."[13] Luther's remark reminds us that reading and thinking about spiritual things are not substitutes for prayer. Prayer is the great school of wisdom because in it we place ourselves under the tutelage of the Counselor who desires to lead us to the fullness of truth (John 16:13). Yet this is no typical experience of education. Here the goal is not greater personal autonomy but more comprehensive personal surrender, not greater capacity for critical thinking but greater readiness for prodigal loving. In prayer we are convinced not by the power of logic and evidence but by the gentleness of love's persistent wooing. Education ripens into formation as we recognize that our prayer is the responding echo of a far more resonant and encompassing prayer—the yearning of God for us that is too deep for words. We were created for life with God, and God's heart is restless until we rest at home with God.

When Philip meets the eunuch, our story tells us, the Ethiopian is "on his way home" (v. 28). This phrase beautifully expresses the movement of prayer, a movement animated by the desire of the heart that draws us away from the far country toward the dwelling place of God. "How lovely is your dwelling place, Lord, God of Hosts. My soul is longing and yearning, is yearning for the courts of the Lord" (Ps. 83:2–3, Grail). It is desire for the "courts of the Lord," more than recollection of the court of the Ethiopian queen, that now draws the eunuch onward. Yet desire alone is not sufficient to find the way home across the desert landscape of our seeking. The warning Goethe's Mephistopheles gives to one of Dr. Faust's students about the dangers of theology also applies to prayer. "When it comes to this discipline, the way is hard to find, wrong roads abound, and lots of hidden poison lies around which one can scarcely tell from medicine."[14] To undertake the great journey home in the literary company of seasoned spiritual guides surely increases our chances of finding our way through the difficult terrain of prayer.

One source of reliable guidance in the ways of prayer is the teaching of the renowned nineteenth-century Russian Staretz (spiritual father) Theophan the Recluse. The wisdom of Theophan was compiled by Igumen Chariton, a monk of the ancient monastery at Valamo in Finland, and is available to us in an anthology titled *The Art of Prayer*.[15] For Theophan the journey home to God in prayer is a journey from the head to the heart, a movement from the tumultuous wilderness of scampering thoughts about God to the holy garden at the center of our personhood where God awaits us. This movement, however, does not involve the abandonment of mind in favor of a more intensely emotional relationship with God. The challenge of prayer is to bring the mind into the heart so that all the mind's God-given powers of imagination and reason can be focused on the one thing necessary. This is the pathway to unceasing prayer, which is not a ceaseless repetition of prayers but an abiding inner posture of standing before God in reverence and hope. Theophan shows that when we finally stand before God with the mind in the heart, prayer ceases to be one activity among many others and becomes instead the single integrating characteristic of our life, a life now at home in the "courts of the Lord." That is why the Recluse can say that prayer is the test, source, driving force, and director of everything.[16] At the same time, Theophan reminds us that the motivation for prayer must be something deeper and more enduring than the quest for personal spiritual profit. "The whole of life, in all its manifestations, must be permeated by prayer. But its secret is love for the Lord."[17]

The way home to God abounds in wrong roads, but there are many right roads as well. These have been scouted and described by other seasoned guides such as Brother Lawrence, whose *The Practice of the Presence of God* shows us how to remain in communion with God simply by "doing for God what we ordinarily do for ourselves."[18] Anthony Bloom's enduring classic *Beginning to Pray* combines great mystical depth with simplicity of expression to prepare the seeker for the "hard, arduous, daring exercise" of prayer.[19] In *Dimensions of Prayer*, Douglas Steere locates the whole endeavor of prayer in a redemptive order already at work in the universe. Here is the basis for full-bodied confidence in the prayer we offer to the God who, Douglas Steere believes, is "far less squeamish than his theological bodyguard."[20] The anonymous author of *The Cloud of Unknowing* would probably concur. This fourteenth-century exploration of contemplative prayer builds on the conviction that the God "whom neither men nor angels can grasp by knowledge can be embraced by love."[21] Thomas Merton's *New Seeds of Contemplation* gathers occasional thoughts by the Trappist monk into thirty-nine short chapters on such subjects as solitude, integrity, detachment, and freedom. Merton's "seeds," falling on a receptive soul, plant the reminder that "we are invited to forget ourselves on purpose, cast our awful solemnity to the winds, and join in the general dance" of Creator and creation.[22]

Receiving a Blessing

With Philip's help the eunuch is able to recognize the healing congruence between his own life and the life of Jesus. Like the eunuch, Jesus was led to a place of pain. Like the eunuch, Jesus had no one to stand between him and the injury about to be done to him. Like the eunuch, Jesus had no offspring. Jesus is someone who, so to speak, has lived inside the eunuch's skin. What power lies in discovering that someone knows our story with such intimacy! And yet, as if this were not sufficient good news, there is more. We are left to wonder what words Philip chose to describe the ineffable mystery of Easter. Here is Paul's effort: "But God raised him high and gave him the name which is above all other names so that all beings in the heavens, on earth and in the underworld, should bend the knee at the name of Jesus and that every tongue should acclaim Jesus Christ as Lord, to the glory of God the Father" (Phil. 2:9–11, JB). God had transfigured the suffering of Jesus into glory. The power of the good news resides in the knowledge not only that God knows our humanity from within but also that in the resurrection of Jesus God has fashioned an utterly new and resplendent destiny for us. The "Good News of Jesus Christ" explained by Philip carries a transforming power that can reshape and renew a person's life. Certainly this was the blessing received by the Ethiopian eunuch. Similar transformation is a possibility for us as well when we embark on the venture of spiritual reading. The eunuch's journey with Philip suggests three aspects of transformation we may experience as a result of time spent with the spiritual classics. They are understanding, acceptance, and joy.

We have seen how the eunuch's engagement with scripture evolves from earnest interest into life-changing understanding. This understanding is not simply intellectual, a cognitive grasp of the text's meaning. Rather, it is an ampler understanding that encompasses both mind and heart and leads to action. When the eunuch begins to understand the convergence of the story of Jesus and his own story, when he realizes that the words of the prophet Isaiah are becoming a word to and for him, he responds: "He ordered the chariot to stop" (v. 38). The eunuch's order to stop the chariot exemplifies the trust and resolve of those who come to understand that God's word is not only a word *about* life but also a word *of* life. It places all our thinking and acting in a new context, the context of the reigning of God in our midst. The eunuch therefore confirms Bonhoeffer's observation that God's word is not simply the dessert after a satisfying meal; God's word is the whole meal or it is nothing at all.

The whole import of God's word cannot be ingested and absorbed in one sitting. The meal is a banquet extending across a lifetime of God's hosting and nourishing us at the table of grace. Sometimes we are ready to try new dishes, and sometimes we seek the comforting aroma of familiar recipes. At times we eat to the point of overindulgence. Often we approach the table reluctantly, as if it were laden with cruets of cod-liver oil. Sometimes we notice delicacies that have long been on the table but never caught our attention. Sometimes we are served insights that prove bitter and difficult to digest. Over time, however, our understanding grows, sometimes slowly and sometimes by great leaps, as we return to the sources of spiritual sustenance in spiritual reading.

We see an example of such growth in the story of the eunuch. His new understanding of the good news leads him to stop the chariot. But this action occurs within the context of a question that reveals there is more for the eunuch to learn. "Further along the road they came to some water, and the eunuch said, 'Look, there is some water here; *is there anything to stop me being baptized?*' " (v. 36, my italics).

The eunuch's question is both poignant and courageous. How often in the past has he asked, "Is there anything to stop me?" only to collide with an unanticipated or immovable barrier. "Is there anything to stop me being married? Is there anything to stop me having children? Is there anything to stop me from being admitted to full membership in the people of God?" The eunuch's question is courageous because even though Philip's description of the good news has roused the Ethiopian's hope, he must still open himself to the possibility that there remains some hidden codicil, some fine print, some impossible condition, that Philip has forgotten to mention. "Is there anything to stop me being baptized?"

Spiritual reading can often help us unearth hidden barriers to our growth. The wisdom of other pilgrims well versed in the terrain of the spiritual journey can open our eyes to the nature of these barriers. Our literary "companions on the inner way" (Morton Kelsey) can also assist us in discerning similarities in the kinds of barriers we have met, or patterns in the way we have responded to them. Moreover, spiritual reading can heighten our sensitivity to the barriers facing the people around us. Do these people have opportunities to ask the difficult, poignant, courageous, or unsettling questions that might open a passage into the new thing God is doing their midst?

That day along the desert road between Jerusalem and Gaza the eunuch learned more than that there were no barriers to prevent his being baptized. He learned that he was fully loved and accepted. Here is the second aspect of transformation in the eunuch's story. Paul Tillich writes: "If only more such moments were given to us! For it is such moments that make us love our life, that make us accept ourselves, not in our goodness and self-complacency, but in our certainty of the eternal meaning of our life."[23] You are accepted! Is this not the good news all people want to hear addressed to them? Is this not the yearning behind all our striving for achievement, status, possessions? Often it is the wounds we receive in childhood that, like the eunuch's scars, cause us to feel unacceptable to the core, a core choked with shame, guilt, anger, and bewilderment. What percentage of the world's violence and hatred derives from experiences of rejection, humiliation, and defeat? What portion of our precious life energy do we expend on trying to show others, and convince ourselves, that we are indeed acceptable?

Not long ago a friend dreamed that he had received an invitation to a special meeting. When he had settled himself at the meeting table, he noticed with some dismay that the few others who had already arrived were world-class musicians. Troubled, he vaguely remembered the content of the invitation—something about forming a new, utterly outstanding double quartet for strings and wind. Just at that moment a person whom he recognized as an internationally known violinist sat down next to him. She greeted my friend with a smile and asked, "Are you good?" How could my friend explain to her (or to any of the others) that he cannot read music and cannot even hold a tune for more than a few measures? A classic performance anxiety dream related to stresses at home or at work? Maybe so. But the question asked my friend by the great violinist transcends any particular circumstance in life: "Are you good?" That is, "Are you acceptable? Do you belong here? Do you deserve my respect and love?"

The answer the eunuch received from Philip was "You are accepted." Little wonder, then, that the Ethiopian "went on his way rejoicing" (v. 39). The eunuch's story gives us insight into the incredible success of the early church's missionary activity. Where the good news was proclaimed, there was joy. Joy, a characteristic response to the experience of God's love, is the third aspect of a transformed life. It is significant that "joy" and "grace" share the same root in Greek. The eunuch reminds us that a graced life is a joyful life.

Spiritual reading brings us in touch with the wellsprings of joy every time an author offers an explanation, a metaphor, or an experience that re-presents for us the nearness of the peaceable kingdom. The kingdom may draw near through wise counsel, new information, clarifying insight, or finding one's own experience mirrored in another's words. These are moments when spiritual reading opens in us a vision of God's life in the world and our life with God, a vision of empowering hope that releases the flow of joy within us. To the Christians in Rome Paul wrote: "May the God of hope bring you such joy and peace in your faith that the power of the Holy Spirit will remove all bounds to hope" (Rom. 15:13, JB). Sometimes our energy for service or mission withers before the many complex forces that furrow the face of humanity. Then it is important to recall the wisdom embodied by the eunuch—that joy is a gift given by the Holy Spirit to burst through the impoverishing limits the world can impose on our hope. In this way joy is itself the power of the Holy Spirit, watering the landscape of human life and making all things new. How characteristic of God that this eunuch, who was without hope of having offspring, may well have returned to Ethiopia and become a progenitor of the Ethiopian Orthodox Church.

Traveling with Confidence

At the beginning, middle, and end of the story of Philip and the Ethiopian eunuch, that is, at each critical turning point in the narrative, the Holy Spirit is at work. It is the Spirit who prepares Philip to embark upon the desert road: "Be ready to set out at noon along the road that goes from Jerusalem down to Gaza, the desert road" (v. 26). It is the Spirit who leads Philip to a life-transforming encounter with the Ethiopian eunuch: "Go up and meet that chariot" (v. 29). And it is the Spirit who carries Philip into the next chapter of his ministry: "Philip was taken away by the Spirit of the Lord. . . . [He] found that he had reached Azotus and continued his journey proclaiming the Good News in every town as far as Caesarea" (vv. 39–40).

So it is with us as we take up spiritual reading along our desert road. It is the Holy Spirit who prepares us by putting us in touch with our hunger for God and our desire for fullness of life. It is the Holy Spirit who guides us toward the author, the book, the chapter, the image or single word that becomes life-giving bread for our journey. And it is the same Spirit who, at the conclusion of our reading, bears us on our way to fresh opportunities for service. Therefore we can travel with confidence, trusting that our encounters with spiritual authors along the way may be unexpected but are never accidental.

Notes

1. *Letter of Aristeas,* ed. Moses Hadas (New York: Harper & Brothers, 1951), para. 139.

2. *Opening the Bible* (Collegeville, Minn.: Liturgical Press, 1970), 27.

3. *Christian Spirituality,* ed. Frank N. Magill and Ian P. McGreal (San Francisco: Harper & Row, 1988).

4. *An Anthology of Devotional Literature,* comp. Thomas S. Kepler (Grand Rapids: Baker Book House, 1977).

5. Douglas V. Steere, *Doorways Into Life* (New York: Harper & Brothers, 1948); E. Glenn Hinson, *Seekers After Mature Faith* (Waco, Tex.: Word Books, 1968).

6. Louis Bouyer, *A History of Christian Theology,* 3 vols. (New York: Seabury Press, 1969).

7. *Christian Spirituality,* 3 vols. (New York: Crossroad, 1986–89).

8. Both works were published by St. Vladimir's Seminary Press in Crestwood, N.Y., in 1979 and 1978, respectively.

9. John the Solitary, "Letter to Hesychius," in *The Syriac Fathers on Prayer and the Spiritual Life,* introduced and translated by Sebastian Brock (Kalamazoo, Mich.: Cistercian Publications, 1987), 87.

10. *The Cost of Discipleship,* trans. R. H. Fuller (New York: Macmillan Co., 1963).

11. See St. Athanasius, *The Life of Antony,* trans. with introduction by Robert C. Gregg (Mahwah, N.J.: Paulist Press, 1980).

12. W. H. Auden, *For the Time Being* (London: Faber & Faber, 1945), 109.

13. *Letters of Spiritual Counsel,* ed. and trans. Theodore G. Tappert, The Library of Christian Classics, vol. 18 (Philadelphia: Westminster Press, 1955), 127.

14. *Goethe's Faust,* trans. with introduction by Walter Kaufmann (Garden City, N.Y.: Doubleday & Co., 1963), 203.

15. *The Art of Prayer: An Orthodox Anthology,* comp. Igumen Chariton of Valamo, trans. E. Kadloubovsky and E. M. Palmer, ed. with introduction by Timothy Ware (London: Faber & Faber, 1966).

16. Ibid., 51.

17. Ibid., 82.

18. Brother Lawrence, *The Practice of the Presence of God,* trans. with introduction by John J. Delaney (Garden City, N.Y.: Doubleday & Co., 1977), 49.

19. Anthony Bloom, *Beginning to Pray* (New York: Paulist Press, 1970), 21.

20. Douglas V. Steere, *Dimensions of Prayer* (New York: Women's Division, Board of Global Ministries, The United Methodist Church, 1962), 69.

21. *The Cloud of Unknowing and the Book of Privy Counseling,* ed. with introduction by William Johnston (Garden City, N.Y.: Doubleday & Co., 1973), 50.

22. Thomas Merton, *New Seeds of Contemplation* (New York: New Directions, 1961), 297.

23. Paul Tillich, "You Are Accepted," in *The Shaking of the Foundations* (New York: Charles Scribner's Sons, 1948), 163.

INDEX

acedia, 96
Allchin, A. M., 11
Ambrose, 21
Amos, 54f.
Antony, 186, 187
Aquinas, Thomas, 21, 68, 74–76, 91
Aristotle, 20, 21, 65, 74–76, 91
Athanasius, 186
Auden, W. H., 187
Augros, Robert M., 26
Augustine, 21, 66–68, 75, 91, 145, 187

Bainton, Roland, 155
Baker, James T., 11
Bamberger, John-Eudes, 36, 37
Barth, Karl, 6, 22, 184
Basil the Great, 21
Beaudin, Lambert, 13
Benedict of Nursia, xiii, 33, 36, 39, 41–46, 130
Benedictine Rule. *See* Rule of Benedict
Berkeley, George, 23
Bernard of Clairvaux, 2, 68, 71–73, 75, 76, 164, 185
Bernstein, Richard, 96
Berrigan, Daniel, 102
Berry, Wendell, 93
Billing, Einar, 88
Blake, William, 12
Bloom, Anthony, 189
Bloy, Leon, 126
Bonaventure, 74, 76
Bonhoeffer, Dietrich, 22, 94, 185
Bouyer, Louis, 184
Bownas, Samuel, 102
Bramachari, 12

Brinton, Howard, 102
Browning, Robert, 173
Bruno, Giordano, 20
Buber, Martin, 165, 169, 170
Bultmann, Rudolf, 22
Bunyan, John, 45, 46
Burgess, Anthony, 94
Buttrick, George, 11

Calvin, John, 88
Carlyle, Thomas, 90
Cassian, John, 75, 130, 132
Catherine of Genoa, 19, 23, 26, 163
Catherine of Siena, 187
Catholic liturgical movement, 2
centering prayer, 129–40
Chalkley, Thomas, 102
Chariton, Igumen, 189
Chenu, M. D., 74
Chesterton, G. K., 93
Chrysostom, John, 21
Cicero, 65, 92
Cistercians, 1–2, 71, 132
Ciszek, Walter, 102
Clarke, Thomas E., S.J., xiv, 101
Claudel, Paul, 133
Clement of Alexandria, 183
Cloud of Unknowing, 130–32, 187, 189
Comte, Auguste, 22
Conferences of John Cassian, 130
Confessions of Augustine, 187
Constantine, emperor, 145
Constitutions of the Society of Jesus, 102, 105, 106, 109
Contemplation and Work, 83–100
Copernicus, 19, 20, 21

Cripps, Arthur Shearly, 4
Cyprian, 20

Dalai Lama, 53, 56, 156
Daniélou, Jean, 22
Dante Alighieri, 76
Dart, Martha, 58
Darwin, Charles, 22, 85
Depew, Chauncey, 90
Didache, 87
Diekmann, Godfrey, xiii, 3
Dinesen, Isak, 34
Donnelly, Doris, xiv, 32

Eckhart, Meister, 58, 89, 185
Ecumenical Institute of Spirituality, 2,
     15, 170, 173
Edwards, Tilden, xv, 141
Eliot, T. S., 35, 125
Ellul, Jacques, 93
Eucharist, 115–28, 154

Farrell, Edward J., xiv, 115
Favre, Pierre, 102, 103
Fénelon, Francis, 169, 174
Fletcher, Joseph, 25
Fogelklou, Emilia, 170
Fox, George, 7, 107, 134, 187
Francis de Sales, 78, 169, 187
Franklin, Benjamin, 90
Friesen, Duane, 153

Galileo, 20
Gandhi, Mohandas K., 4
Gardiner, Percy, 17
Gardner, Edmund, 23
Gethsemani, Abbey of, 8, 11, 162
Gödel, Kurt, 26
Goethe, J. W. von, 188
Graham, Aelred, 2, 14
Greeley, Andrew, 26
Greene, Gwendolen, 162, 163, 167–
     69
Gregory of Nazianzus, 21
Gregory of Nyssa, 21, 185
Gregory the Great, 21, 42, 68, 69, 75
Guardini, Romano, 90
Gutiérrez, Gustavo, 183

Haughton, Rosemary, 11
Heard, Gerald, 170
Hegel, G. W. F., 23
Heisenberg, Werner, 26
Herwegen, Ildephonse, 14
Heschel, Abraham Joshua, 5, 52, 54, 58
Hesiod, 87
hesychastic traditions, 73, 81
Hibbert, Gerald, 58
Hinson, E. Glenn, 11, 161, 184
Hocking, Raymond, 163
Hocking, William Ernest, 164
Hound of Heaven, 165
Hughes, Gerard, 102
Huvelin, Abbé, 23, 163

Ignatius of Loyola, 77, 78, 101–10,
     113
Illich, Ivan, 88, 92
Irenaeus, 20, 141
Isaac, Abba, 130–32

James, William, 85
Jerome, 21, 87
Jesus, 17, 66, 105, 107, 117–21, 136,
     143–45, 178, 184, 185, 190
John XXIII, pope, 5, 12, 169
John the Baptist, 66
John Cassian. *See* Cassian
John of the Cross, 56, 104, 187
John the Solitary, 184
Jones, Rufus, 164
Julian of Norwich, 55, 187
Jung, C. G., 26
Jungmann, Joseph A., 14
Justin Martyr, 20

Kane, Leslie, 34
Kant, 18, 23
Keating, Thomas, 36, 129
Kelly, Thomas, 7, 18
Kelsey, Morton T., xiii, 15, 26, 192
Kepler, Johannes, 21
Kepler, Thomas S., 183
Kierkegaard, Søren, 18, 56, 92
Kilduff, Tom, 173
King, Martin Luther, Jr., 186
Kuhn, T. S., 26

Lawrence, Brother, 189
Leclerq, Jean, O.S.B., xiv, 2, 3, 41, 45, 63
lectio divina, 41, 42
Lewis, Clarence I., 164
Lindbergh, Anne Morrow, 36
Loisy, Alfred, 163
Lonergan, Bernard J. F., 22
Lucretius, 87
Luecke, Richard, xiv, 83
Luther, Martin, 88, 89, 94, 187, 188
Lynch, James, 40

Maria Laach monastery, 2
Maritain, Jacques, 92
Marx, Karl, 22
Marx, Michael, 14
Mary, 66, 76
Mather, Cotton, 89
Merton, Thomas, xiii, xiv, 1–12, 78–81,
    96, 125, 131, 132, 135, 162, 170, 182,
    184, 190
Modernist Movement, 15, 163
Moffitt, John, 11
Mogabgab, John, xv, 177
Montefiore, Claude, 171
Moore, Paul, 52
Morton, James, 61
Mother Teresa, 58
Mozart, W. A., 6

Nelson, John Oliver, 11
Niebuhr, Reinhold, 11, 45
Nouwen, Henri J. M., 26, 57, 168, 187

O'Brien, Tim, 147
Olsen, Tillie, 34
Opus Dei, 10
Origen, 142

Palmer, Parker, 94
Paul VI, pope, 129, 131, 133
peacemaking, 141–59
Péguy, Charles, 95
Pennington, Basil, O.C.S.O., xiv, 3, 36,
    129
Pennington, Isaac, 125, 134
Petre, Maude, 170, 172
Philokalia, The, 187

Picard, Max, 127
Pieper, Josef, 96
Pinter, Harold, 36
Plato, 20, 65, 76
Pliny, 65

Quakers. *See* Society of Friends

Rahner, Karl, 22
Rich, Adrienne, 34
Richardson, John, 102
Ricoeur, Paul, 33, 37
Rodgers, Daniel, 90
Royko, Mike, 84
Rule of the Master, 43
Rule of Benedict, xiv, 33–49, 67, 87, 88,
    90, 130

Sagan, Carl, 61
Saint Joseph's Abbey, xiii, 131
Sandburg, Carl, 83, 84
Schutz, Roger, Brother, 52, 58
Schweitzer, Albert, 169
Scotus, Duns, 91
Second Vatican Council, xiv, 2, 12, 15
Seneca, 65
Shaw, Robert, 62
Skinner, B. F., 22
Smith, John, 102
Snyder, Ross, 57
Society of Friends, 7, 9, 12, 16, 58, 101,
    124, 129–40
Sorg, Rembert, 88
Spencer, Herbert, 22
Spiritual Exercises, 101–14
spiritual reading, 177–95
Stanciu, George, 26
Statuta ecclesiae antiqua, 87
Steere, Dorothy, xiii, 138, 164, 166, 167,
    171
Steere, Douglas V., xiii, xiv, xv, 1–12,
    15–17, 19, 23, 27–29, 33, 34, 46, 57–
    59, 85–87, 91, 93, 97, 102, 122–27,
    132, 133, 137, 138, 161–76, 184,
    189
Story, Thomas, 102
Sullivan, Emmanuel, S.A., 5
Symeon the New Theologian, 187

Taizé Community, 52, 58
Tawney, R. H., 89
Taylor, A. E., 18
Teilhard de Chardin, Pierre, 6
Teresa of Avila, 78, 187
Tertullian, 20
Theophan the Recluse, 188
theoria, 64
Thomas à Kempis, 187
Thomas, Lewis, 37
Thurman, Howard, 58, 170, 187
Tillich, Paul, 11, 169, 170, 192
Tracy, David, 95
Trappists, 1
Tyrrell, George, 163, 165, 166

Una Sancta Movement, 12
Underhill, Evelyn, 15–17, 27, 28, 30, 125, 167, 175, 232

Van Buren, Mary Lou, xiv, 51
Van Dusen, Henry P., 52, 62
von Hügel, Friedrich, xiii, xv, 15–19, 23, 25–29, 161–76
von Hügel, Gertrud, 165, 166, 171

Ware, Kallistos, 184
Watts, Alan, 78
Way of a Pilgrim, The, 187
Webb, Clement, 170
Weber, Max, 88
Weems, Renita J., 186
Weigel, Gustave, 102
Whitehead, Alfred North, 164
Williams, Paul, 39
Woolman, John, 103–13, 187

Zen Buddhism, 2, 11, 81